THE ULTIMATE JOB SEARCH SURVIVAL GUIDE

PAUL L. DYER

PETERSON'S
Princeton, New Jersey

About Peterson's

Peterson's is the country's largest educational information/communications company, providing the academic, consumer, and professional communities with books, software, and online services in support of lifelong education access and career choice. Well-known references include Peterson's annual guides to private schools, summer programs, colleges and universities, graduate and professional programs, financial aid, international study, adult learning, and career guidance. Peterson's Web site at petersons.com is the only comprehensive—and most heavily traveled—education resource on the Internet. The site carries all of Peterson's fully searchable major databases and includes financial aid sources, test-prep help, job postings, direct inquiry and application features, and specially created Virtual Campuses for every accredited academic institution and summer program in the U.S. and Canada that offers in-depth narratives, announcements, and multimedia features.

Visit Peterson's Education Center on the Internet (World Wide Web) at www.petersons.com

Copyright © 1998 by Paul L. Dyer

Library of Congress Cataloging-in-Publication Data

Dyer, Paul L., 1955–
    The ultimate job search survival guide / Paul L. Dyer
      p.   cm.
  Includes bibliographical references and index.
  ISBN 0-7689-0009-3
  1. Job hunting.   I. Title.
HF5382.7.D94 1998
650.14—dc21
                                        98-11994
                                           CIP

Composition and design by Peterson's

Printed in the United States of America

10 9 8 7 6 5 4 3 2 1

In loving memory of Bill Dyer
my one and only true hero.

DEDICATION

· ·

To Carol and Callie, who each day demonstrate
that the grace from the One who calls is more real
than the rocks and trees.

Acknowledgements

How marvelous that by writing about discovering career treasure, I've stacked it a mile high in my own life. For this I must thank God because it is Grace that makes all good things possible.

I am deeply humbled when I think of the many people to whom I owe a debt of gratitude. Of course, listing all of these people is impossible, and selecting just a few is more than a little daunting, but I will try. My sensitive and loving father taught me to challenge every idea before accepting it, and my never-say-die mom serves as a powerful role model for facing the world with courage. My brother Joel showed me that following your dreams is perhaps the most practical of all of life's possible courses. I would not be who I am, let alone able to write this book, without their love.

I must also express my appreciation for the guidance and support of the many mentors and colleagues I've had the great pleasure of knowing through the years including Mike Knight, Bill Frederickson, Bob and Joyce Hogan, Bob Smither, and all of my former colleagues at Dow's Center for Employee and Organizational Assessment. To my longtime friends Brian Rice and Kevin Meeks, thank you for always believing in me, and for never letting me take myself too seriously.

I could not have written this book without the direct assistance of others. I am especially grateful for Judy Siklosi's typing help and Cindy Aycrigg's copyediting on early drafts. Finally, my editor Erika Heilman's patience and insight made this book much better than it would otherwise have been.

CONTENTS

. . . .

Chapter 14   Special Job Search Journeys   227

It's Exactly the Same but Different • Dual-Career Families—The Challenges of
Relocation • It Wasn't Supposed to Be Like This: Outplaced at Midlife •
Moving From a Military to a Civilian Career • Every Job Search is a Unique
Journey

APPENDICES

INDEX

INTRODUCTION

Imagine yourself standing by the ocean. You can hear the peaceful cry of several seagulls floating effortlessly overhead as the two-foot waves gently greet the shore. You smell the salt air and the early sun already feels warm. At any other time, you would find this scene peaceful, but not this morning. This morning you feel anxious, maybe even a little more than anxious. Surveying the horizon, you no longer hear the sounds of the ocean; indeed, you stop hearing much of anything except your own doubts.

The appointment to lead the queen's annual treasure hunt surprised you. But when the queen speaks, people listen; and in a few hours you will begin a journey to the other side of the world. Her instructions were easy to understand: "Go find treasure; gold, silver, or diamonds are acceptable." The journey may take months. Although you possess considerable talent and a unique set of skills and abilities, none of your previous experiences prepared you for the task of sailing a ship, for months, across this seemingly endless expanse of water. There seem to be hundreds of questions about provisions, sailing strategy, how to set and maintain the course, and how to manage the crew. And how will you contend with those sea monsters you overheard several drunken sailors talking about last night? These concerns are anything but unfounded. You personally know of brand new captains, like yourself, who ended up running aground, careening into barrier reefs, or sinking to the bottom of the ocean as the result of some terrible storm.

As the captain, you came here this morning to examine the sailing ship that will carry you to your destination. You suddenly notice a salty old character standing on the dock next to the mooring. As you approach the old sailor, you notice he is wearing the insignia of a captain. You strike up a conversation and learn that he has successfully captained many voyages, never losing a ship or a crew member, and always reaching his desired destination. Clearly, he *knows* how to sail. Unfortunately, a recent accident on shore blinded the captain.

Late last night, the rugged seaman heard through the old-sailor grapevine that you would set sail later today, and he came here this morning to make you an offer. Although he cannot pilot your ship, for the opportunity to return to the open sea, he will teach you all that he knows about selecting a destination to meet your desires and about safely navigating the ocean's perils. At the very moment you eagerly accept his offer, you notice that you can once again hear the seagulls and the waves.

Careers are journeys. Each of us begins our career journey in search of some sort of treasure. Of course, in the real world, no monarch will commission you to find this treasure. Instead, circumstances such as corporate downsizing or simple dissatisfaction will provide your motivation to enter the ocean called the job market. Also, only you can determine what kind of treasure is worth your job hunting effort. You must make numerous strategic decisions about where and how to look for your next job, and about how to best present yourself to potential employers. And like the drunken sailors' tales of sea monsters, the job market can indeed present perils; particularly for the

unprepared. Fortunately, *The Ultimate Job Search Survival Guide's* offer is just like that of the old captain. Listen to the advice contained in this book, and much more importantly, apply this advice, and you will learn how to skillfully sail toward your ideal job. Now get ready to begin a journey guaranteed to deliver rich rewards.

PART

1

CHOOSING YOUR PERFECT CAREER

CHAPTER

1

GETTING STARTED

· ·

*"I find the great thing in this world is not so much where we
stand as in what direction we are moving: To reach the port of
heaven, we must sail sometimes with the wind and sometimes
against it—but we must sail, and not drift, nor lie at anchor."*
Oliver Wendell Holmes

YOUR JOURNEY

Your ideal job exists, and if you learn a number
of specific job searching skills you can find it.
The Ultimate Job Search Survival Guide will take
you through a step-by-step journey of self-
discovery where you will master each of these
skills. Through this process, you will discover
how to choose a richly rewarding career and
how to skillfully navigate the job market so that
you can secure your ideal job.

In the brief sailing story in the introduction, you saw that a newly appointed captain's
fears greatly diminished upon learning that an
experienced captain would both provide an
understanding of the journey's many requirements and teach the necessary sailing skills

needed to find treasure. It's not hard to imagine
that the new captain will soon develop the
maritime skills needed to qualify as a skillful
solo traveler. This is also my goal for you.
Although I will stand on the bridge with you
during your job search voyage, the responsibility for (and ultimately the wonderful reward of)
the journey is yours alone. ***In your career
journey, you are the captain.***

WELCOME TO THE NEW WORLD OF WORK

No one's job is secure. Not any more. Until
recently, an unspoken psychological contract
existed between the employer and the employee.

3

In essence, the contract implied that if a worker exhibited loyalty and would forgo his or her personal goals for the good of the organization, the organization would, in turn, "take care" of the employee. In short, loyalty begat loyalty. While a spectacular career was certainly not guaranteed, the worker knew that the job was secure.

Robert Roger is a consultant and author with Developmental Dimensions International. His description of his father's work life nicely contrasts yesterday's world of work with today's.

My father worked for the same company for forty-two years. When he retired, he received a gold watch, his pension, and full medical coverage for life. He never considered working anywhere else, knowing that if he performed well in his job, there would be periodic increases in responsibility and pay as well as a job he could count on to support his family. Even today, more than two decades after his retirement, my father still speaks frequently about "his" company and its successes and failures over the years. A very clear bond of trust existed between my father and the company that employed him. Consequently, the organization received maximum effort and commitment from a talented, dedicated employee, and my father received security and the knowledge that he was appreciated by his employer.

As Dorothy said upon her abrupt arrival in Munchkinland, "We're not in Kansas any more, Toto." Downsizing, rightsizing, restructuring, total quality management, teaming initiatives, and dramatic demographic shifts have forever changed organizations and, as a result, individuals' careers. No longer do you graduate from college, get a good job, give the company your loyalty, retire, do some stuff you always wanted to do, and die. Of course, with today's realities you will still die, but you almost certainly will not work for one company for your entire career. In fact, experts now estimate that the typical worker will change jobs between eight and twelve times during a career. Whether you believe organizations began these initiatives primarily in reaction to global marketplace realities or simply because of corporate greed, the plain fact remains: careers in today's world of work barely resemble our father's and mother's.

Along with the tens of thousands forced into job hunting by corporate restructuring, many others voluntarily enter this turbulent job market to begin the job search journey. The disappearance of the psychological contract from the world of work is the catalyst for many to leave dissatisfying jobs. Since only the most naive now believe that organizations will "take care" of them, many workers are asking if their current jobs make sense. They may have thought about the value of their work before. But with today's reality, why wait until the boss calls them into the office for that fateful closed-door meeting? Their thinking goes like this: "If security no longer exists and loyalty is often rewarded with a pink slip, why not try to do something that I really want to do?"

If it were easy, everyone would do it

Locating the *right job* requires a clear understanding of one's vocational identity as well as a thorough knowledge of the job market. Even though these two tasks may take considerable effort, simply discovering what you would like to do and where you may be able to do it are by no means a guarantee of securing that position. Getting the right job also requires effective use of the following job searching skills: networking, telephoning techniques, letter and résumé writing, and interviewing. Additionally, because the campaign may take several months and involve many activities, successful job searching often demands efficient administrative skills to keep track of these activities.

Thanks, but no thanks

By the way, I should also mention that not all employers will be delighted to see you. Think how unpleasant it is to have your dinner, a movie, or a romantic interlude interrupted by calls from telemarketers. You may receive several of these calls a week. A little irritating, aren't they? Well, some of the decision makers you will encounter during your job hunt are approached numerous times each day by job seekers, many of whom are poorly prepared and have no possibility of "fitting" with the needs of the organization. As you might imagine, these decision makers learn quick ways, sometimes quite abrupt, to say, "Thanks, but no thanks."

In other words, you will encounter a lot of rejection during your job search. Since you are human, you hate rejection. Since you will encounter rejection, and since you hate rejection, you will want to engage in job seeking activities that reduce the chance of encountering rejection. Makes sense. Unfortunately, as you will see in Chapter 9, low rejection job seeking strategies are *by far* the least effective methods of finding employment.

Put me in, coach, I'm ready to play

You are a talented and skilled individual. Your God-given talents, formal education, and work experiences qualify you to make valuable contributions to the world of work. While your skills may need enhancing to get the job you want, you are certainly employable. You know how to play the work game; it's getting off the bench and on the field for which you may be unprepared. While educational institutions and corporate training departments spend billions of dollars teaching people how to do things, it is likely that no one has ever taught you how to choose a career or effectively conduct a job search.

DEVELOP A WINNING ATTITUDE: THE WIND IN YOUR SAILS

Given these realities, it is not too difficult to imagine a job search that begins with a good deal of fanfare and high aspirations soon turning into an effort that feels like drudgery and is marked by discouragement. But job finding absolutely does not have to be this way! Here are three reasons why. First, there are many good jobs out there; despite the number of job seekers, employers often find it very difficult to locate the right person for their employment needs. Put simply, high demand for qualified workers exists. You will learn how to find these opportunities in Chapter 9. Second, since most people are ill-equipped for job searching, if you learn and practice the skills contained in this book, you will possess a significant competitive advantage over the vast majority of job seekers. While this book will not actually find you a job, it will provide you with information and job searching skills to help you secure the employment situation you believe is best for you. Third, choosing a career and finding a new job can represent one of the greatest opportunities in anyone's working life. Indeed, many people choose to view the employment-seeking process as a very positive experience. The right job can be a significant source of not only income but personal fulfillment as well. Seeking new employment through *The Ultimate Job Search Survival Guide*'s exercises and processes provides you with an opportunity to clearly identify your vocational identity, to evaluate your career objective in light of this identity, and to seek the best possible fit between your vocational identity and a job opportunity from the world of work. Regardless of your employment situation, you will learn career management skills that will serve you throughout your working life.

As you go about the "job" of finding a job, nothing will be more important than developing and maintaining a positive attitude. A positive, winning attitude will not only make your job search a more pleasant experience but also will actually increase your chances of finding the right kind of job situation quickly. Psychologists often refer to the "Pygmalion effect" or the "self-fulfilling prophecy" when describing the power that thoughts have in determining behavior. That is, as you think, so will you become. Nowhere is this concept more true than in the job hunting arena. If you believe that you are a valuable person, someone who will be an asset to some organization, then you will be. Self-confidence is key to your success; believe in yourself and others will believe in you too.

The good news is that while you cannot govern the job market or change your past, you can control your attitude. Your attitude is *your choice*. And remember, attitudes, both positive and negative, show. Every potential employer prefers an upbeat, positive job candidate to the proverbial sad sack. Many interviewers are looking to hire candidates with a "winning attitude." You can do a number of things that ensure that you will maintain a positive attitude even when job searching presents situations that challenge you. The next few pages present ten practical ideas that will assist you in building and maintaining your own unique "winning attitude."

Remember, the power is in doing these ten ideas, not reading about them. . . so please do them!

Ten ideas for developing and maintaining a winning attitude

1. Operate with an internal locus of control.

Determining your locus of control is essentially answering the question: "Who runs your life?" Some people, with an internal locus of control, believe that by hard work, skill, and training they can improve their career management. Others, with an external locus of control, believe that chance, luck, and the behavior of others determine their career destiny.

Those who possess an internal locus of control will be more successful in a job search campaign than those with an external locus of control. You can affect what happens to you through your own actions. This book will equip you to make solid career choices and to conduct the job search; however, the responsibility for

FIGURE 1
Example of Affirmations List

I am a winner	I am a loving spouse
I never give up	I overcome adversity
I am a loving parent	I am a good leader
I am very creative	I am sensitive to those who have physical needs
I have courage to try new things	I can be counted on to do what I say I will do
I am a good speaker	I am a good friend
I can see the talent of others	I am willing to help others
I encourage others	

managing your career in general, and this campaign specifically, belongs solely to you.

2. Cultivate and rely upon your social support.

We have all heard it said that no one is an island. Social psychologists have known for some time that those who rely upon the support of others when faced with life's challenges experience less stress, for shorter periods of time, than those who do not.

As you begin your job search campaign, make a list of all of the resources you can draw upon for social support. Your friends, family, clubs, churches, neighbors, and others who may have recently changed jobs or careers can all serve as reservoirs of support. Contact some of these resources, and discuss your feelings about beginning to look for work or about changing careers. Realize you are not the first person to go through this experience. As you interact with these people, you are likely to learn of others who have successfully navigated these waters in the past. Their experiences will provide useful insights, you will learn that you are not alone, and that others are concerned and interested in you.

3. Exercise regularly.

Health-care experts know that exercise reduces the negative effects of future stress. In other words, exercise is good preventative medicine. Exercise also will improve your attitude, increase your resistance to disease, and create a more confident self-image. Your schedule may never be more flexible than during the time you look for a new position; this schedule provides a terrific opportunity to begin an exercise program.

4. Evaluate your accomplishments, skills, abilities, and talents.

You are a unique person. No one has your personality, your set of skills and abilities, nor the identical set of experiences you have. Over the years, you accomplished many things that demonstrated your value as a person and as an employee. The first part of this book, Choosing Your Perfect Career, provides ideas to consider regarding career choice and a number of exercises for conducting a thorough self-assessment. This assessment will assist you in identifying your values, articulating your life's purpose, recognizing your marketable job skills, discovering your vocational identity, and building a career objective that will serve as your primary target for the job search campaign.

5. Recognize the job search realities.
You may have to work harder at finding the right job than you ever worked while in a job. A number of factors outside your control may impact your job search. Concentrate on those factors that you can impact, and recognize and accept those that you cannot. While each job search situation is unique and contains a number of important elements, the following four factors will play significant roles in creating your job search reality.

FIGURE 2
An Interesting Career Path

- Lost job, 1832
- Defeated for legislature, 1832
- Failed in business, 1833
- Elected to legislature, 1834
- Sweetheart died, 1835
- Had nervous breakdown, 1836
- Defeated for speaker, 1839
- Defeated for nomination for Congress, 1843
- Elected to Congress, 1846
- Lost renomination, 1848
- Rejected for land officer, 1849
- Defeated for Senate, 1854
- Defeated for nomination for vice president, 1856
- Defeated again for Senate, 1858
- Elected president of the United States, 1860
- Abraham Lincoln's Career Path

Reprinted with permission from *Outplace Yourself*, Charles H. Logue, 1993 (published by Adams Media Corp.).

- *How well you conduct your job search*—Both the quality of your efforts and the amount of time you spend on your job search will help determine the outcome. Getting started as early as possible, following the ideas presented in this book, and treating your job search as a full-time job will result in quicker and better results.

- *The condition of the job market and geographical limitations*—You will learn how to determine the condition of the job market in Chapter 8. There may be a surplus or shortage of your skills available in the job market, the general economic conditions of your geographic area of interest may be poor or good, or your industry may be depressed or booming. You did not create these market conditions, and there is little you can do to change them. Additionally, if you are in a dual-career situation, you will probably limit your job search to one particular geographic area.

- *Your salary and job level*—In general, the higher paying the job the longer one should expect to spend on the job search. A commonly cited rule of thumb for managerial positions states that for every $10,000 in income, expect to spend about one month on the search. Your search may take even longer depending upon other factors, such as the two mentioned above.

- *Good fortune*—Earlier, I made the point that having an internal locus of control is more likely to result in a successful job search campaign (the right job situation for you) than having an external locus of control.

Although this is certainly true, no one can deny that luck, or good fortune, can play a role.

We have all heard the phrase "being in the right place at the right time." Someone *will* win the lottery, but this fact is obviously not the best basis for building your long-term financial plan. However, good and bad things do sometimes happen for no apparent reason; this truth constitutes a part of your job search reality. Yet you dramatically increase your chances of being able to seize an opportunity if you take charge of your actions and do your homework. As Jonas Salk said, "Chance favors the prepared mind."

6. Use positive affirmations to develop positive inner thoughts.
Positive self-talk impacts both the way we feel about ourselves and our behavior. Sometimes negative patterns develop, subtly, over time. Little statements like "you dummy," or "knowing me, I'd probably blow it," can have a very big and negative impact on your self-image and how you are perceived by others. In addition to perceptions, self-talk affects performance. Research has shown that athletes who engage in negative self-talk such as "don't miss it" are less successful than athletes who say to themselves, "I'll make this shot."

Make a list of 15 to 20 positive statements about yourself and your situation; for example: "I am a valuable person," "I am a great problem solver," "I will find just the right job for me." (See more examples in Figure 1.) Find a quiet and private place, such as a spare bedroom, a

park, or your car. At least once a day, recite these affirmations out loud. Commit them to memory, and rehearse them silently several more times during the day. If you feel negative during the course of your job search, realize this is normal. Redirect your attention to more positive thoughts, and use your personal positive affirmations.

7. Realizing change may be painful, but it often yields very positive results.
You can view your job search as a problem or as a challenge you will overcome or even as an opportunity to enhance your career. People generally resist all forms of change. However, as is often said, the only constant is change. Although the ultimate destination of your career journey is never a certainty, one truism bears noting: Careers seldom follow a simple, straight path. View this change as a given, and as a challenge you will face with confidence and dogged determination. The preceding example (Figure 2) serves as powerful testimony to what this kind of approach can accomplish.

8. Be proactive.
As the old saying goes, "Plan your work and work your plan." Your "work" is to locate suitable employment. Chapter 9 will give you a comprehensive framework for building your job search campaign strategy. But even before you go about building your strategy, you can determine now to begin your campaign soon, develop daily plans that move you toward your

> *"We're all faced with a series of great opportunities brilliantly disguised as impossible situations."*
>
> Charles R. Swindoll

career goals, and recognize that effort given often equals results received.

9. Behave like a winner.

Sports psychologists have demonstrated that a number of mental attitudes correspond to performance. Among others, my good friend Dr. David Cook, a leading sports psychologist who has worked with professional baseball and basketball players as well as numerous golf pros, has shown that these mental attitudes not only relate to performance on the athletic field but also to performance in corporate environments. Although many attitudes are important in terms of both self-esteem and performance, Cook believes "confidence is the cornerstone to performance." In a nutshell, it is important to behave like a winner.

10. Develop a terrific job search campaign.

Knowing that you possess a *great* game plan represents one of the best ways to insure your self-confidence and consequently to cause you to behave like a winner. Don't settle for a second-rate job search campaign strategy. Decide that you will develop a great job search plan and that you will follow through on all of the steps.

One other important point: if you are not working, you are not unemployed (or soon to be unemployed). You have a full-time job called "looking for the best possible job." If you treat your job search this way and dedicate yourself to following the processes laid out in this book, you will greatly enhance your chances of meeting your career objective in a timely fashion.

C H A P T E R

2

Your Career Destination and Vocational Identity

· ·

"That which you are seeking is causing you to seek."
Zen Buddhist Meditation

IT'S TIME TO DREAM

So, what do you want to be when you grow up? Sound like a childish question? It's not. It's a wonderful question. Before we grew up and learned that reality gets in the way of dreams, we were eager to answer this inquiry with thoughtfulness and creativity. My 6-year-old daughter wants to be "a part-time doctor and a full-time singer." Good for her! Fortunately, her occupational aspirations are unencumbered by concerns over money, education, and perhaps most important, the expectations of others. Her peers have not yet assigned a social status to various occupations and her mother and I haven't laughed at her desires. Without these encumbrances she can focus on the most important word in the question: *want.*

While I will ask you to think about a number of issues that may profoundly affect your life, this chapter's primary focus is on your heart, not your head. For the time being, please forget emotionless black-and-white analysis, financial realities, and what others expect from you. Instead, as you read Part 1, please—earnestly, candidly, and openly—ask yourself, "What is it that I *want*, desire, enjoy, *love* to do?"

If you answer this question from your heart, you will learn that when it comes to choosing careers, "What do you want to be when you grow up?" was the right question all along.

The journey begins

So, whether outplacement, choice, or some other circumstance brought you to this point, you have just launched your career journey. But where are you going, and how are you going to get there? You must choose a destination—but how? In the story in the Introduction, the new captain doesn't yet know where he is going, but at least he knows what he is seeking. The queen commissioned him to search for treasure, and only gold, silver, or diamonds would do. But in the career journey, what represents the treasure? How successful can your career journey be if you don't know what you're looking for, let alone where to look? You're not even sure if this sort of inquiry is worthwhile. More than once you've said to yourself, "Hey, what's the big deal? Why not just get a job like everybody else and forget about these 'what's-life-all-about?' questions?"

It's about time

A worker spends an average of 2,080 hours per year on a 40-hour-a-week job. The average middle manager works 55 to 60 hours per week or about 3,000 hours per year. We all work a lot, but why do we work? One bestselling career book suggests that companies' and individuals' goals are exactly the same, with each seeking to make as much money as possible in as short an amount of time as possible. This goal, the book suggests, "allows you to do the things you really want to do with the rest of your time." This is a *very* bad idea because your time is not unlimited. After work, throw in another 2,000 or so hours for sleeping, then mow the yard, wash a few dishes, vacuum the carpet, go to the dentist, pick up the cleaning, buy the groceries, change the oil in the car, and do your taxes. *Now* you

can begin to think about doing the things you really want to do with the rest of your life. One important fact cannot be escaped: *your time is finite.*

The amount of time available to you each year to "do the things you really want to do" is severely limited by lots of life's demands, such as the list of chores in the previous paragraph. But another very important, and quite immovable, time constraint exists. In addition to annual limitations, the length of your life is also bounded; you won't live forever. So, even without considering daily time-consuming obligations, for most of us, working 83,200 hours (during a forty-year career) solely to make "as much money as possible" still makes little sense.

Think of your life span as a savings account at a bank. Assume that you can draw out as much time as you want from the savings account, but you cannot exceed, or add even a single second, to the total amount. Now, assuming you will spend 8 hours sleeping each night, ask yourself, "Do I really want to spend one half of the remaining amount of time available from my account in my current career?" If so, terrific! If not, since life is pretty brief, you should seek to make your life's work a major part of what you really want to do with the rest of your life. Either way, I believe that all of us can benefit from wrestling with the old "what's-life-all-about?" question, and there are few better times to stop and reevaluate your life than at the beginning of your job search.

I believe that a "money only, money now" philosophy is the primary reason that the typical Fortune 500 company lasts only forty-two years (about thirty years less than the average person's life span), as well as why more than 50 percent of workers report that they are unhappy in their careers. Both organizations and individuals need a higher purpose, a reason for being, to serve as a guide for their day-to-day activities. In most cases, money alone just won't cut it.

LIFE'S PURPOSE

Before you get too worried (in some cases, too excited), let me assure you that I will not, and indeed cannot, tell you what your purpose in life is or should be. But it's a very important issue, perhaps the most important issue, for you to consider when thinking about your career. By life's purpose, I mean your reason for existing, the center of your motivation, your supreme value. All other values are subordinate to, and ordered by, this purpose. When you have a clear understanding of your purpose, you have a guide or beacon to help order all of life's activities.

So why is formally defining your life's purpose so important in the job search process? Well, it's important for a couple of reasons. First, deciding what life is about and then linking this decision to your career simply makes a lot of sense, since you will spend more time at work than you will spend engaged in any other single activity. Second, if you clearly understand your purpose, then you are *much* more likely to discover your ideal career destination and you will be able to manage your job search campaign accordingly. Along with exercises and discussion of your work and personal values, the next chapter will also give you a process for formally defining your life's purpose and then writing your *life's mission statement*. This statement serves as a word picture reflecting your purpose.

CAREER DESTINATIONS

Just as with a ship's journey, career journeys ultimately arrive at destinations. After you arrive at your destination, you walk down the plank, look around, and assess whether this is a good place, a bad place, or, like most destinations, somewhere in between. Unlike sailing, however, career destinations come in two distinct forms: your *ideal* career destination and your *chosen* career destination.

Ideal destination

Your ideal career destination already exists; you do not select it, it selects you. It is outside of you. Although you may never have seen your ideal destination, you have an inner sense of what it must be like. You have received a number of clues throughout your life about where it resides. Your ideal destination calls you to a particular course of action. But to discover it, you must listen. Remember the times you've been really excited about some project or work? You remember, when you lost track of time. It was fun. And you were good at it too; you knew it—and so did others. Remember? These were times when you engaged in the kinds of activities that are found in abundance at the site of your ideal destination. This notion of an ideal destination is sometimes referred to as one's *calling*. I believe that everyone has a calling and that only by listening to and answering the call will you find satisfaction with your career. This calling is relentless; just as magnetic North is to the compass. No matter what career destination you choose, your ideal destination will continue to call you, to pull you toward it. Dissatisfaction with your career is one of the strongest indicators of this tugging from your ideal destination.

Chosen destinations

On the other hand, whether or not you listen to the clues coming from your ideal destination, you will choose some career destination. Indeed, you are free to choose any career destination you wish, based upon any criteria you like. This chosen destination or decision is inside of you.

This choice of destination represents your career objective. Defining a clear career objective requires that you select both a type of job (what to do) and an industry (where to do it). As the captain, you must make these choices and set the course in order to begin the journey. Unfortunately, it is possible for you to choose a destination that causes you to arrive at a place that barely resembles your ideal destination. I assume, however, that if you knew where your ideal destination lies, you would define your

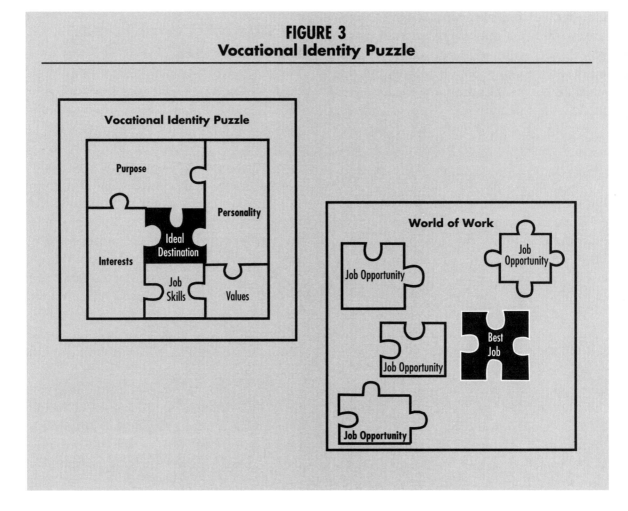

FIGURE 3
Vocational Identity Puzzle

career objective in a fashion that would lead you directly to that spot.

Career treasure

In its simplest form, finding the ideal career destination is merely selecting the career that allows you to do the things you most want to do and to accomplish the things you most want to accomplish. Although discovering your destination is seldom as easy as this sentence suggests, the payoff makes the search extremely worthwhile. The purpose of your career journey is straightforward: find *career treasure.*

Fortunately, finding career treasure is not an all-or-nothing experience. You'll find out how much career treasure is available after you arrive at your chosen destination. Although all work yields some treasure, one chosen destination is not as good as any other chosen destination. Career destinations have relative value determined by the amount of career treasure you're able to collect. The closer your chosen destination is to your ideal destination, the more career treasure you will receive.

So, what's the treasure? Unfortunately, I can't tell you because you have to decide for yourself. What I can tell you is that you will find a *great deal of career treasure* when you choose a destination that is similar to your ideal destination. I can also tell you that the more career treasure you find, the more satisfied with your career, and with your life, you will be. Although your ideal destination has already been created, no one can tell you where it is. You must discover it yourself. Okay, so where do you begin in order to discover your ideal destination? While I don't have any idea about where your ideal destination is, I do know that it will fit your *vocational identity* and will further your life's purpose. Thus, finding your ideal destination starts with clearly understanding your vocational identity.

VOCATIONAL IDENTITY

Webster defines identity as "the distinguishing character or personality of an individual." This "distinguishing character" as it relates to job preference is your *vocational identity*. You were created as a unique individual, full of potential, and hard-wired to enjoy activities that move you toward your ideal destination. A reporter once asked George Burns, the venerable entertainer, about the secret to his long and successful life. He replied simply, "Fall in love with what you do for a living." You will fall in love with what you do for a living when you choose a career destination, a job, and an industry that reflect your vocational identity.

You can think of your vocational identity as a puzzle made up of several pieces. As Figure 3 shows, five internal factors work together to create a person's vocational identity: life's purpose; values; knowledge, skills, and abilities; personality; and vocational interests.

FIGURE 4
Puzzle Pieces and Diagnostic Questions

Puzzle Piece	Question
Life's Purpose and Values	What really matters to you?
Skills and Abilities	What do you really do well?
Personality and Vocational Interests	What type of person are you?

The next three chapters provide ideas and self-assessment exercises so that you can evaluate each of the puzzle's pieces in your life. Each time you complete one of these exercises, I will ask you to record the results on the Vocational Identity Summary (VIS) found in Appendix A. Please take a moment to turn to Appendix A and scan the summary page. As you can see, the VIS allows you to capture a great deal of information about who you are. You will make use of this summary page many times during the course of reading this book and working through the exercises. I am certain that you will find the VIS an invaluable tool as you decide upon your career objective and throughout the course of the job search campaign.

As a way of giving you a first pass at thinking about your vocational identity puzzle, I grouped the puzzle pieces using three simple diagnostic questions. Please take a few minutes to read each question and then reflect upon your answers.

Notice in Figure 3 that the center of the puzzle contains the final piece: a person's ideal destination. When empty, the space for the puzzle's final piece is shown darkened. Only by finding a job opportunity from the world of work that closely matches the ideal destination

can the puzzle be completed. (In Chapter 6 you will define your career objective based upon what you learn about your vocational identity in Chapters 3, 4, and 5.) In general, finding the "best job" represents your career objective. By "best job" I am referring to the one job and industry, within a given job market, that most closely matches your ideal destination. Because your career objective will steer your job search campaign, it is very important that this objective is a clear reflection, or shorthand version, of your vocational identity. Finding your best job furthers your life's purpose, is consistent with your values, makes use of your skills, and fits your personality and interests.

To discover your vocational identity, do not begin by asking "What am I trained or skilled at doing?" or "What is it that I should do?" While these are reasonable questions to ask as you refine your career objective, they can lead you far astray of your ideal destination if they are your first line of thinking. At the beginning you should begin by dreaming, by asking yourself, "What is it that I really *want* to do?" Find someone who loves his career, and you will find someone who very closely matched his vocational identity to a job.

I visualized the Grail a shining light,
Perceptible from any vale in which
I and my helpers struggled. It would be
A constant beacon, milestone in the sky,
Signally far
Calling to goal.
I did not comprehend that it could function
Only by flashing back light from me. Its gleam
Existed, but in partnership with mine,
And I had launched the search a blind man,
Nothing within myself to guide the way,
No silver in my soul to match the blaze
Of what I sought, nor did I test the peaks
That would forever bar me from my goal
Till I broke through with force and fortitude
To conquer them and in my victory
Conquer myself as well.

Trevor Blythe
Fictional character
in James Michener's novel *Journey*

3

IDENTIFY YOUR VALUES AND LIFE'S PURPOSE

"This is the true joy in life, the being used for a purpose you consider a mighty one, the being a force of nature rather than a feverish, selfish clod of ailments and grievances complaining that the world will not devote itself to making you happy."
George Bernard Shaw

IT'S ALWAYS A QUESTION OF VALUES

"Should we move to Cincinnati? How about the kids? It's not exactly the job I want, and we really love it here—but, oh, the money." Maybe you have faced this sort of dilemma before; if not, you probably will. At various points in our lives, we all face important career choices. Whether deciding upon a college major, changing careers, or choosing which job offer to accept, we must select a path. The baseball legend and sometime philosopher Yogi Berra once advised, "When you come to the fork in the road, take it." Indeed, life's forks in the road demand decisions. Even a decision not to choose will lead to an outcome. Because the competing alternatives can offer widely different benefits and costs, we often find career decisions extremely complex. But how will you balance all the competing issues as you decide what really matters to you? Upon what criteria will you base your decisions?

In order to achieve real satisfaction with your career, your career choices *must* include careful consideration of your core values and purpose. At the heart of almost all career dissatisfaction rests a choice to follow a direction that proved inconsistent with a person's values and purpose. Whether a person fails to carefully consider his or her own values or uses someone else's values (for example, society's or a parent's) to make career decisions, the result is the same: dissatisfaction.

19

ASSESSING YOUR VALUES AND PURPOSE

When you answer the question "What really matters to you?" your vocational identity puzzle moves one piece closer to completion. You began answering this question fairly casually in the last chapter. Over the next several pages you will have an opportunity to answer the question in much more depth. First you will learn more about three specific types of values. Exercise 1 asks you to evaluate a number of general or personal values and to rank order these values. While these personal values certainly affect your work, they also have implications that pertain to every facet of your life. Exercise 2 assesses values that are more specific to the world of work. Exercise 3 asks you to think about the kind of working environment that makes up your ideal job. After you complete the values assessment, the fourth exercise in the chapter gives you a step-by-step process for evaluating your purpose and writing your *life's mission statement*. If you think through the issues in this exercise carefully, and work through the steps with candor, I know you will find it an important and valuable experience. If you then put your mission statement into practice, you will find it life-changing, moving you closer to both career and life satisfaction.

You will find the results from these exercises useful for two primary purposes. First, by helping you build an accurate picture of your vocational identity, they provide valuable information as you make career choices and write your career objective. Second, you should also use the results from the assessments as a template against which you can evaluate the job offers you will receive. I'll say more about this in Chapter 12, but basically these results, along with the exercises in Chapters 4 and 5, form a checklist for you to use when determining whether a job is right for you. As with most of the exercises in the book, I will ask you to record your results from three exercises on the Vocational Identity Summary found in Appendix A.

Tell it like it is

Finding satisfaction in your career rests on making choices that are consistent with what you truly value. Results produced in light of what *should* be valued are, at best, irrelevant and at worst, you will soon see them as idealistic words with no practical application. If you have ever observed a mission statement upon the wall of a corporation that bears no resemblance to actual practice or what really matters to its leaders, you know what I'm talking about. Defining your core values and writing a mission statement based upon what a company wished it believed, instead of what it truly believes, quickly builds cynicism within the organization and will do the same in your personal life. If you operate from a "what-*should*-be-my-values-and-purpose" perspective rather than what your heart actually feels is important and genuinely desires, you will construct a picture of your vocational identity that is untrue. If you then set a career objective based upon this false picture of your vocational identity, you create a recipe *guaranteed* to deliver career dissatisfaction.

Instead, to gain genuine benefit from these exercises you must complete them while focusing on what truly is. If making money is more important to you than spiritual fulfillment, say so. When you complete the exercises from a truthful and candid perspective, you build an accurate picture of your vocational identity.

Exercise 1 will take you about 10 minutes to complete; Exercise 2, about 20 to 30 minutes; and Exercise 3, about half an hour.

EXERCISE 1
Personal Values
Self-Assessment

• •

Below you will find a list of twenty-two items. The list contains items that many people "value" in their lives. We all encounter situations each day, in our personal lives and in the world of work, that require us to make choices that involve these sorts of issues. Remember, a decision not to choose is still a choice that leads to real outcomes.

The items are arranged in no particular order. **STEP 1:** Read completely through the list, pausing 5 to 10 seconds to think about each item. **STEP 2:** List next to the (Other value) item any additional items that you feel are important in terms of your personal values but are not found on the list. **STEP 3:** Go through the list a second time. This time find the item that is *most important to you*. Place a 1 to the left of this item. **STEP 4:** Go through the list a third time, selecting your next most important value, and write the number 2 to the left of this item. Continue this process until all items are rank ordered (1 = most important).

_____ Accomplishing great things		_____ Spiritual fulfillment	
_____ Marriage		_____ Economic status	
_____ Financial security		_____ Love of self	
_____ Being well regarded in the community		_____ Friendship	
_____ Geographic location		_____ Knowledge and wisdom	
_____ Love		_____ Freedom	
_____ The environment		_____ Being recognized by others for your achievements	
_____ Music		_____ Art and beauty	
_____ Family relations (other than marriage)		_____ Peace of mind and serenity	
_____ Discretionary time		_____ (Other value)_____	
_____ Exciting and adventuresome activities		_____ (Other value)_____	
_____ Equal opportunity for all people		_____ (Other value)_____	
_____ Pleasurable experiences			

STEP 5: After completing your ranking, turn to the Vocational Identity Summary Page in Appendix A and record your top 5 (most important) and bottom 5 (least important) Personal Values in the spaces provided.

EXERCISE 2
World of Work Values
Self-Assessment

• •

Many values can be met through your work. Exercise 2 takes you through a five-step process to evaluate which of these work-related values are most important in your life. When met, these values add much satisfaction to your career. While you may feel that many, or even most, of the values in this exercise are important, you will be asked to choose which of these values is *most* important. The exercise presents five value groups, each containing nine statements. Just as in everyday life, in each of the five value groups several of the values will probably compete for your attention. Remember, these are factors that you will be looking for as you evaluate various career and job opportunities.

STEP 1: Five groups of statements (value groups) appear below. Each of these groups contains nine statements. Beginning with Value Group 1, rank each statement in terms of its importance in your career. Within each group, the most important statement should receive a rating of 1 and the least important a 9. After completing the rankings for Value Group 1, move on to groups 2 through 5. Since there are five value groups you will have 5 ones, 5 fours, etc. An example of a ranking for the first value group is shown below.

IMPORTANT: You should have no ties. Within each value group each statement should have a unique number (1 through 9).

Example
Value Group 1:
Importance in My Ideal Job
Rank order, 1 = most important, 9 = least important

1. Being able to help others	2
2. Pursuing new ideas	3
3. Solving complex problems	4
4. Freedom and independence	1
5. Working with a well-respected organization	7
6. Financial rewards	8
7. Workplace that is conveniently located	9
8. Working with a talented group of people	6
9. Working on many different tasks	5

Value Group 1:
Importance in My Ideal Job

1. Being able to help others	
2. Pursuing new ideas	
3. Solving complex problems	
4. Freedom and independence	
5. Working with a well-respected organization	
6. Financial rewards	
7. Workplace that is conveniently located	
8. Working with a talented group of people	
9. Working on many different tasks	

Value Group 2:
Importance in My Ideal Job

10. Being able to make a real difference in people's lives	
11. Creating beauty	
12. Not working on routine tasks	
13. Absence of control from others	
14. Recognition for my achievements	
15. Making a lot of money	
16. Having the kind of traveling schedule I want	
17. Working in a team environment	
18. Every day presenting new and different kinds of challenges	

Value Group 3:
Importance in My Ideal Job

19. Making the world a better place	
20. Being unconventional	
21. Building strategic plans	
22. A good deal of autonomy	
23. An important job title	
24. Being financially secure	
25. Geographic location	
26. Building quality relationships with coworkers	
27. Exciting and adventuresome activities	

Value Group 4:
Importance in My Ideal Job

28. Concern about the welfare of others	
29. Solving problems that do not have clear answers	
30. A great deal of intellectual stimulation	
31. Being held accountable for results, but able to do it my way	
32. Working in a competitive environment	
33. Job security	
34. A nice office and other amenities	
35. Daily working with the general public	
36. Changing responsibilities to keep my interest	

Value Group 5:
Importance in My Ideal Job

37. Adding spiritual meaning to life	
38. Turning different, even unusual, ideas into reality	
39. Treating complex work problems like a chess game to be mastered	
40. Not being told how to do things	
41. Influencing others	
42. Working in a safe environment	
43. An organized workplace	
44. Having good relationships with my coworkers	
45. A lot of variety	

STEP 2: First, place your ranking for each item in the boxes provided below. Next, add all the ranking scores together within each category to achieve a total score for each of the nine values categories: social concerns, creative opportunity, intellectual stimulation, freedom and independence, status and prestige, security and economic benefit, the work environment, social relations at work, and variety at work.

Value	Item number	Your ranking (1-9)
SOCIAL CONCERNS	1	
	10	
	19	
	28	
	37	
	Total Score=	

Value	Item number	Your ranking (1-9)
STATUS AND PRESTIGE	5	
	14	
	23	
	32	
	41	
	Total Score=	

Value	Item number	Your ranking (1-9)
CREATIVE OPPORTUNITY	2	
	11	
	20	
	29	
	38	
	Total Score=	

Value	Item number	Your ranking (1-9)
FREEDOM AND INDEPENDENCE	4	
	13	
	22	
	31	
	40	
	Total Score=	

Value	Item number	Your ranking (1-9)
INTELLECTUAL STIMULATION	3	
	12	
	21	
	30	
	39	
	Total Score=	

Value	Item number	Your ranking (1-9)
SECURITY AND ECONOMIC BENEFIT	6	
	15	
	24	
	33	
	42	
	Total Score=	

Value	Item number	Your ranking (1–9)
THE WORK ENVIRONMENT	7	
	16	
	25	
	34	
	43	
	Total Score=	

Value	Item number	Your ranking (1–9)
SOCIAL RELATIONS AT WORK	8	
	17	
	26	
	35	
	44	
	Total Score=	

Value	Item number	Your ranking (1–9)
VARIETY AT WORK	9	
	18	
	27	
	36	
	45	
	Total Score=	

STEP 3: Record the total scores from each of the nine value categories in Step 2 in the second column on the following page.

STEP 4: Next, give the lowest score (total scores from Step 2) your number one ranking in column three, your next lowest score a number two ranking, and so on until you have ranked each value category 1 through 9. The highest total score receives a ranking of 9. (If one or more of the categories are tied, reread the items within each of those categories; then simply rank the categories.)

Overall Ranking of World of Work Values

Value	Overall Value Score (Total score from Step 2)	Overall Ranking of Values
Social Concerns		
Creative Opportunity		
Intellectual Stimulation		
Freedom and Independence		
Status and Prestige		
Security and Economic Benefit		
The Work Environment		
Social Relations at Work		
Variety at Work		

STEP 5: After completing your ranking, turn to the Vocational Identity Summary in Appendix A and record your top five (most important) and bottom four (least important) Work Values in the spaces provided.

EXERCISE 3
Your Best Friend's Questions
About Your Ideal Job

• •

The last chapter began by saying "it's time to dream." This exercise asks you to do just that—to dream about your ideal job. Of course, with dreams you can create any ideas and images you like. So, imagine that you recently located your *ideal* job. You never thought you could enjoy any situation and position as well as you do this one.

Now think about the person who is your *very best* friend. This best friend just heard that you have a new job and sent you a note asking you to describe this new job. In the note this friend asked several questions about your new position.

You are now sitting down to write a return letter answering each of your best friend's questions. (Use the space provided or an extra sheet of notebook paper to answer the questions.)

- Where is your new position and company located? Why is this so ideal?

- How would you describe this ideal company?

- What do the company's facilities look like?

- What kind of corporate culture and management style are found in this company?

- Tell me about your work environment: how much travel do you do, how do they make decisions about promotions, what are the other workers like?

- What is your new boss like?

- What is your compensation and what kind of benefits do you have?

- What is the *single best thing* about your new job?

Unlike the other exercises, you will not record any information from Exercise 3 on the Vocational Identity Summary page. You will return to this page after you receive a job offer as one of the means of evaluating the offer. More will be said about this exercise during the discussion regarding negotiating in Chapter 12.

WRITING YOUR LIFE'S MISSION STATEMENT

As you read the next several paragraphs, I'd like to ask you to become very involved. Please do not simply read the words, but instead try to visualize the images as vividly as possible. At the end of several of the sentences you will see the word **PAUSE** written in bold type as this one is. When you see **PAUSE**, stop your reading for about 15 to 30 seconds, and perhaps as many as 60 seconds for the last paragraph. Close your eyes and think about the images around you. What does the room look like? What is the temperature? How do you feel at this moment? What color is the carpet? The more detail you add to this exercise, the more powerful it will become for you.

The telephone call

It's 8:30 a.m., and you just poured a second cup of coffee. You're feeling particularly harried this morning. Details, deadlines, and customer demands have never been greater in this job. You ran out of the house fairly quickly this morning, stopped by the cleaners, dropped off the kids at school, and then fought the traffic on I-something or other. Now you're surveying your surroundings. The computer printout is lying on your desk waiting for your evaluation, the copy machine is buzzing in the outer office, you need to read three interoffice memos and write two others, and you know that plenty of phone mail messages need your attention as soon as possible. **PAUSE**

Just as you start to look through your in-box, the telephone rings on your direct line. Answering it, you're surprised to hear your physician's voice. As you greet each other with typical pleasantries, you feel mildly nervous, wondering why the doctor would call you personally. **PAUSE**

After the greeting the doctor gets right down to business. It seems your results from the company's required routine physical are anything but routine. Indeed, your tests indicate that although you have no symptoms, you have advanced cancer—likely terminal. You immediately feel certain the tests' results are wrong. Surely, they mixed up your test tube with someone else's. But as the doctor calmly describes the results in detail and asks you to come into the office immediately, it slowly begins to sink in. You knew that life would end someday, but not now, not this soon. **PAUSE**

As you hang up the phone, you realize that you must begin to tell your loved ones and friends. As you consider the list of people you must contact, you think first of your spouse and your children, then of siblings and parents. Then coworkers and other friends from the community and religious organizations to which you belong come to mind. Suddenly, you start to evaluate your life as you have never evaluated it before. How have you spent your time? If they were completely honest, what would each of the people on your contact list say about their interactions with you? What have your actions said about what is most important to you? To what have you dedicated your life—for what purpose? **PAUSE**

Although facing life's finiteness head-on is always somewhat uncomfortable, I hope that as you reflected upon the preceding scenario you were able to feel a sense of satisfaction with your current life. Many people don't, however. Unfortunately, most of us do not consider such weighty matters on a daily basis. In fact, our rushed lives seem to drive our actions more than our inner purpose, with the urgent pushing out the important—the proverbial tail wagging the dog.

The fact that life is finite, coupled with the fact that some things mean more to you than others, makes creating a meaningful life's mission statement an extremely valuable undertaking. By carefully considering the things that matter most to you and weighing their relative value, you can make choices about how you spend your time, interpret events—in short, direct your life. Earlier in the chapter I said that you should not complete the exercises in terms of what your values should be but rather what your values truly are. I did not mean that you should not think about how you would like to construct your future. Indeed, writing a personally significant mission statement hinges primarily on your success in capturing a vision for your future that is consistent with your core values. As the old saying goes, "Aim at nothing and you're bound to hit it." However, if you go about your day-to-day activities in a manner consistent with this vision, then you will move toward this desired state. As you listen carefully for clues to your ideal career destination, you will find that some of the strongest indications of its origin are found in the sense of purpose that already resides inside you.

Careers are but one of life's important pursuits

As I said in the last chapter, I will not tell you what your purpose should be. I will, however, suggest several things for you to think about as you consider your purpose. All of us have a number of activities and relationships that engage our efforts. We play the roles of parent, child, worker, leader, and lifelong learner, among others. I call the effort we expend in these various roles "life's pursuits." You, and only you, decide which pursuits are most important to you, what you hope to achieve, and the amount of time and energy you will invest in each pursuit. You cannot avoid these choices.

I feel strongly that defining one's purpose is the most important endeavor that any of us take on. Why? Because every action in which we engage reflects our purpose, whether we've given it much thought or not. Our purpose may be clear or unclear, structured or haphazard, recognized or strange. Regardless, how we elect to spend our time and the activities in which we choose to participate demonstrate our values and our current purpose. From deciding whether or not to coach the Little League team to selecting a presidential candidate for whom to vote to choosing a career, our purpose serves as the guide to our behavior.

Below you will find a seven-step process for identifying your purpose and writing your life's mission statement. Regardless of which other activities and exercises you participate in or which questions you ask when choosing a career or deciding about a particular job, you should always test these choices against your mission. Ask yourself this simple but important question: "Is this choice consistent with my mission?" If not, make a different choice. In the end, you can rest in the comfort of knowing you are a person of integrity who lives in harmony with those things most vital to you.

The first five steps in Exercise 4 will take about an hour or so for you to complete. In the fifth step you will create a draft of your mission statement. I suggest you stop at the end of this fifth step for two days to think about the drafted statement. As you begin, you should find a quiet place to work on this exercise where you will not be interrupted. Find as peaceful a spot as possible that will allow you to contemplate deeply.

EXERCISE 4
A Step-by-Step Process
for Defining Purpose

Step 1: Identify pursuits and desired outcomes for each pursuit

Each day you engage in a variety of activities, such as going to the grocery store, making deposits at the bank, going to work, and making choices that affect your home life. Each of these activities connects to a larger issue. These larger issues are life's pursuits. For example, you may leave work a little early to make the school play in which your son or daughter has a part. You are probably not attending the production for its theatrical quality. Instead, you are going to support your child and family. In this example, going to the play is an activity connected to the pursuit of Home and Family.

Following is a list of eight of these larger issues or pursuits. Read through this list of pursuits. If you need more categories, create them. If a category does not fit your needs, simply disregard it. Then take 30 seconds or so and think of yourself in the future; imagine yourself toward the end of your life.
PAUSE

Next, consider each pursuit. Do not merely think about it, but attempt to feel deeply what you hope you have accomplished in each of these pursuits during the course of your life. For each pursuit, describe in a sentence or two what you have accomplished at the end of your life. Be candid, genuine, and write from a heartfelt perspective.

Example of Completed Step 1 from Exercise 4

Pursuit	Statement: What I Accomplished (My Desired Outcome)
Home and Family Life	I actively made my family my number one priority. I showed my love to my family by my actions as much as my words. Each member of my family achieved more and is happier because of my encouragement.
Work and Career	I accomplished as much, in quantity and quality, as I possibly could using the gifts that God gave me.
Personal Pursuits	I did and continue to do some exercises and play some music every day.
Material Pursuits	I have all the material things I need and learned to want things that are consistent with my values.

Pursuit	Statement: What I Accomplished (My Desired Outcome)
Health	I have been and continue to be healthy. I continue to take care of myself through exercise and healthy eating.
Relationships	I've tried to treat people the way I wish to be treated. I have deep, long-lasting relationships with a number of people. They know that I can be counted on to help whenever a need arises.
Community	I participate in the community. I help make (my town) a better place to live and to raise families. One of the primary ways I accomplish this is through being a good neighbor.
Spiritual and Religious	I continue to seek to become the man God desires for me to be.

Step 2: Transfer your responses to the Mission Statement Worksheet

Now, please transfer the pursuits that pertain to you to the Mission Statement Worksheet that follows. Next, also transfer the one- or two-sentence description of your desired outcomes for each of these pursuits.

Step 3: Identify the life role and the key relationships related to each pursuit

Each pursuit involves you, of course, but it almost always involves others, too. For the second part of this exercise you should identify key people related to each of your major pursuits and your relationships, or the roles you play, with those people. For example, if you are married and have children, then your spouse and children are key people tied to the home and family life pursuit. Your role with your spouse is either husband or wife and is parent with your children. At work you may play the role of boss, worker, engineer, etc. The important point is to connect the roles you play to the key relationships you identify.

First, try to identify at least one key relationship for each of your pursuits and write the name of the person in column 3 on the Mission Statement Worksheet. You may not always be able to come up with a key relationship for every pursuit. If not, you may wish to think of the pursuit as *me focused* (see example). After identifying a key relationship, list in column 4 the role that you play in this pursuit with this person.

Step 4: Construct statements for each person

Once again, place yourself forward in time, near the end of your life. Begin with the first person listed as a key relationship in column 3. Construct a statement that you deeply desire this person would make about you toward the end of your life. After writing this statement, move on to the next key relationship on the worksheet and do the same. Continue this process until you've written statements for each relationship.

Step 1: My Pursuits

Pursuit	Statement: What I Accomplished (My Desired Outcome)
Home and Family Life	
Work and Career	
Personal Pursuits	
Material Pursuits	
Health	
Relationships	
Community	
Spiritual and Religious	
Other	
Other	

Example

Mission Statement Worksheet

My Pursuits	Desired Future Outcome	Key Relation-ships	Life Role	Statement from Key Relation-ship
Home and Family Life	I actively made my family my number one priority. I showed my love to my family by my actions as much as my words. Each member of my family achieved more and is happier because of my encouragement.	Kathy	Husband	He has always been faithful, placing my needs above his.
		Lisa	Father	He encouraged me to become everything I could be and undoubtedly loves me unconditionally.
		Bill	Brother	His faith in me caused me to believe in myself.
Work and Career	I accomplished as much, in quantity and quality, as I possibly could using the gifts that God gave me.	Joe	Colleague	I have always been able to count on him to give me an honest reading of his thoughts. He supported me in many ways.
Material Pursuits	I have all the material things I need and learned to want things that are consistent with my values.	Kathy	Husband	He carefully comanaged our finances so that we felt secure, could provide for our children, and were able to give to others.
Spiritual and Religious	I continue to seek to become the man God desires me to be.	Lisa	Father—Spiritual Guide	He gave me an appreciation for the love of God and the need to lean on Him first and myself second.

Mission Statement Worksheet (Exercise 4)

My Pursuits	Desired Future Outcome	Key Relation-ships	Life-Role	Statement from Key Relation-ship

Step 5: Write your Mission Statement

When you are confident that you have considered all the pursuits in life that are vital to you and that you have completed the Mission Statement Worksheet for each pursuit, you are ready to draft your life's mission statement. Read over your worksheet. On a sheet of notebook paper, write a draft of a statement that captures your purpose. Although you can write the statement in any format you wish, it should be exciting and inspirational; be creative, be sincere, and be very, very honest with yourself.

You should now put the statement away for two days. I suggest that you show it to no one; but over the next two days periodically think about the issues you considered in the first five steps. The following page shows two examples of mission statements.

Examples
Life Mission Statements

Randy

To strive everyday to achieve the highest goals and values in both my personal and my business life. To always take full responsibility and be aware of how my daily actions are perceived by my wife and sons so they will be proud of how I contributed to their lives. I will live my life so that if I find out that today is my last, I would have no regrets.

Susan

To nurture a relationship with God, communicate to Him daily in prayer, and recognize and appreciate His blessings.

To celebrate the joyousness that my family brings me by connecting with my parents and my brother weekly.

To build emotional intimacy and trust with my boyfriend by facing challenging issues head-on.

To confront the future.

To control less and listen more.

To work less and live more.

To create the unimagined.

To have more solitude.

To broaden my circle of friends.

To volunteer my time to someone who desperately needs it.

To sacrifice something selfish.

To challenge my fears and grow from the discomfort.

To enjoy a higher quality of life by maintaining optimum health.

To preserve the child in me by daring to ask bold questions, acting silly, playing when I shouldn't, taking naps, indulging in treats, and breaking the rules.

To laugh and dream daily.

Step 6: Wait two days, and then review your statement

After two days, find a quiet, contemplative place once again. Reread your statement. People often ask, "How do you know when it's finished?" First of all, it's never completely finished. You can and should modify it anytime your heartfelt desires create a need to change it. When evaluating the usefulness of the statement, you should ask yourself these two questions: "Does the statement provide both *guidance* and *direction*?" and "Does it genuinely provide real *inspiration* for my life?" If the answers to these questions are no, or if the statement does not get to you at the core of your being, please write it again. Continue to rewrite the statement until you can respond positively to these two questions. When you answer yes to these statements you have created a meaningful mission statement and should move on to Step 7.

> **"Man is a mystery: if you spend your entire life trying to puzzle it out, then do not say that you have wasted your time. I occupy myself with this mystery, because I want to be a man."**
>
> Fyodor Dostoevsky

Step 7: Record your mission statement on the vocational identity summary page

As with most of the self-assessment exercises, please turn to the VIS in Appendix A and write your mission statement in the space provided. Remember, this statement provides guidance. You should evaluate all career questions, indeed all decisions, in light of your purpose.

You've done a great deal of important work in this chapter. By identifying your core values and defining your purpose, you answered the first question introduced in Chapter 2: "What really matters to you?" You filled the first, and the most significant, piece of the Vocational Identity puzzle. In Chapter 4, you will fit the next piece into the puzzle when you answer the question "What do you do really well?"

C H A P T E R

4

Recognize Your Marketable Job Skills

"Let each man pass his days in that
wherein his skill is greatest."
Sextus Propertius

MARKETING YOUR
VOCATIONAL IDENTITY

Why do companies hire employees? The answer is pretty simple: to further their aims. When the Acme Widget company needs to design new products it hires engineers, to build the new widgets it hires production people, to sell the widgets it hires salespeople, and so forth. It seeks out people with knowledge and skills and the right traits to perform a job in a way that causes the organization to succeed. Throughout the first three chapters I encouraged you to dream about what you really want to do; to find a career about which you feel real passion. You will certainly find that same theme running through this chapter as well. However, as you move to fill in the job skills piece of the voca-

tional identity puzzle, you will need to integrate your desires and talents with the needs of the marketplace.

Because potential employers won't hire you simply because you're excited about a particular career, pose the question presented above in a more personal way: "Why will a company hire me?" If you elect to try self-employment, I'll discuss this option in Chapter 13, change the question slightly and ask "Why will customers do business with me?" Looking sincerely at a job interviewer and enthusiastically exclaiming, "I want this job because I believe it is close to my ideal destination and will deliver a lot of career treasure!" will almost certainly not land you the position. Employers will hire you for one reason only: the benefit you will bring to the company. One of the primary ways you will deliver benefits to a company, or to customers, is through your knowledge and job skills. So, understanding what skills you possess, and then presenting them in an appealingly package to potential employers, is an essential part of getting a job.

But my goal for you, and I hope by now your goal as well, is not merely to provide techniques to help you find a job, but instead, to assist you in finding the *best* job; the job that most closely mirrors your vocational identity. This chapter will indeed give you exercises and advice about identifying and then marketing your job skills to potential employers. But along with these activities you will also find an exercise that provides additional clues as to the location of your ideal career destination by helping you find your treasure-yielding skills.

JOB SECURITY STILL EXISTS

Given all the recent restructuring and downsizing and the end of the psychological contract, as mentioned in the first chapter, most people think that job security no longer exists. That's simply not true. Job security definitely exists—you'll just find it in a new location. Instead of finding job security inside the confines of some corporation, you'll find it in the marketplace—if you possess the right skills. The new job security equation in Figure 5 plainly makes the point. For people with the right transferable skills and the ability to market those skills, the future is incredibly bright, the opportunities endless. For those few who still cling to the old notion that "the company will take care of me," rough waters are very possibly ahead. I feel strongly that regardless of the career path you select, you should constantly

seek opportunities to improve your skills. Whether through formal education or other training, or through particular job experiences, better skills equal better opportunities. Regardless of how you develop them, remember the value of learning the higher-order skills.

WHAT ARE JOB SKILLS?

Before I give you a definition of job skills, let me say that you have quite a few of them. Most people feel that they really don't possess a lot of marketable job skills. This feeling comes primarily from a misunderstanding of what is meant by *job skills*. Not surprisingly, without a proper understanding of what job skills really are, the vast majority of people find it difficult to identify and subsequently package their marketable job skills for potential employers. However, as you will see as you go through the skill-identification exercises in this chapter, you do possess a good number of useful and marketable job skills.

Let me start defining job skills by telling you several things they are not. Job skills are not abilities. Abilities are innate potential to perform. For example, if your IQ is high, this is an ability, not a skill. Abilities are wonderful, but they do not necessarily translate into useful or marketable benefits to organizations. Let's take the

FIGURE 5
The New Job Security Equation

JOB SECURITY ≠ SOME COMPANY
JOB SECURITY = MARKETABLE JOB SKILLS
+ JOB-FINDING SKILLS

high IQ example a little further. Besides being bright, suppose you have very good fine motor skills; that is, you can manipulate small objects quite well. Let's also assume you are very mechanical and inquisitive about scientific matters. Given these things, you probably have the ability to become a surgeon. However, if your Aunt Mildred needs her gallbladder removed next week, chances are that she probably will not call on your services. Why? Because even though you most likely have the ability, without attending medical school, participating in an internship, etc., you have not developed the skills necessary to perform surgery on Aunt Mildred or anyone else.

The second and perhaps most common mistake made by people attempting to identify their job skills is confusing traits with skills. If you are energetic, seek achievement, enjoy taking risks, and are outgoing, good for you. While these characteristics represent important traits that significantly affect both your work performance and your career satisfaction, they are not job skills. These traits or behaviors come from your personality, and I will discuss them in much more detail in the next chapter.

So what are job skills? First, people acquire the knowledge and behaviors known as job skills; they are not innate abilities. Second, organizations need many of these particular bits of knowledge and behaviors and are willing to pay for them. I think it's useful to consider three types of job skills: job-specific skills, transferable skills, and treasure-yielding skills.

Job-specific skills

Sometimes called technical skills, these learned behaviors are specific to particular jobs and occupations. For example, a physical therapist providing electrical stimulation therapy to a patient demonstrates the use of a job-specific skill. These skills are only transferable when the job requirements in one occupation are identical in another occupation. These skills can be very useful and potentially quite valuable to employers; however, their marketability is often limited to a narrow range of jobs. In many cases, employees can quickly learn job-specific skills; for example, the skill and knowledge needed to complete paperwork specific to some company's requirement. In this sort of case the economic value of this skill is not great.

Transferable skills (marketable skills)

While some job skills are only useful for a particular job, company, or occupation, most job skills are useful in other settings. If you can transfer a job skill used in one setting to a different setting or context, that skill is a *transferable skill*. If you possess the skill to persuade others, for example, this is a transferable skill because it is useful in a wide variety of occupational settings. I also refer to these as marketable skills because many different employers fervently seek the benefits these skills bring to their organizations. In addition to their marketing value, because these skills are useful in a variety of settings, transferable skills provide you with one of the primary tools necessary to change careers.

Sydney Fine, while working for the Department of Labor, developed the best-known scheme for categorizing job tasks. His method places all skills into one of three categories: data, people, or things. The *Dictionary of Occupational Titles* uses this scheme to classify the task requirements of more than 20,000 jobs.

Figure 6 shows his method for organizing skills. Take a moment to survey the table. Which skills do you possess? Which ones are you using on your current or last job? Which ones do you really enjoy using?

The data, people, things model makes several very good points about transferable skills. As you can see, skills exist in lower-to-higher orders. The lower the number, the more complex the skill. Each more complex skill requires mastery of the less complex skills plus new knowledge and learning. In other words, gaining higher-level job skills is somewhat like climbing a ladder. In order to reach the top of the ladder, you must climb each of the lower rungs along the way. Several valuable things make acquiring higher-level skills worthwhile. In general, the more complex the transferable skills you possess, the less competition you will have for jobs, the more compensation you will receive, and the more freedom your employer will (or should) give you to operate on your own.

Identifying your transferable skills

The vast majority of people find that while the data, people, things model provides insight into understanding transferable skills, it does not provide sufficient detail for self-assessment purposes. Developing a clear understanding of your skills is a critical element in completing the vocational identity puzzle. Exercise 5 presents you with a list of 100 transferable skills. Your task for this exercise is to determine how well you perform each of these skills.

You may be saying something like a young man I know as he considered dramatically changing his career path in his late twenties: "Well, I'm very good at persuading others, in fact I have been extremely successful in sales, but you know what? I've *really* hated every minute I've spent in that career." Good point— no, mega point. Of course, being good at something and enjoying it are certainly two different issues. However, in this first skills activity you should not try to determine whether or not you enjoy using these skills or whether you would like being involved in a career where you would make use of them. You'll get to those issues later. In Exercise 5 you will simply generate an inventory of your transferable skills. The point of this exercise is to help you recognize the many job skill resources you have to draw

FIGURE 6

Data	People	Things
0—Synthesizing	0—Mentoring	0—Setting up
1—Coordinating, Innovating	1—Negotiating	1—Precision working
2—Analyzing	2—Instructing	2—Operating, Controlling
3—Analyzing	3—Supervising	3—Driving, Operating
4—Compiling, Computing	4—Diverting, Persuading	4—Manipulating
5—Copying	5—Speaking, Signaling	5—Tending
6—Comparing	6—Serving, Taking Instructions, Helping	6—Feeding, Offbearing

upon. You can market to potential employers any of your transferable skills you choose.

Please read the list of 100 transferable skills below. In the Performance Rating column, rank yourself in terms of how well you believe you perform each skill (1 being the lowest score and 5 being the highest). Use the five-point scale below to determine your ratings. You should not rate yourself against anyone else or against any standard. Simply decide how much of the skill *you* feel you possess. Do *not* consider whether you enjoy using the skill at this point or whether you will seek a job that requires use of the skill. **Important:** You should rate no more than 20 skills with a 5. You may use as many of the other numbers as you like.

EXERCISE 5

	Marketable Skills Assessment			Treasure-Yielding Checklist (from Exercise 6)							
1 = cannot perform this skill **2** = perform this skill at a low level **3** = perform this skill at a moderate level **4** = perform this skill at an above-average level **5** = perform this skill at a high level; it's one of my strongest skills				**Achievement Number**							
#	**Transferable Skill**	**Performance Rating**		**1**	**2**	**3**	**4**	**5**	**6**	**7**	**Total**
1	Acting, entertaining, amusing others	1 2 3 4 5									
2	Administering activities and programs	1 2 3 4 5									
3	Agricultural knowledge and skills	1 2 3 4 5									
4	Analyzing information	1 2 3 4 5									
5	Anticipating/visualizing the future	1 2 3 4 5									
6	Asking questions of people	1 2 3 4 5									
7	Building things	1 2 3 4 5									
8	Building and maintaining rapport with others	1 2 3 4 5									
9	Calculating numbers	1 2 3 4 5									
10	Carpentry skills	1 2 3 4 5									
11	Classifying and organizing information	1 2 3 4 5									
12	Coaching others	1 2 3 4 5									
13	Compiling information	1 2 3 4 5									
14	Computer programming	1 2 3 4 5									
15	Construction of buildings	1 2 3 4 5									
16	Coordinating meetings and events	1 2 3 4 5									
17	Coping with stress	1 2 3 4 5									
18	Correspondence with others	1 2 3 4 5									

Marketable Skills Assessment		Treasure-Yielding Checklist (from Exercise 6)							

1 = cannot perform this skill
2 = perform this skill at a low level
3 = perform this skill at a moderate level
4 = perform this skill at an above-average level
5 = perform this skill at a high level; it's one of my strongest skills

Achievement Number

#	Transferable Skill	Performance Rating	1	2	3	4	5	6	7	Total
19	Counseling others for improvement	1 2 3 4 5								
20	Creating new solutions	1 2 3 4 5								
21	Dealing with scientific data	1 2 3 4 5								
22	Dealing with difficult people	1 2 3 4 5								
23	Decision making	1 2 3 4 5								
24	Delegating to others	1 2 3 4 5								
25	Demonstrating ideas or products	1 2 3 4 5								
26	Designing systems to manage information/ data	1 2 3 4 5								
27	Developing plans to reach objectives	1 2 3 4 5								
28	Editing others' writing	1 2 3 4 5								
29	Evaluating and screening people for selection	1 2 3 4 5								
30	Evaluating the effectiveness of program and projects	1 2 3 4 5								
31	Event promotion	1 2 3 4 5								
32	Expediting or handling materials	1 2 3 4 5								
33	Expense budgeting	1 2 3 4 5								
34	Facilitating group discussion	1 2 3 4 5								
35	Financial investing	1 2 3 4 5								
36	Finding missing information	1 2 3 4 5								
37	Fixing mechanical things	1 2 3 4 5								
38	Following directions	1 2 3 4 5								
39	Foreign language skills	1 2 3 4 5								
40	Fund-raising	1 2 3 4 5								
41	Generating new ideas	1 2 3 4 5								
42	Giving advice as a consultant	1 2 3 4 5								
43	Handling many interruptions	1 2 3 4 5								
44	Inspecting equipment and other objects	1 2 3 4 5								
45	Interpersonal skills	1 2 3 4 5								
46	Interviewing	1 2 3 4 5								
47	Inventing new things and ideas	1 2 3 4 5								
48	Keeping financial records	1 2 3 4 5								

| | | | Marketable Skills Assessment | | | | Treasure-Yielding Checklist (from Exercise 6) | | | | | | | |

1 = cannot perform this skill
2 = perform this skill at a low level
3 = perform this skill at a moderate level
4 = perform this skill at an above-average level
5 = perform this skill at a high level; it's one of my strongest skills

Achievement Number

#	Transferable Skill	Performance Rating	1	2	3	4	5	6	7	Total
49	Knowledge and skills with animals	1 2 3 4 5								
50	Leading by persuading others to follow your vision	1 2 3 4 5								
51	Library research	1 2 3 4 5								
52	Listening	1 2 3 4 5								
53	Making charts, diagrams, and figures	1 2 3 4 5								
54	Making financial decisions	1 2 3 4 5								
55	Managing people	1 2 3 4 5								
56	Managing customer complaints	1 2 3 4 5								
57	Managing records	1 2 3 4 5								
58	Meeting new people	1 2 3 4 5								
59	Monitoring accuracy	1 2 3 4 5								
60	Motivating/inspiring others	1 2 3 4 5								
61	Musical skills—playing an instrument, singing, or conducting	1 2 3 4 5								
62	Negotiating	1 2 3 4 5								
63	Networking with people	1 2 3 4 5								
64	Number manipulation	1 2 3 4 5								
65	Operating equipment and machinery	1 2 3 4 5								
66	Painting, refinishing	1 2 3 4 5								
67	Persuading people	1 2 3 4 5								
68	Physical handling of materials	1 2 3 4 5								
69	Picking up subtle meaning in written or spoken words	1 2 3 4 5								
70	Presenting plans to others	1 2 3 4 5								
71	Problem solving	1 2 3 4 5								
72	Public speaking	1 2 3 4 5								
73	Putting together agendas	1 2 3 4 5								
74	Putting mechanical things together	1 2 3 4 5								
75	Reading through large quantities of information	1 2 3 4 5								
76	Recruiting people to join an organization	1 2 3 4 5								
77	Remembering things accurately	1 2 3 4 5								

Marketable Skills Assessment		Treasure-Yielding Checklist (from Exercise 6)							

1 = cannot perform this skill
2 = perform this skill at a low level
3 = perform this skill at a moderate level
4 = perform this skill at an above-average level
5 = perform this skill at a high level; it's one of my strongest skills

Achievement Number

#	Transferable Skill	Performance Rating					1	2	3	4	5	6	7	Total
78	Researching information	1	2	3	4	5								
79	Resolving conflicts among others	1	2	3	4	5								
80	Searching for the causes of problems	1	2	3	4	5								
81	Selling products or services	1	2	3	4	5								
82	Serving others	1	2	3	4	5								
83	Setting up equipment	1	2	3	4	5								
84	Sewing or weaving	1	2	3	4	5								
85	Solving disputes between people	1	2	3	4	5								
86	Sorting or filing	1	2	3	4	5								
87	Statistical analysis	1	2	3	4	5								
88	Strategic planning for organizational needs	1	2	3	4	5								
89	Supervising subordinates	1	2	3	4	5								
90	Synthesizing, integrating different parts into a whole	1	2	3	4	5								
91	Teaching/instructing	1	2	3	4	5								
92	Understanding human interactions	1	2	3	4	5								
93	Understanding organizational politics	1	2	3	4	5								
94	Using numerical data	1	2	3	4	5								
95	Verbalizing ideas	1	2	3	4	5								
96	Visualizing new ways of doing things	1	2	3	4	5								
97	Working long hours	1	2	3	4	5								
98	Working with details	1	2	3	4	5								
99	Working with children	1	2	3	4	5								
100	Writing reports	1	2	3	4	5								

After completing this exercise, turn to the Vocational Identity Summary (VIS) page in Appendix A and record your 20 strongest skills. Begin with those items rated 5, then move on to those rated 4, and so forth until you reach 20. If you have too many of one number, e.g., ten 5s and twenty-three 4s, simply rank order the skills you feel you perform the best, 1 through 20 and record on the VIS.

After completing Exercise 5, you now have a reasonable idea about what kind of transferable skills you have to draw upon. But as the statement from the young man (who was terrific at sales but disliked it enormously) shows, there is more to career satisfaction than just doing something well. Frankly, this young man's experience is somewhat unusual. A remarkable correlation exists between doing things well and enjoying them. While it's not at all clear whether people usually enjoy things because they do them well, or whether they do things well because they enjoy them, the fact remains that people often find enjoyment and proficiency together in the world of work. One of the best ways to discover the transferable skills you most enjoy using is to explore times in the past when you used them to accomplish something particularly significant to you.

Treasure-yielding skills (marketable + enjoyable job skills)

You are unique and full of special talents. In your past, you have shown these talents to the outer world. "When was that?" you ask. When you think back to your moments of greatest achievement, you will identify times you made use of the transferable skills you most enjoy practicing, the skills the world most needs to receive, and the times when you were engaged in activities that yielded an abundance of career treasure. By systematically studying these past achievements, you will discover patterns of skills that you use again and again to create these meaningful and significant times in your life. And here is the best part. Once these treasure-yielding skills are identified and you

decide to use them to demonstrate your special excellence, you will create a better future.

Occasionally, when I take an individual or a group through an exercise to identify their past achievements, people feel as though they really haven't accomplished anything great. Oh, but you have. The first thing you must do to successfully identify your treasure-yielding skills is disregard what others feel is important. Others' feelings are simply irrelevant in this process. During Steps 1 through 3, you must think primarily with your heart. If you tend to be highly analytical, evaluating information against objective standards, suspend that practice until you get to Step 4. In this activity, you should define an achievement's degree of greatness by how *you feel* about the event. Exercise 6 provides a method to identify these achievements and then extract the transferable skills used in bringing them about.

The experiences you identify as achievements can come from any period in your life. They may range from helping someone home with groceries when you were in grade school to hitting a home run in Little League to starting up a new manufacturing plant to winning a Senate seat. Your task is to identify events in your life that you consider important, valuable, and enjoyable—achievements that have a sense of joy and satisfaction attached to them.

A question people often ask is "Why should I spend time learning about what I really love to do—don't employers just want useful job skills?" Good question. As you will see when you get to the end of Exercise 6, you will evaluate your achievements against a list of transferable or marketable skills. In fact, it's the same list you used to determine your skill resources in Exercise 5. The two exercises deliver different results, however: what you *can do* versus what you *want to do*. While Exercise 5 provides you with a list of your marketable capabilities, Exercise 6 gives you a list of transferable skills that are not only marketable, but that you love to use and result in achieving things you consider important.

EXERCISE 6
Treasure-Yielding Skills Assessment

Step 1: List your achievements

Think back over your life. What do you consider an important achievement? What life events delivered satisfaction and joy and do you feel pride in remembering? On a sheet of notebook paper, write down a couple of words or a short phrase that captures the first event you recall. This does not mean that this is your most important achievement, just the one that came to mind first. Continue this process until you have generated at least ten to twelve achievements. If you have difficulty thinking of achievements, divide your life into ten-year chunks: e.g., 1 year old to 10 years old, 10 to 20 years old, etc. Try to identify several achievements for each of these time periods. Spend about 30 minutes on this step.

Step 2: Prioritize your list

As a next step, review the list of achievements you created in Step 1. Now spend a few minutes prioritizing the achievements. Of the ten to twelve achievements on this list, which seven hold the most significance for you? Place a check mark next to the seven achievements you feel are most significant. Next, find the achievement about which you feel the most pride and satisfaction and place the number 1 beside it. Continue this process until you have rank ordered your seven most significant achievements.

Step 3: Write the story

On seven sheets of notebook paper, you will now write a brief description of your seven most significant achievements. For the first achievement on your list, write the words or phrase describing the event at the top of the first page. Next, write a one- or two-paragraph description of the achievement by answering the following four questions:

- When did the achievement occur?
- What actions did I take and what did I accomplish?
- What hurdles or barriers did I overcome?
- Why do I consider this an achievement?

Continue this process until you describe the remaining six achievements. Here is a sample of an achievement story.

Example

Leading the sales force in sales and profit in the same month

Although this achievement occurred more than fifteen years ago, it is still fresh in my mind. I was part of a straight-commission sales force in the retail furniture business. Our store had twenty-four salespeople— the best in the business. I was taught that good salespeople sell the product—not the price. However, we were allowed to deeply discount the furniture in order to make the sale. There were a lot of sales contests, cash and other prizes for the salesperson who sold the most furniture each month. We also received prizes for the salesperson who delivered the most profit. Although this store had been in business for more than thirty years, no salesperson had ever delivered the highest sales and the highest profit in the same month. That is, until I did it. I don't think I ever worked harder, but I really enjoyed being able to show that you can sell the product and deliver high volume at the same time.

Step 4: Find your treasure-yielding skills

Read the first achievement story you created. Now, return to the marketable skill list you used in Exercise 5. Once again, go down the list of 100 transferable skills. Each time you encounter a skill you used in the course of completing this achievement, place a check in the column labeled 1. Next, read the second story and place a check in column 2 each time you find a skill you used during this achievement. Continue this process for the remaining five stories.

Now, for each skill, add the check marks across the table to obtain a total number of check marks for that skill. Here is an example.

Marketable Skills Assessment			**Treasure-Yielding Checklist (from Exercise 6)**							
1 = cannot perform this skill **2** = perform this skill at a low level **3** = perform this skill at a moderate level **4** = perform this skill at an above-average level **5** = perform this skill at a high level; it's one of my strongest skills			**Achievement Number**							
# **Transferable Skill**	**Performance Rating**		**1**	**2**	**3**	**4**	**5**	**6**	**7**	**Total**
1	Acting, entertaining, amusing others	1 2 3 4 5		√	√		√	√	√	5
2	Administering activities and programs	1 2 3 4 5	√		√					2

The transferable skills that receive the largest number of check marks represent your treasure-yielding skills. These skills are highly marketable. You demonstrated your special excellence when using them. These skills are one of the most significant indications of where your ideal destination lies. You've enjoyed using these skills in the past and they led you to important and enjoyable achievements; they will do the same in the future.

Alternate Step 4: Identifying treasure-yielding skills with others

If you have difficulty identifying which skills are present in your achievement stories, try the following. Find two or three friends who would be willing to spend about 30 minutes to an hour assisting you in this process. Give them a quick overview of the procedure and hand them each a copy of the transferable skills checklist. Read your first achievement story out loud and ask them to go through the skill list, placing a check in the column labeled number 1 to indicate the skills they believe you used in the story. Then repeat this process until you've read all seven stories to your friends. At the end of the seventh story, have your friends total the check marks. Next, your friends should read out loud the skills they believe you used most to create your achievement. Last, ask them to give you the skill checklist for your records.

Incidentally, if these friends or colleagues express interest in identifying their own treasure-yielding skills, let them know that this process works well in a group setting. Just start at the beginning and have everyone go through all the steps.

Step 5: Record your results

Identify your twenty transferable skills most associated with delivering career treasure. In descending order, find the skills with the largest number of checks. Once again, turn to the Vocational Identity Summary in Appendix A and record your twenty top treasure-yielding skills. In case of ties, simply decide which of the skills you enjoy using the most and rank the items in that order.

Step 6: My favorite transferable skill

As a last step, review the twenty transferable skills recorded on the VIS. Of these twenty skills, which is your absolute favorite skill to use? Write this skill on the "Favorite Skill" line on the VIS.

PACKAGING YOUR SKILLS FOR POTENTIAL EMPLOYERS

Now you know what you *can do* (transferable skills) and what you *want to do* (treasure-yielding skills). As you begin to market the job search product (you), you will need to present these skills in a way that quickly conveys the benefits an employer will receive by hiring you. Behavioral science experts know that *past behavior is the best predictor of future behavior.* By reviewing your résumé and by conducting a job interview, employers attempt to take advantage of this fact. They assume that the kind of benefits you've delivered in the past to other employers will translate into similar benefits for them in the future. Pretty simple idea, and one that holds true.

Thus, employers want to see past accomplishments that demonstrate future potential; they are not particularly interested in what happened to you in grade school. I must emphasize that Exercise 7 is perhaps the *most useful* activity in the book. When you complete this activity, you will possess about fifteen accomplishment statements. These statements provide a very powerful method for summarizing your work accomplishments in a way that demonstrates your potential benefit to employers;

and this is the reason businesses hire people. The output from this exercise will prove valuable in Chapter 7, as you make your résumé one guaranteed to deliver job interviews, and in Chapter 10, as you suit up to perform very well in the job interview. The result: job offers.

EXERCISE 7
Writing Your Work Accomplishments
(Packaging the benefits of your transferable skills to potential employers)

Step 1: Identify potential accomplishments

Determining which of our past work activities constitute an "accomplishment" represents the first part of this three-part process. Unlike earlier exercises, others' opinions matter a great deal in this activity. Remember, in this exercise you must demonstrate how your past work behaviors will add value to a new employer.

To begin, you should get several pages of notebook paper. List all the jobs you have held over the last five to ten years. If you are a new graduate, list part-time and summer work, as well as clubs and academic experiences. Figure 7 lists ten questions regarding your past work experiences. Thinking about the first job on your list, simply read the first question in Figure 7. Before you go on to the next question, jot down a quick note regarding any past event that comes to mind. Repeat this process for each of the remaining nine questions. You will use these notes to build a preliminary list of your work accomplishments in Step 2.

FIGURE 7
Work Accomplishment Questions

1. Did you increase sales?
2. Did you decrease costs?
3. Did you design and/or implement a new work process or system?
4. Did you introduce new products or services?
5. Did you receive any special awards?
6. Did you make a job or work process easier or more efficient?
7. Did you train or develop others?
8. Did you do a job with fewer resources (people/money/equipment)?
9. Did you solve a long-standing work problem?
10. Did you create or participate in any technological improvements?

Step 2: Build a preliminary list of your accomplishments (the OAR method)
In Step 2, you will construct a preliminary list of your work accomplishments. It is not important that each of your accomplishments is earth shattering, life changing, or company saving. Few of us have such experiences from which to draw. The important thing is that you begin to demonstrate to potential employers that you will add value to their current situation. Each work accomplishment should contain the following three key elements:

The Three Key Accomplishment Elements
(OAR Method)

- **Opportunity for improvement**—The conditions that existed that created the company's need and provided the opportunity for you to improve the situation. What situation did you face that required you to respond in a special way? Essentially, you can think of this as a statement of the problem.
- **Activities you engaged in to seize this opportunity**—Description of your work behavior in response to the business need—in other words, the answer to the question "What did you do about this opportunity for improvement?"
- **Results**—As a direct result of your activities, what benefits—such as increased profits, decreased costs, increased speed, etc.—did your organization receive? *Important:* Benefits should be stated quantitatively whenever possible; e.g., percentage improvement, dollars, etc.

Begin Step 2 by reviewing the first note you created during Step 1. Next, create three columns on a sheet of notebook paper and label the top of the columns: Opportunities, Activities, and Results. Attempt to identify each of the above three key elements for that experience, and then briefly summarize each element in the three columns. If you successfully identify all three elements, you possess a likely candidate for a work accomplishment. Repeat this process for each note from Step 1. Here is an example.

Opportunity	Activities	Results
I was asked to create a new marketing campaign for men's apparel.	I wrote a detailed plan and sold the ideas to management.	We experienced an 8% increase in sales over the previous year.

Step 3: Write your work accomplishment statements
Now it's time to refine your list and to put it in a final format to use in conversations and in writing cover letters and your résumé. Each of your final work accomplishment statements should:

1. Begin with an action verb
2. Describe the activities in which you engaged to seize the opportunity and to make things better than they were before

3. Demonstrate how your activities added value; that is, provided benefit to the organization (stated quantitatively whenever possible)

4. Be only one sentence long

To begin, review the first work experience from the OAR list you created in Step 2. Create one sentence that summarizes all three elements. To help find an appropriate verb, turn to page 52, on which begins a list of hundreds of action verbs.

When describing results, you should remember to show how your activities benefited the company. To effectively demonstrate benefits, your statements should describe the results in one or more of the following ways:

1. Dollars saved (number of dollars, or percentage improvement)

2. Improved processes (such as percent faster, need for fewer people, improved quality, percent increased customer satisfaction scores, etc.)

3. Increased dollars earned (amount of new revenue, better profit margins, etc.)

Example
Accomplishment Statements

- Proposed and created a new marketing campaign for men's apparel that resulted in an 8 percent increase over the previous year's sales.
- Conducted a special study to determine the best site for locating a new branch office; the new site met all company needs and was purchased at 18 percent below company average for that area.
- Identified three sources of waste in the welding department, which resulted in $15,000 in annual savings.
- Redesigned work flow process in dishwasher door assembly, which reduced manufacturing time by 16 percent.
- Provided leadership for restructuring task force, which reduced the head count by 8 percent and increased productivity by 18 percent.
- Redesigned sales force from geographic organization to type of customer organization. Increased market share by 5 percent within first nine months.
- Coordinated plantwide safety team and achieved lowest OSHA reportables and lowest accident rate in last five years.
- Designed and directed research aimed at building state-of-the-art industrial strength ceramics. Time to market was six months ahead of schedule and 10 percent under budget.
- Suggested and implemented new ideas in purchasing, which resulted in reducing the amount of time in processing orders by 50 percent.

Step 4: Record your Statements

Record your final work accomplishment statements on a sheet of notebook paper. You will refer back to this list numerous times throughout the book, particularly when writing your résumé and preparing for the job interview, so please put it in a safe place.

Action Verbs for Accomplishment Statements

Accelerated	Approached	Cataloged	Considered
Accepted	Appropriated	Celebrated	Consolidated
Accommodated	Approved	Centralized	Constructed
Accomplished	Arbitrated	Chaired	Contemplated
Accounted	Arranged	Challenged	Consulted
Achieved	Ascertained	Championed	Consummated
Acquired	Assembled	Changed	Contracted
Acknowledged	Assessed	Charted	Contributed
Acted	Assigned	Checked	Controlled
Activated	Assimilated	Circulated	Converted
Adapted	Assisted	Clarified	Convinced
Added	Attained	Classified	Cooperated
Addressed	Attended	Cleaned	Coordinated
Adjusted	Attracted	Closed-up	Copied
Administered	Audited	Coached	Corrected
Admired	Augmented	Collaborated	Correspondent
Adopted	Authorized	Combined	Counseled
Advanced (to)	Automated	Communicated	Created
Advertised	Averted	Compared	Credited
Advised	Avoided	Compiled	Criticized
Advocated	Awarded	Completed	Cultivated
Affected	Balanced	Composed	Cut
Agreed	Benefited	Compounded	Danced
Aided	Boosted	Computed	Debated
Allocated	Bound	Computerized	Decentralized
Altered	Bought	Conceived	Decided
Amplified	Broadened	Conceptualized	Decorated
Analyzed	Budgeted	Conciliated	Decreased
Answered	Built	Concluded	Defined
Anticipated	Calculated	Condensed	Delegated
Applied	Called	Conducted	Delivered
Appointed	Capitalized	Conferred	Demonstrated
Appraised	Carried (out)	Confined	Designated
Apprised	Carved	Conserved	Designed

Detailed	Effected	Formed	Informed
Detected	Elaborated	Formulated	Initiated
Determined	Eliminated	Found	Innovated
Developed	Emphasized	Founded	Inspected
Devised	Employed	Framed	Inspired
Diagnosed	Enacted	Freelanced	Installed
Diagrammed	Encouraged	Fulfilled	Instigated
Dictated	Enforced	Fund-raised	Instituted
Differentiated	Engaged	Gardened	Instructed
Dimensioned	Engineered	Gathered	Insured
Directed	Enhanced	Gave	Integrated
Disapproved	Enjoined	Generated	Interested
Disbursed	Enlarged	Got	Interpreted
Discharged	Enlisted	Governed	Intervened
Disciplined	Ensured	Graduated	Interviewed
Discovered	Entertained	Grouped	Introduced
Discussed	Enumerated	Guided	Invented
Dismantled	Equipped	Had (responsibility	Inventoried
Dispatched	Exercised	for)	Invested
Dispensed	Expanded	Halved	Investigated
Displaced	Expedited	Handled	Joined
Displayed	Expended	Harmonized	Judged
Disposed	Experimented	Headed	Justified
Disapproved	Explained	Helped	Kept
Dissected	Expressed	Hired	Keynoted
Disseminated	Extended	Hosted	Landscaped
Distinguished	Extracted	Hypothesized	Launched
Distributed	Fabricated	Identified	Laid (out)
Diversified	Facilitated	Illuminated	Learned
Diverted	Familiarized	Illustrated	Lectured
Documented	Favored	Imagined	Led
Doubled	Figured	Implemented	Licensed
Drafted	Filed	Improved	Lifted
Dramatized	Financed	Improvised	Lightened
Drew (up)	Fired	Inaugurated	Liquidated
Drove	Finished	Incorporated	Listened
Dug	Fixed	Increased	Located
Earned	Focused	Indexed	Logged
Edited	Followed	Induced	Made
Educated	Forecasted	Influenced	Maintained

Managed	Oriented	Protected	Replaced
Manipulated	Originated	Proved	Reported
Manned	Overcame	Provided	Represented
Manufactured	Overhauled	Publicized	Requested
Marketed	Oversaw	Published	Required
Mastered	Packed	Purchased	Researched
Maximized	Painted	Put (together)	Reshaped
Measured	Packaged	Questioned	Resolved
Mechanized	Participated (in)	Raised	Respected
Mediated	Penetrated	Reached	Responded
Memorized	Perceived	Read	Restored
Mentored	Performed	Realized	Restricted
Merchandised	Personalized	Reasoned	Restructured
Merged	Persuaded	Rebuilt	Retailed
Met	Photographed	Received	Retrieved
Minimized	Piloted	Recognized	Returned
Mixed	Pinpointed	Recommended	Reversed
Mobilized	Pioneered	Reconciled	Reviewed
Modeled	Planned	Reconstructed	Revised
Moderated	Played	Recorded	Revitalized
Modernized	Positioned	Recruited	Revived
Modified	Postulated	Rectified	Rewarded
Molded	Predicted	Redirected	Risked
Monitored	Prepared	Redesigned	Routed
Motivated	Prescribed	Reduced (losses)	Safeguarded
Moved	Presented	Reestablished	Salvaged
Navigated	Presided	Referred	Sang
Negotiated	Prevented	Refined	Satisfied
Nominated	Printed	Regulated	Saved
Notified	Probed	Rehabilitated	Scanned
Observed	Problem–solved	Reinforced	Scheduled
Obtained	Processed	Rejected	Screened
Occupied	Procured	Rejuvenated	Secured
Offered	Produced	Related	Selected
Opened	Profited	Remembered	Sensed
Operated	Programmed	Rendered	Separated
Optimized	Projected	Renegotiated	Served
Orchestrated	Promoted	Renewed	Serviced
Ordered	Proofread	Reorganized	Set
Organized	Proposed	Repaired	Settled

Set up	Streamlined	Tested	Understood
Sewed	Strengthened	Theorized	Understudied
Shaped	Structured	Tightened	Undertook
Shared	Studied	Told	Unearthed
Shipped	Submitted	Took (charge,	Unified
Showed	Subordinated	instructions, over)	United
Shut (down)	Succeeded	Traced	Unraveled
Signed	Suggested	Tracked	Updated
Simplified	Summarized	Traded	Upgraded
Simulated	Superseded	Trained	Uplifted
Sketched	Supervised	Transacted	Used
Slashed	Supplied	Transcribed	Utilized
Sold	Supplemented	Transferred	Vacated
Solicited	Supported	Transformed	Validated
Solved	Surpassed	Translated	Verbalized
Sorted	Surveyed	Transmitted	Varied
Sought	Sustained	Traveled	Verified
Spearheaded	Symbolized	Treated	Vitalized
Specified	Synergized	Triggered	Washed
Spoke	Synthesized	Trimmed	Weighed
Sponsored	Systematized	Tripled	Wholesaled
Staffed	Tabulated	Troubleshot	Widened
Staged	Tailored	Turned (around)	Withdrew
Standardized	Talked	Tutored	Withstood
Started	Taught	Typed	Won
Stimulated	Team–built	Typeset	Worked
Stipulated	Tended	Umpired	Wrote
Straightened	Terminated	Uncovered	Wrought

If you have difficulty quantifying your accomplishments

People often have difficulty with the results portion of the OAR method. Many people I've worked with will at first write statements such as "Developed new quality program." This is not an effective accomplishment statement. First of all, it tells the reader nothing about why the writer undertook the effort. Second, and by far most important, it does not communicate how the action benefited the organization. I usually ask the author of such a statement to read it to me. I then look at the author and ask "So?" or "So what?" I've noticed that my simple question usually produces a good deal of frustration on the part of the author. He or she typically first replies with something like "Well, it made things better," or "It's hard to quantify." I then ask "Well, how do you know this was useful to the organization?" For your work accomplishment statements to be effective, you absolutely must continue to ask the "So?" or "How-do-you-know-this-matters?" questions until you can answer them.

After my initial inquiry, people will usually rework their early statements and return to get my feedback on revised accomplishment statements. Sometimes the second draft of the statements powerfully encapsulates their accomplishments. More often than not, however, the second draft contains statements that look something like "Developed new program that improved the company's quality." Again I ask "So?" or "By how much?" You see, this statement still does not tell the reader how the company benefited from the action. In the end the statement should read more like this: "Developed a new quality program that reduced rejects by 5 percent and saved more than $3,500 in scrap cost each quarter." Now the reader gets it. It's clear what the writer did, and it's also clear

> "We may affirm absolutely that nothing great in the world has been accomplished without passion."
>
> Georg Wilhelm Friedrich Hegel

why the company cares. In many cases you'll have to estimate the quantitative results. Contacting former work colleagues may help in establishing estimates of the impact of your actions. In any event, estimating is perfectly acceptable as long as you are reasonably accurate and can defend your numbers.

It may take you a while before you complete this exercise. That's just fine. You will gain significant competitive advantage over other job seekers by sticking with this process. In the end, you will have at your disposal fifteen to twenty extremely powerful statements valuable in a variety of job-hunting circumstances.

You have so far identified the values most important to you, the skills that you *can* use, and those skills you *most enjoy* utilizing. You also created a powerful list of accomplishment statements to capitalize upon during the job search. It's now time to ask the last question: "What type of person are you?"

5

Assess Your Personality and Vocational Interests

"By the work one knows the workman."
Jean La Fontaine

WHO ARE YOU ANYWAY?

Remember those band kids in high school? And how about the jocks or the people in woodworking shop? Some kids actually enjoyed biology class, and others found the Young Entrepreneurs' Club or Junior Achievement thrilling. There were some, even in the midst of the self-centeredness that usually accompanies adolescence, that gave their time to help others by volunteering at the hospital, coaching younger kids, or serving as the resident student counselor. You probably participated in one of these activities, or fell into another easily identifiable group.

I, of course, didn't attend your high school, and you may have graduated much earlier or much later than 1973; nevertheless, I know

these groups were there. While some of your high school colleagues were active in several of the groups I just mentioned, I'm also sure that most concentrated their time within a single group or perhaps two. Personality explains why these groups exist in every high school and why certain people are drawn toward them. I am not referring to the most common usage of the word, such as "she has a marvelous personality," or "he has a lot of personality." Instead, I'm using the word the way psychologists use it: to mean patterns of behavior or traits. If you know an individual's personality traits, you can make a very good guess as to the kind of group in which he or she will find the most interest and enjoyment, and will be best able to exhibit talent. As you will soon see, not only is this true in high schools everywhere, it is even more true in the larger world of work.

Some like it hot—and some don't

The idea that different people have different personality types is hardly new. For example, the early fourth-century Greek philosopher Theophrastus wrote stories that featured "characters" such as the Coward, the Flatterer, the Boor, etc. Theophrastus' basic assumption is the same as that of modern personality psychologists: people behave the same across a variety of different situations. The trick is to accurately identify the traits that exist in all of us and, for our purpose here, relate these traits to the choice of career.

You may be asking something like "Doesn't my personality change in different situations or at different times in my life?" Well, no, it generally doesn't. In fact, we all demonstrate the stability of personality traits when we describe each other. Here is a quick demonstration. Think of someone that you know well. Now, before reading further, get a piece of paper and jot down at least ten adjectives that describe him or her; e.g., careful, happy, shy, etc.

Using everyday language, you just began describing someone's personality. You couldn't do this if traits changed depending upon the situation. If I tell you about my friend who is *outgoing, creative,* and a *likable* person who *enjoys taking risks,* I'm telling you about how he consistently behaves across a wide variety of situations. I am absolutely certain that he will not wake up tomorrow morning and decide to be *shy, practical, unfriendly,* and *cautious.*

So where do these traits come from? Some of the most interesting information about the origins of personality comes from studies of identical twins. These studies show that identical twins have many incredibly similar ways of behaving in adulthood; even when different parents raise each twin, in very different geographical locations. It's becoming more and more obvious that we inherit our personality traits. Yes, you were born that way. This does not mean that the environment or the situation you find yourself in is irrelevant. Your economic status, parents, siblings, even the time in history in which you live, all certainly contribute to the kind of person you are. However, by and large, you inherited your personality traits. In a nutshell, your personality develops very early, doesn't change across situations, and is an extraordinarily powerful predictor of how you will behave in variety of settings.

PERSONALITY TRAITS AND CAREER CHOICE

What does this have to do with selecting a career? A great deal! Along with knowing what is most important to you (values) and what you do well (knowledge and skills), personality assessment completes the personal portion of your vocational identity puzzle. By assessing your personality, you answer the "What-type-of-person-are-you?" question posed in Chapter 2. You reveal who you are by the behavior patterns, or traits, you exhibit to others. Years ago, psychologists distinguished between personality and interests. This is no longer true. Today we know that vocational interests and personality represent the same thing: your traits. In the last few years, psychologists have learned that whenever we observe, evaluate, or categorize one another, our description always falls

FIGURE 8
Personality/Vocational Interests Types

Type	Description
Realistic	Realistic types enjoy mechanical activities, the outdoors, working with animals, and athletics. They often do not like formal education and are more concerned with the practical than the theoretical. They consider themselves mature, persistent, and dependable. They sometimes have difficulty expressing themselves verbally and often feel they do not possess good interpersonal skills.
Investigative	Investigative types enjoy science and other intellectual activities. They like to search out creative solutions to problems and explore possibilities. They do not like repetitive and routine tasks. They see themselves as being good at math and science.
Artistic	Artistic types enjoy both observing and creating artistic expression. They often write poetry, music, draw or paint, participate in drama, or spend time writing. They dislike ordered or controlled activities.
Social	Social types are concerned about the welfare of others. This type does not define a person's degree of introversion and extroversion. Social types can be either outgoing or shy or reserved; their distinguishing characteristic is that they seek out helping others.
Enterprising	Enterprising types are assertive and competitive and seek status. They do not like to spend time systematically analyzing information or creating theories about why things are the way they are; they prefer to take action to achieve their goals. They think of themselves as good leaders and able to persuade others.
Conventional	Conventional types appreciate order. They seek out activities that allow them to exercise their natural bend toward organization. They like to organize numbers, records, or other materials and operate in a systematic fashion.

into about five or six categories. These categories are personality traits.

The Holland theory

John Holland provides the most respected, and by far the most complete, way of using personality to make career decisions. Over the next few pages I will summarize his theory. If you would like a more detailed look at his ideas you should read his classic book *Making Vocational Choices: A Theory of Vocational Personality and Work Environments* (second edition), from Prentice Hall, Inc. Here are the basics presented in three major points.

The RIASEC Model

First, each of us can be described by one of six personality types: *Realistic, Investigative, Artistic, Social, Enterprising,* and *Conventional* (RIASEC). Figure 8 briefly describes some of the typical behaviors of each type in the RIASEC model. A little later I will show you one way of identifying which of these types best fits your personality. For now, as you look over Figure 8, ask yourself which type description sounds most like you. As a way to become more familiar with the types, try this little activity. Reread the chapter's opening paragraph. Try to categorize

FIGURE 9
High School Groups and Personality

Personality Type	Opening Paragraph Examples
Realistic	athletes and woodworking shop kids
Investigative	those who enjoyed biology
Artistic	band kids
Social	volunteers—hospital, coaching younger kids
Enterprising	Young Entrepreneurs Club—Junior Achievement
Conventional	no example

each of the groups mentioned. Which of the six type descriptions do you feel best describes the band kids, the jocks, the young entrepreneurs, etc.? After you classify the groups, compare your answers to Figure 9.

RIASEC classifies both people and work environments

The second major point is that, just like individuals, work environments also fall into the RIASEC categories. No other approach to personality type classifies both individuals and careers. Investigative work environments exist, for example, just as Investigative people do. The same is true for the other five types. This idea makes the RIASEC theory the most complete of all approaches to using personality to make career choices. By matching your personality type to a work environment of the same type you will go a very long way toward finding your ideal career destination, one that closely mir-

rors your vocational identity, one that provides a wealth of career treasure.

The reason that different work environments fall into the RIASEC categories is because every career is full of people with a particular personality type. In other words, a Realistic work environment has primarily Realistic personality types employed in it. Most important, people whose personality type matches their work environment type experience happier *and* more successful careers than when this isn't true. The hexagon on the following page reveals two other valuable insights from the RIASEC theory.

1. *The farther other types are away from your type on the hexagon, the less like you they are.* For example, if you are an Artistic type, you will probably have the least amount of interest in Conventional activities and careers. In the same way, Conventional types typically will have little interest in Artistic endeavors. You can see that these types are on opposite sides of the hexagon.

I recall working with a young mechanical engineer who had just graduated from a prominent Michigan university. Mechanical engineering is very much a Realistic type of occupation. He made good grades while in college and had worked for about a year with one of the Fortune 500's twenty largest firms. Unfortunately, he was quite miserable in his job. After assessment, we learned that Social kinds of interests dominated his personality. He could not have been more misplaced in terms of occupational choice. He decided to major in mechanical engineering in college because "my father said this is good field and convinced me to pursue it." Although he was bright enough to do well in a school subject that he didn't care for, he clearly was not

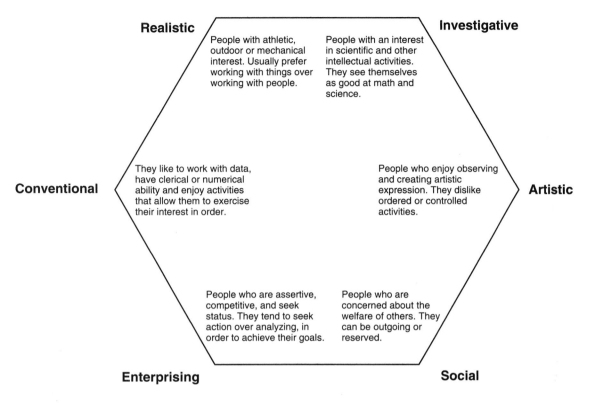

Realistic — People with athletic, outdoor or mechanical interest. Usually prefer working with things over working with people.

Investigative — People with an interest in scientific and other intellectual activities. They see themselves as good at math and science.

Conventional — They like to work with data, have clerical or numerical ability and enjoy activities that allow them to exercise their interest in order.

Artistic — People who enjoy observing and creating artistic expression. They dislike ordered or controlled activities.

Enterprising — People who are assertive, competitive, and seek status. They tend to seek action over analyzing, in order to achieve their goals.

Social — People who are concerned about the welfare of others. They can be outgoing or reserved.

going to succeed in a long-term engineering career. After gaining a better understanding of his vocational personality and his own values, he left engineering and returned to school to pursue a teaching career, an occupational choice quite consistent with his personality type.

2. *The closer on the hexagon other types are to your type, the more like you they are.* The two types on each side of your type are most similar to your type. For example, if you are an Artistic type, Social and Investigative interests are likely to represent your next most similar personality. This fact can be very important in career choice. Let's stay with our example a bit longer. Suppose, as an Artistic type, your skills and motivation lie in creating artwork through painting. However, you find either your values or circumstances demanding that you make a steady

income. While some artists receive regular income, many do not. By looking at career opportunities located on either side of the Artistic type, you may identify a satisfying alternative to painting. For example, notice that the Social type is next to the Artistic type on the hexagon. One of the primary Social occupations is teaching. Perhaps you might like to seek an opportunity to teach art while pursuing your own creations in your spare time.

Your three-letter personality code

The third major point you'll need to understand when applying vocational personality to your life has to do with the complexity of both people and work environments. People are simply too complex for only one letter, or type description, to represent them. When fully exploring your type, you'll be defined by a three-letter personality code; for example, ASI or ECR, among hundreds of other possible combinations. The first letter of the code indicates your primary personality type. The second and third letters represent secondary vocational interests that modify your primary type.

The Guide to Occupational Exploration Model of Interests

In its *Guide to Occupational Exploration*, the U.S. Department of Labor created another scheme for classifying vocational interests and work environments. As you can see from Figure 10 on the following page, the Department of Labor's twelve categories easily map onto the RIASEC scheme. Again, regardless of what you call these personality factors, they exist, and as you will learn in Chapter 6, they will provide you with a great deal of assistance as you explore career options.

ASSESSING YOUR VOCATIONAL PERSONALITY

At this point you're probably asking two questions: "How do I assess my vocational personality?" and "How do I match it to jobs in the real world?" To answer the first question, I developed a process for my clients and students to use as a start in identifying their vocational personality; you'll find it here as Exercise 8. The process is easy to follow, but will take a little time; most people spend about 30 minutes to an hour in completing the exercise.

While you'll find this process useful, if you would like a more thorough vocational personality assessment, here are two resources. First, I highly recommend John Holland's Self-Directed Search from Psychological Assessment Resources, Inc. (PAR). The SDS Specimen Set includes the Self-Directed Search personality assessment, the Occupations Finder (a list of careers arranged by RIASEC classification), and three other booklets: *You and Your Career, Educational Opportunities Finder,* and the *Leisure Activities Finder.*

Psychological Assessment Resources, Inc.
Box 998
Odessa, FL 33556
800-331-8378 (toll free)

The Strong Interest Inventory (SII) provides another very good way to learn about vocational personality. As with the Self-Directed Search, the SII provides a three-letter vocational personality code called a General Occupational Theme (GOT) code. In addition, this assessment will show you how your results compare to many specific jobs. Unlike the SDS, however, you will have to find a career counselor to administer this assessment. Almost all colleges provide some career counseling, and many will administer the SII and help you interpret the results.

Before you get started identifying your vocational personality, I will take a moment to address the second question about matching your personality to occupations. After you complete a thorough self-assessment, your next course of action is exploring various career options. Clearly, your vocational personality is a valuable tool in this endeavor. Job experts have made vocational personality particularly useful by classifying thousands of occupations using the RIASEC model. When an ASI person

FIGURE 10
Comparison of Holland Types and U.S. Department of Labor Interests Factors

Holland Type	U.S. Department of Labor: Guide for Occupational Exploration
Realistic	**Plants and Animals:** Interest in activities involving plants and animals, usually in an outdoor setting.
	Protective: Interest in the use of authority to protect people and property.
	Mechanical: Interest in applying mechanical principles to practical situations, using machines, handtools, or techniques.
	Industrial: Interest in repetitive, concrete, organized activities in a factory setting.
	Physical Performing: Interest in physical activities performed before and audience.
Investigative	**Scientific:** Interest in discovering, collecting, and analyzing information about the natural world and in applying scientific research findings to problems in medicine, life sciences, and natural sciences.
Artistic	**Artistic:** Interest in creative expression of feelings or ideas.
Social	**Accommodating:** Interest in catering to the wishes of others, usually on a one-to-one basis.
	Humanitarian: Interest in helping others with their mental, spiritual, social, physical, or vocational needs.
Enterprising	**Selling:** Interest in bringing others to a point of view through personal persuasions, using sales and promotion techniques.
	Leading-Influencing: Interest in leading others through activities involving high-level verbal or numerical abilities
Conventional	**Business Detail:** Interest in organized, clearly defined activities requiring accuracy and attention to detail, primarily in an office setting.

meets an ASI environment, or an RCI person meets an RCI environment, for example, it's often a beautiful thing. But sometimes it isn't. Why? Because although personality is a very good predictor of career satisfaction, it doesn't explain everything.

When I suggest vocational interest assessment as part of a career choice process to my clients, I often hear remarks like this: "I took an interest test one time and it said I should be a forest ranger. That's not even close; I *definitely* don't want to be a forest ranger." By saying this, these clients are showing that they believe the results are pretty inaccurate. This generally is not the case. Once again, let's consider the example of a person who disbelieves results showing that "forest ranger" is a good match with his or her personality. Although the person feels no connection with the forest ranger option, this career probably does match his or her personality. So, if the person's personality fits the job, why does the person feel so uncomfortable with the forest ranger career? Most likely, when the individual combined the other pieces of the vocational identity puzzle with the personality results, forest ranger truly didn't match. Perhaps the person values high income and status, or he or she will not use treasure-yielding skills as a forest ranger. Personality is a vitally important element in making good career choices, but no more so than values and skills.

Here is the point. To find career treasure, you must consider *all* of the pieces of your vocational identity puzzle *simultaneously.*

In Chapter 6, I will present methods for exploring careers that include matching your personality to work environments; we will also consider the rest of your vocational identity. For now, to identify your vocational personality code in order to complete your vocational identity puzzle, follow the directions in Exercise 8.

EXERCISE 8
Assessing Your Vocational Personality

Step 1: Adjectives

Beginning with the work of Gordon Allport in 1936 and continuing through today, psychologists have shown that whenever we observe, evaluate, or categorize one another, we use everyday language to describe personality traits. Below are ten groups of adjectives. Read the adjectives in Group 1 and select the adjective most like you and place a 3 next to this word. Now, of the five remaining words in Group 1, select the adjective that best describes you and give it a 2 ranking. Do the same for the third most descriptive word, giving it a 1. When finished with the adjectives in Group 1 you will have rank ordered the three words that best describe you. Three of the words will have no rankings. Go through this same procedure for the remaining nine groups.

Group 1

Code	Adjective	Rank
R	Mechanical	
I	Scientific	
A	Creative	
S	Caring	
E	Competitive	
C	Accommodating	

Group 2

Code	Adjective	Rank
R	Athletic	
I	Philosophical	
A	Different	
S	Helpful	
E	Persuasive	
C	Rule following	

Group 3

Code	Adjective	Rank
R	Animal-loving	
I	Inquisitive	
A	Expressive	
S	Supportive	
E	Adversarial	
C	Organized	

Group 4

Code	Adjective	Rank
R	Dependable	
I	Abstract	
A	Unorganized	
S	Outgoing	
E	Action-oriented	
C	Careful	

Group 5

Code	Adjective	Rank
R	Reliable	
I	Scholarly	
A	Sensitive	
S	Congenial	
E	Status seeking	
C	Structured	

Group 6

Code	Adjective	Rank
R	Handy	
I	Careful	
A	Overly-rosy	
S	Personable	
E	Confident	
C	Systematic	

Group 7

Code	Adjective	Rank
R	No nonsense	
I	Complex	
A	Risk-taking	
S	Courteous	
E	Lively	
C	Submissive	

Group 8

Code	Adjective	Rank
R	Outdoor loving	
I	Theoretical	
A	Hasty	
S	Warm	
E	Business-oriented	
C	Tried-and-true	

Group 9

Code	Adjective	Rank
R	Bashful	
I	Thoughtful	
A	Unconventional	
S	Spiritual	
E	Witty	
C	Dutiful	

Group 10

Code	Adjective	Rank
R	Rugged	
I	Self-reliant	
A	Inventive	
S	Reliable	
E	Resilient	
C	Detail-oriented	

Step 2: Selecting a description

Step 2 presents the same personality type descriptions you read earlier in the chapter. However, now you should read each description once again and rank order the top three descriptions that best describe you: 3 = most similar, 2 = next most similar, and 1 = somewhat similar.

Type Descriptions

Type	Description	Rank
Realistic	Realistic types enjoy mechanical activities, the outdoors, working with animals, and athletics. They often do not like formal education and are more concerned with the practical than the theoretical. They consider themselves mature, persistent, and dependable. They sometimes have difficulty expressing themselves verbally and often feel they do not possess good interpersonal skills.	
Investigative	Investigative types enjoy science and other intellectual activities. They see themselves as enjoying and being good at math and science. They like to search out solutions to complex problems and explore possibilities.	
Artistic	Artistic types enjoy both observing and creating artistic expression. They often write poetry, music, draw or paint, participate in drama, or spend time writing. They dislike ordered or controlled activities and are often unconventional.	
Social	Social types are concerned about the welfare of others. This type does not define a person's degree of introversion and extroversion. Social types can be either outgoing or reserved; their distinguishing characteristic is that they seek out helping others.	
Enterprising	Enterprising types are assertive and competitive and seek status. They do not like to spend time systematically analyzing information or creating theories about why things are the way they are; they prefer to take action to achieve their goals. They think of themselves as good leaders who are self-confident and able to persuade others.	
Conventional	Conventional types appreciate order. They seek out activities that allow them to exercise their natural bend toward organization. They like to organize numbers, records, or other materials and operate in a systematic fashion.	

Step 3: Occupational themes

As with the adjectives in Step 1, this step presents you with ten groups. The groups contain occupational themes extracted from the U.S. Department of Labor's *Guide for Occupational Exploration*'s List of Interest Areas, Work Groups, and Subgroups. Rank order the three occupational themes that sound most interesting to you. **IMPORTANT:** Do not try to determine if you would like to spend your career in any of these occupations, or whether or not you believe you are qualified for any particular occupation. Simply decide which occupation in Group 1 is most interesting and give it a 3 rating, the next most interesting a 2, and the next a 1. Then move on to the remaining nine groups of occupations and do the same thing.

Group 1

Code	Occupation	Check
R	Forestry and logging	
I	Theoretical research	
A	Creative writing	
S	Teacher	
E	Salesperson	
C	Bookkeeping	

Group 2

Code	Occupation	Check
R	Emergency responding—e.g., fire fighter	
I	Medical sciences—medicine/surgery	
A	Performing	
S	Nurse	
E	Entrepreneur	
C	Auditing	

Group 3

Code	Occupation	Check
R	Farming	
I	Life sciences—study plants	
A	Entertaining	
S	Religious work	
E	Intangible sales	
C	Accounting	

Group 4

Code	Occupation	Check
R	Sports	
I	Medical sciences—dentistry	
A	Arts and crafts	
S	Counseling and social work	
E	Public relations	
C	Financial detail	

Group 5

Code	Occupation	Check
R	Law and order—e.g., police officer	
I	Technological science	
A	Composing music	
S	Nursing	
E	Business management—hotel	
C	Budget and financial control	

Group 6

Code	Occupation	Check
R	Mechanical engineering	
I	Medical sciences—veterinarian	
A	Performing dance	
S	Therapy—physical therapist	
E	Negotiating contracts	
C	Secretarial work	

Group 7

Code	Occupation	Check
R	Operating equipment	
I	Life sciences—study animals	
A	Directing drama	
S	Child care	
E	Real estate sales	
C	Records processing	

Group 8

Code	Occupation	Check
R	Woodworking	
I	Medical sciences—general	
A	Creating visual art	
S	Counseling—psychologist	
E	Broadcasting—newscaster	
C	Computer operation	

Group 9

Code	Occupation	Check
R	Machinist	
I	Laboratory work—with plants and animals	
A	Working with crafts	
S	Barber and beauty services	
E	Business administration	
C	Financial auditing	

Group 10

Code	Occupation	Check
R	Truck Driving	
I	Laboratory work—physics or geology	
A	Editing	
S	Guide services	
E	Law—attorney	
C	Statistical reporting	

Step 4: Calculating your scores

This step explains how to calculate scores for each of the four previous steps: adjectives (Step 1), type descriptions (Step 2), and occupational themes (Step 3). In every case you will record your score for each of these three steps on the Summary Scoring Table (see page 69). Before calculating your scores, find the Summary Scoring Table and briefly review it. Now, move on to scoring each step. You may find it helpful to use a calculator.

a. Adjectives that describe me (from Step 1)

First, add up the total score for the R (Realistic) adjectives in all ten groups and record that number in the table below. If a word received no rating, give it a 0 score. For example, if you gave the adjective *mechanical* a 1 ranking and *rugged* a 2, but left all other R adjectives blank, then your total R score = 3 for Step 2. Next do the same for the I, A, S, E, and C adjectives. The maximum score for any type in Step 2 is 30.

Adjectives from Step 1	Total score	Ranking
R—Realistic		
I—Investigative		
A—Artistic		
S—Social		
E—Enterprising		
C—Conventional		

Next, rank the top three adjective scores by total score. In other words, rank the factor that received the largest number of points a 3, the next largest number a 2, and the next a 1. If two or more tie, e.g., Factor 3 = 20 and Factor 4 = 20, reread the adjectives in those categories and then just rank order the factors. Now, on the line titled *adjectives*, record this ranking on the Summary Scoring Table on page 69.

b. Selecting a type description (from Step 2)

As with Step 1, just record your ratings on the Summary Scoring Table on the *type descriptions* line.

c. Occupational themes that sound interesting to me (from Step 3)

You score the occupations section just as you did the adjectives. First, add up the total score for all R occupations and record that number in the table below. If an occupational theme received no rating, give it a 0 score. For example, if you gave the occupation *farming* a 1 ranking and *truck driving* a 2, but left all other R occupations blank, then the total R score = 3 for Step 3. Next, do the same for the I, A, S, E, and C occupations. The maximum score for any type in Step 3 is 30. Once again, if two or more categories tie, e.g., Realistic = 20 and Conventional = 20, reread the occupations in those categories and then simply rank the types.

Occupations from Step 3	Total score	Ranking
R—Realistic		
I—Investigative		
A—Artistic		
S—Social		
E—Enterprising		
C—Conventional		

Next, rank the top three occupational theme scores by total score. Just as with the adjectives, rank the type that received the largest number of points a 3, the next largest number a 2, and the next a 1. Now, record this ranking on the Summary Scoring Table on the line titled *occupations*.

Summary Scoring Table

Steps	Ranking Scores (1–3)					
	R	I	A	S	E	C
Adjectives (Step 1)						
Type Descriptions (Step 2)						
Occupations (Step 3)						
Total Scores						

Step 5: Determine your code

You're now ready to determine your vocational personality code using the RIASEC model. On the last row of the Summary Scoring Table, total the scores for each column. Begin with the R column and then total the scores for the I, A, S, E, and C columns. Looking at the total line in the Scoring Table, select the type (RIASEC) that received the highest score and record this letter on the first line below. Next, select the next highest number and record this letter on the second line. Finally, after finding the type receiving your third highest score, write it on the third line below.

My Vocational Personality Code _____ _____ _____

What about ties in the total score? If you find a tie among the total scores, you are probably interested in several categories about evenly. For this exercise, reread the type descriptions in Step 3.

Make sure you agree with your ratings, and use the ranking as your personality code. You should also get a copy of the Self-Directed Search from PAR, and verify your type.

Step 6: Record your Vocational Personality Code on the VIS
As with most of the book's exercises, record your three-letter code on the Vocational Identity Summary.

Another perspective on personality (MBTI Type)®*

The Myers–Brigg Type Indicator, or MBTI, supplies the most popular method of describing personality today. In recent years, tens of thousands of people from virtually every walk of life have learned their MBTI classification. With results often referred to simply as Type, the MBTI looks at personality by evaluating preferences—a much different perspective than the Holland approach. Katherine Cook Briggs and her daughter Isabell Briggs Myers developed the MBTI. Katherine Cook Briggs constructed a theory of personality in the 1920s—

FIGURE 11

MBTI TYPE TABLE

ISTJ	ISFJ	INFJ	INTJ
ISTP	ISFP	INFP	INTP
ESTP	ESFP	ENFP	ENTP
ESTJ	ESFJ	ENFJ	ENTJ

about the same time the famous German psychologist Carl Jung was working on his own theory. Impressed by Jung's ideas, she later integrated many of them into her own theory. In 1942, Isabell Briggs Myers put together a paper-and-pencil test to measure personality in an effort to assist in occupational placement in support of the war effort.

*Myers-Briggs Type Indicator and MBTI are registered trademarks of Consulting Psychologists Press.

FIGURE 12

Dimension	Description
Extroversion(E)————Introversion(I)	Our source of energy. Whether we become refreshed by being around others (E) or by spending time alone (I)
Sensing(S)————Intuition(N)	The kinds of information we attend to; how we take in data. Whether we prefer to gather data (S) or we look within for information (N)
Thinking(T)————Feeling(F)	The way we go about making decisions once we have the information. Whether we analyze (T) or go with our heart (F)
Judging(J)————Perceiving(P)	Our lifestyle or work habits. Whether we prefer order and structure (J) or more spontaneity (P)

Today, the MBTI is widely used for many activities, including career counseling, team building, management development, and relationship counseling. To understand what Briggs and Myers meant by preferences, try this activity. Take out a sheet of notebook paper. Now, write your name, but use your nonpreferred hand. Next, write your name using your preferred hand (the hand you usually use). On the back of the paper, draw a vertical line down the center of the page. On the left-hand side, write down words that describe how you felt when you wrote with your nonpreferred hand. Finally, on the right-hand side of the page, jot down words describing your feelings when you wrote with your preferred hand. Words like *awkward, strange, difficult,* or *odd* often surface when describing the nonpreferred condition. On the other hand (yes, I noticed the pun), people often use words such as *natural, easy, fun,* or *fast* when describing writing their name with their preferred hand. This little exercise nicely captures the essence of what it means to operate in accordance with your preferences.

The MBTI assesses four kinds of preferences, or dimensions. You will find these preferences and brief descriptions shown in Figure 10. Using each end of the four dimensions, you can build a four-by-four matrix that creates sixteen Types, as seen in Figure 11.

The good news and the bad news

The MBTI can supply a wealth of insight. However, unlike the Holland approach, it does not classify organizations by type; thus, it doesn't offer a comprehensive theory for making career decisions. I think of MBTI Type as somewhat like the manual focus on an old 35-millimeter camera (before auto-focus cameras were made).

> Oh, fortune and fame
> such a curious game.
> Perfect strangers can call you
> by name
> And pay good money to hear
> *Fire and Rain*
> again and again and again
> Oh, some are like summer,
> coming back every year
> Got your baby,
> got your blanket,
> got your bucket of beer.
> I break into a grin
> from ear to ear
> and suddenly it's perfectly clear.
> That's why I'm here
> Singing tonight, tomorrow,
> and every day
> That's why I'm standing
> That's why I'm here.
>
> James Taylor

If I took a picture of you using this kind of camera, I would need to focus the lens manually to get a picture that accurately represents you. I believe the MBTI, like focusing the camera lens, can certainly help sharpen the vocational identity picture. However, you should not rely solely on MBTI Type to make a career selection.

Obviously, I've given you a very brief introduction to the kinds of behaviors measured by the MBTI. If you would like to learn more about your MBTI Type (and I recommend that at some point you do), here are a couple of resources for you. First, you can find a professional career counselor or psychologist to administer the MBTI. It's widely available and the majority of counselors have some experience with the MBTI. Second, you may wish to take the Keirsey Temperament Sorter survey. This assessment is available for free on the Internet. The survey consists of seventy questions requiring an A or B answer. The survey automatically scores your survey and provides you with results using the four letters from the MBTI system. You may find some of the questions a little frustrating because you'd like to have a third choice. Just remember to go with your first response based upon what is usually true about you.

The Keirsey Temperament Sorter Internet address

http://www.kiersey.com

We've come to the end, so now we can begin

You've spent a lot of time and effort, and in some instances considerable emotional capital, in completing your vocational identity puzzle. You should feel proud of yourself. You have just invested in a worthwhile venture—you. You may have learned little new information in the process and simply confirmed earlier ideas about yourself. More likely, you discovered an important thing or two along the way, and perhaps you had one of those AHA! experiences that will change your life. You now know what you can do, and what you really enjoy doing. You identified what is truly important to you, and articulated your purpose in life. You understand your personality much better, and you're beginning to see how all of these issues interconnect. You are now ready to put it all together, to explore the possibilities, to set a career objective aimed at discovering your ideal destination. If you do, you will spend your 80,000+ lifetime hours of work engaged in activities that you enjoy—and even love. You will contribute to your own life and to the lives of others in ways that matter to you and in ways that will matter to them as well. You, my friend, will find career treasure.

6

Explore Options and Define Your Career Objective

*"Finding the right work is like discovering
your own soul in the world."*
Thomas Moore

ONCE UPON A TIME

In 1980 the country was in the midst of a deep economic recession—that is, most of the country. In a few states, such as Oklahoma, Texas, and Louisiana, something remarkably different from a recession was taking place. A number of factors, including fear of worldwide oil shortages; producers' speculation that the government would deregulate deep natural gas, thereby creating rapid and huge price increases; and bank corruption all worked together to fuel an oil and gas (O & G) industry boom. In many ways the boom was not unlike the Gold Rush. Prices for everything from housing to food spun out of control. For those on fixed incomes,

this rapid inflation presented difficulties. But for anyone in the O & G industry, the boom–related inflation was insignificant, given their newfound wealth. And in 1980 virtually everyone in the O & G industry became wealthy almost instantly.

Like many young men in Oklahoma in 1980, Joel, a 22-year-old construction worker and college dropout, decided to "get in the oil business." Leaving his job laying prefabricated stone, he joined several friends in a new business and learned how to check the legal records necessary to purchase or lease mineral rights. His income doubled overnight and continued to increase rapidly. Even when the inevitable oil bust came along and washed out most of the newcomers, Joel managed not merely to "hang on," but to prosper economically as a result of his intelligence, hard work, and fate. He moved to Boulder, Colorado, and continued checking O & G records, working steadily. But all was not well. While others were amazed by his career's good fortune, he felt unfulfilled, frustrated, and bored; and with each passing day he disliked his work a bit more.

In about 1990, a decade after his entry into the O & G industry, he asked me to assist him in finding a different kind of career. As he worked through the self-assessment process, the reasons for his discontent became obvious. He had little interest in money, disliked administrative tasks, and was drawn to social causes and artistic expression. Standing in a dusty courthouse in Elk City, Oklahoma, 8 hours a day, poring over old records to assist in an oil and gas company's acquisition of more wealth was exactly wrong—for Joel.

After values, skills, and personality assessment and a good deal of introspection, Joel decided he wanted to be a journalist. He liquidated his assets, took a photography course, and bought a good deal of photography equipment. Using some of the same skills he developed when asking farmers to sign an O & G lease, he contacted the environmental group The Nature Conservancy. He persuaded the group that he was the right choice to travel the country for one year as a staff photographer. Although he made little money, he was in love—in love with following his vocational identity. After the year was up, he returned to Boulder. Because of his Nature Conservancy experience, he landed a position as a staff photographer for a weekly paper. After a few months, in addition to serving as a staff pho-

tographer, he began contributing small articles to the paper. About one year later, he became an assistant editor; a few months later, a senior editor. He then decided he wanted to write a book. He did. His book, *Harvest of Rage*, traces the beginnings of the militia movement in America. Because of his knowledge of the militia and domestic terrorism, he was featured on CBS's *48 Hours* and *Nightly News*, ABC's *Evening News*, NBC's *Today*, and National Public Radio. In addition, his publisher nominated his book for the Pulitzer Prize.

This story is no fairy tale. It is the true story of one man's ongoing career journey. Do you think Joel is a success? If so, when did he become successful? While the recent notoriety and public accolades are nice, they were not this journalist's objective. His public success is merely a by-product of listening to the calling from his ideal destination. He began reaping incredible career treasure the day he stopped checking oil and gas records and jumped in an old Ford van and began traveling the U.S., taking pictures. That was the day he began pursuing activities that were consistent with his vocational identity. That was the day he became successful.

CAREER EXPLORATION

The previous four chapters of Part 1 focused primarily on you. These chapters asked you to examine yourself, to identify the issues and people most important to you, to discover the things you do best and most enjoy doing, and to assess your personality. As you completed the VIS page, like an artist painting a portrait, you created a picture of your vocational identity. Your vocational identity is only 50 percent of the career treasure equation, however. You'll find the other 50 percent when you match your vocational identity to a career. During the self-assessment process, a person occasionally meets with a EUREKA! type of experience, finding the perfect career almost as if by magic. Although this doesn't happen often, it does happen. In these cases, learning more about oneself, coupled with one's existing knowledge of the world of work, is enough to reveal a career objective. I hope this was your experience. If so, move on to Chapter 7 and start preparing for the job hunt. If not, do not fear. You'll find plenty of direction and ideas in this chapter to assist you in exploring career options.

Career exploration is *not* job market research

Career exploration involves gathering information about various career options, evaluating how well these options match your vocational identity, selecting one of the options, and then setting a goal to find employment within your selected option. *Job market research*, on the other hand, is the process of gathering information about the location of jobs that meet your career goal and about the companies where these jobs exist. While the goals of career exploration and the goals of job market research are considerably different, job hunters and career-book authors alike often confuse these two efforts.

Figure 13 shows that while the type of information sources are the same, the questions, goals, and outcomes of the two activities are quite different. Career exploration prepares you to make a career choice. Job market research prepares you to begin a job search. In both cases, you will find information through books, the Internet, and, most important, through people. However, while the types of resources are the same, the kinds of information you're

FIGURE 13
Career Exploration vs. Job Market Research

Career Exploration		
Goal	**Question to Answer**	**Sources of Information**
Career Choice: Select a career that matches my vocational identity	What career best matches my vocational identity (values and purpose, knowledge and skills, and personality)?	Publications Internet People *Career Exploration:* The Informational Interview
Market Research		
Goal	**Questions to Answer**	**Sources of Information**
Job Search: Locate employment opportunities that match the career I selected during Career Exploration	What is available that meets my career objective? What company information is useful? What salary should I expect?	Publications Internet People *Networking:* The Advice and Information Interview

after and the specific sources are quite different. Because you'll probably need to engage in both types of efforts to find your ideal job, this chapter shows you how to explore career options, and Chapter 8 presents strategies and resources for conducting job market research.

The career exploration process

Some people do seem to just fall into their ideal job. I assume, however, that since you're still reading this chapter, you'd appreciate a systematic approach for making a career choice. The following presents a straightforward five-step method for exploring career options. If you already have a strong desire to explore some particular occupation . . . great! You may still find walking through the first step, Select Careers to Explore, useful for confirming your choice, or for adding additional careers to the mix for further exploration. Either way, the other four steps will assist you in learning more about particular careers, deciding how well a particular occupation fits your vocational identity, and writing a career objective.

STEP 1: SELECT CAREERS TO EXPLORE

Obviously, you cannot gather information about all possible careers. For example, the *Dictionary of Occupational Titles* lists more than 20,000 jobs. In order to begin your in-depth exploration, you must select a smaller and more manageable number from the total of all possible careers. Thankfully, you don't have to do this by flipping a coin or throwing darts, because you already know the basic characteristics of the career you're seeking—the characteristics that match your vocational identity. The ques-

tion is, how do you locate the careers that have these characteristics? Fortunately, careers can be organized by skill requirements and by personality type. In other words, careers that require similar transferable skills can be grouped together. Job experts usually refer to these groups as job families. Similarly, Holland's RIASEC model (Chapter 5) serves as a good scheme for grouping jobs of similar personality type. These groupings make career exploration much more manageable. Here is a procedure you can use to select careers you would like to explore further.

How to Select Careers to Explore

1. Remember what you've always known
2. Review groups of jobs with similar skill requirements (job families) and select those that are most interesting
3. Examine jobs with similar personality requirements (RIASEC groups) and select those that are most interesting
4. Select the career(s) you would like to explore further

In the next few pages, I will provide you with a detailed explanation of how to accomplish each of the four parts in this procedure. During each part, you will make decisions about which careers most interest you. Each time you make one of these decisions, write your choices on the Career Exploration Worksheet that follows.

a. Remember what you've always known— Let's get started with listening to what your heart tells you. Pause just a minute to consider, and then complete, the following two statements:

FIGURE 14

	Career Job Families (Grouped by Skill Requirements)
1	Executive, Administrative, and Managerial Occupations
2	Engineers, Surveyors, and Architects
3	Natural Scientists and Mathematicians
4	Agricultural, Forestry, and Fishing Occupations
5	Teachers, Counselors, Librarians, and Archivists
6	Health Diagnosing and Treating Practitioners
7	Registered Nurses, Pharmacists, Dietitians, Therapists, and Physician Assistants
8	Health Technologists and Technicians
9	Writers, Artists, and Entertainers
10	Technologists and Technicians, Except Health
11	Marketing and Sales Occupations, Including Clerical
12	Administrative Support Occupations, Including Clerical
13	Service Occupations
14	Agricultural, Forestry, and Fishing Occupations
15	Mechanics and Repairers
16	Construction and Extractive Occupations
17	Production Occupations
18	Transportation and Material Moving Occupations
19	Handlers, Equipment Cleaners, Helpers, and Laborers

Over the years, I've often wondered if I should consider _____ as a career for me.

Regardless of my skills, or practicality, or whether I would even consider it as a career for myself, for me the single most interesting job in the whole world is_____.

Record your responses to these statements on the Career Exploration Worksheet.

b. Review groups of jobs with similar skill requirements and select those which are most interesting—By grouping jobs with simi-

lar skill requirements, the Department of Labor organized the *Dictionary of Occupational Titles'* 20,000 jobs into nineteen job families. Figure 14 shows these nineteen job groups. As you read through them, ask yourself "Which jobs sound better than others?" Of these nineteen job families, which *two* interest you the most? Write the two job families you find most interesting on the space provided on the Career Exploration Worksheet.

Next, review the World of Work table. Also prepared by the Department of Labor, this breaks down the nineteen job families into 209 jobs. This breakdown lists and defines seventeen occupational characteristics and requirements for each of these jobs. Once again, as you look through the table, ask yourself "Which of these jobs appears most interesting?" Of the 209 jobs, which *five* jobs hold the most interest for you? As before, record these five jobs on the Career Exploration Worksheet on page 89.

THE WORLD OF WORK

	Job requirements								Work environment			Occupational characteristics					
	1. Leadership/persuasion	2. Helping/instructing others	3. Problem solving/creativity	4. Initiative	5. Work as part of a team	6. Frequent public contact	7. Manual dexterity	8. Physical stamina	9. Hazardous	10. Outdoors	11. Confined	12. Geographically concentrated	13. Part-time	14. Earnings	15. Employment growth	16. Number of new jobs, 1984–95 (in thousands)	17. Entry requirements
Executive, Administrative, and Managerial Occupations																	
Managers and Administrators																	
Bank officers and managers	•	•	•	•	•	•						•		H	H	119	H
Health services managers	•	•	•	•	•	•								H	H	147	H
Hotel managers and assistants	•	•	•	•	•	•								[1]	H	21	M
School principals and assistant principals	•	•	•	•	•	•								H	L	12	H
Management Support Occupations																	
Accountants and auditors			•	•	•							•		H	H	307	H
Construction and building inspectors			•	•	•	•	•			•				M	L	4	M
Inspectors and compliance officers, except construction			•	•	•	•	•			•				H	L	10	M
Personnel, training, and labor relations specialists	•	•	•	•	•	•								H	M	34	H
Purchasing agents	•		•		•	•								H	M	36	H
Underwriters			•											H	H	17	H
Wholesale and retail buyers	•	•	•	•	•									M	M	28	H
Engineers, Surveyors, and Architects																	
Architects			•	•	•	•	•							H	H	25	H
Surveyors	•				•		•	•		•				M	M	6	M
Engineers																	
Aerospace engineers			•	•	•							•		H	H	14	H
Chemical engineers			•	•	•									H	H	13	H
Civil engineers			•	•	•									H	H	46	H
Electrical and electronics engineers			•	•	•									H	H	206	H
Industrial engineers			•	•	•									H	H	37	H

[1]Estimates not available.
[2]Less than 500.

	Job requirements								Work environment			Occupational characteristics					
	1. Leadership/persuasion	2. Helping/instructing others	3. Problem solving/creativity	4. Initiative	5. Work as part of a team	6. Frequent public contact	7. Manual dexterity	8. Physical stamina	9. Hazardous	10. Outdoors	11. Confined	12. Geographically concentrated	13. Part-time	14. Earnings	15. Employment growth	16. Number of new jobs, 1984–95 (in thousands)	17. Entry requirements
Mechanical engineers			•	•	•									H	H	81	H
Metallurgical, ceramics, and materials engineers			•	•	•									H	H	4	H
Mining engineers			•	•	•									H	L	2[2]	H
Nuclear engineers			•	•	•									H	L	1	H
Petroleum engineers			•	•	•							•		H	M	4	H
Natural Scientists and Mathematicians																	
Computer and Mathematical Occupations																	
Actuaries			•	•							•	•		H	H	4	H
Computer systems analysts	•	•	•	•	•							•		H	H	212	H
Mathematicians			•	•										H	M	4	H
Statisticians			•	•										H	M	4	H
Physical Scientists			•	•										H	M		H
Chemists			•	•										H	L	9	H
Geologists and geophysicists			•	•	•				•			•		H	M	7	H
Meteorologists			•	•	•									H	M	1	H
Physicists and astronomers			•	•										H	L	2	H
Life Scientists																	
Agricultural scientists			•	•										1[1]	M	3	H
Biological scientists			•	•										H	M	10	H
Foresters and conservation scientists		•	•	•	•			•	•	•				H	L	2	H
Social Scientists, Social Workers, Religious Workers, and Lawyers																	
Lawyers	•	•	•	•	•	•	•							H	H	174	H
Social Scientists and Urban Planners																	
Economists			•	•										H	M	7	H
Psychologists		•	•	•		•								H	H	21	H
Sociologists			•	•		•								H	L	2[2]	H
Urban and regional planners	•		•	•	•	•								H	L	2	H
Social and Recreation Workers																	
Social workers	•	•	•	•	•	•								M	H	75	H
Recreation workers	•	•	•	•	•	•	•	•			•		•	L	H	26	M

[1] Estimates not available.
[2] Less than 500.

	Job requirements								Work environment			Occupational characteristics				
	1. Leadership/persuasion	2. Helping/instructing others	3. Problem solving/creativity	4. Initiative	5. Work as part of a team	6. Frequent public contact	7. Manual dexterity	8. Physical stamina	9. Hazardous	10. Outdoors	11. Confined	12. Geographically concentrated	13. Part-time	14. Earnings	15. Employment growth	16. Number of new jobs, 1984–95 (in thousands)	17. Entry requirements
Religious Workers																	
Protestant ministers	•	•	•	•	•	•								L	[1]	[1]	H
Rabbis	•	•	•	•	•	•								H	[1]	[1]	H
Roman Catholic priests	•	•	•	•	•	•								L	[1]	[1]	H
Teachers, Counselors, Librarians, and Archivists																	
Kindergarten and elementary school teachers	•	•	•	•	•	•	•	•						M	H	281	H
Secondary school teachers	•	•	•	•	•	•		•						M	L	48	H
Adult and vocational education teachers	•	•	•	•	•	•	•	•					•	M	M	48	H
College and university faculty	•	•	•	•	•	•							•	H	L	-77	H
Counselors	•	•	•	•	•	•								M	M	29	H
Librarians	•	•	•	•	•	•		•					•	M	L	16	H
Archivists and curators			•	•	•									M	L	1	H
Health Diagnosing and Treating Practitioners																	
Chiropractors	•	•	•	•	•	•	•							H	H	9	H
Dentists	•	•	•	•	•	•	•							H	H	39	H
Optometrists	•	•	•	•	•	•	•							H	H	8	H
Physicians	•	•	•	•	•	•	•						•	H	H	109	H
Podiatrists	•	•	•	•	•	•	•							H	H	4	H
Veterinarians	•	•	•	•	•	•	•	•	•					H	H	9	H
Registered Nurses, Pharmacists, Dietitians, Therapists, and Physician Assistants																	
Dietitians and nutritionists	•	•	•	•	•	•								M	H	12	H
Occupational therapists	•	•	•	•	•	•	•							[1]	H	8	H
Pharmacists	•	•	•	•	•	•					•			H	L	15	H
Physical therapists	•	•	•	•	•	•	•	•						M	H	25	H
Physician assistants	•	•	•	•	•	•	•							M	H	10	M
Recreational therapists	•	•	•	•	•	•	•	•		•				M	H	4	M
Registered nurses	•	•	•	•	•	•	•	•	•				•	M	H	452	M
Respiratory therapists	•	•	•	•	•	•	•							M	H	11	L
Speech pathologists and audiologists	•	•	•	•	•	•								M	M	8	H
Health Technologists and Technicians																	
Clinical laboratory technologists and technicians			•		•		•					•		L	L	18	[3]

[1]Estimates not available.
[3]Vary, depending on job.

	Job requirements								Work environment			Occupational characteristics					
	1. Leadership/persuasion	2. Helping/instructing others	3. Problem solving/creativity	4. Initiative	5. Work as part of a team	6. Frequent public contact	7. Manual dexterity	8. Physical stamina	9. Hazardous	10. Outdoors	11. Confined	12. Geographically concentrated	13. Part-time	14. Earnings	15. Employment growth	16. Number of new jobs, 1984-95 (in thousands)	17. Entry requirements
Dental hygienists		•		•	•	•	•						•	L	H	22	M
Dispensing opticians		•	•	•	•	•	•							M	H	10	M
Electrocardiograph technicians		•	•		•	•	•							[1]	M	3	M
Electroencephalographic technologists and technicians		•	•		•	•	•							[1]	H	1	M
Emergency medical technicians	•	•	•	•	•	•	•	•	•		•			L	L	3	M
Licensed practical nurses		•			•	•	•	•					•	L	M	106	M
Medical record technicians					•						•			L	H	10	M
Radiologic technologists		•			•	•	•		•					L	H	27	M
Surgical technicians		•			•	•	•							L	M	5	M
Writers, Artists, and Entertainers																	
Communications Occupations																	
Public relations specialists	•		•	•	•	•								H	H	30	H
Radio and television announcers and newscasters	•	•		•	•	•							•	L	M	6	H
Reporters and correspondents	•		•	•	•	•								[1]	M	13	H
Writers and editors	•		•	•	•						•		•	[1]	H	54	H
Visual Arts Occupations																	
Designers			•	•	•	•	•							H	H	46	H
Graphic and fine artists			•	•			•								H	60	M
Photographers and camera operators			•	•		•	•						•	M	H	29	M
Performing Arts Occupations																	
Actors, directors, and producers			•	•	•	•	•	•				•	•	L	H	11	M
Dancers and choreographers			•	•	•	•	•	•				•	•	L	H	2	M
Musicians			•	•	•	•	•	•				•	•	L	M	26	M
Technologists and Technicians Except Health																	
Engineering and Science Technicians																	
Drafters			•			•						•		M	M	39	M
Electrical and electronics technicians			•	•		•								M	H	202	M
Engineering technicians			•	•		•								M	H	90	M
Science technicians			•	•		•								M	M	40	M
Other technicians																	
Air traffic controllers	•	•	•		•						•			H	L	[2]	H

[1]Estimates not available.
[2]Less than 500.

	Job requirements								Work environ-ment			Occupational characteristics				
	1. Leadership/persuasion	2. Helping/instructing others	3. Problem solving/creativity	4. Initiative	5. Work as part of a team	6. Frequent public contact	7. Manual dexterity	8. Physical stamina	9. Hazardous	10. Outdoors	11. Confined	12. Geographically concentrated	13. Part-time	14. Earnings	15. Employment growth	16. Number of new jobs, 1984-95 (in thousands)	17. Entry requirements
Broadcast technicians			•		•	•					•			M	H	5	M
Computer programmers			•		•						•			H	H	245	H
Legal assistants				3	•	3								M	H	51	L
Library technicians		•			•	•	•						•	L	L	4	L
Tool programmers, numerical control			•				•		•					M	H	3	M
Marketing and Sales Occupations																	
Cashiers		•				•	•					•	•	L	H	566	L
Insurance sales workers	•	•	•	•		•							•	M	L	34	M
Manufacturers' sales workers	•	•	•	•		•								H	L	51	H
Real estate agents and brokers	•	•	•	•		•				•			•	M	M	52	M
Retail sales workers	•	•		•		•							•	L	M	583	L
Securities and financial services sales workers	•	•	•	•		•							•	H	H	32	H
Travel agents	•	•	•	•		•								1	H	32	M
Wholesale trade sales workers	•	•	•	•		•								M	H	369	M
Administrative Support Occupations, Including Clerical																	
Bank tellers				•	•							•	•	L	L	24	L
Bookkeepers and accounting clerks				•								•	•	L	L	118	L
Computer and peripheral equipment operators			•		•		•					•		L	H	143	M
Data entry keyers					•		•					•		L	L	10	L
Mail carriers					•	•	•			•				M	L	8	L
Postal clerks					•	•	•	•				•		M	L	-27	L
Receptionists and information clerks		•			•	•						•	•	L	M	83	L
Reservation and transportation ticket agents and travel clerks		•	•		•	•						•		M	L	7	L
Secretaries				•	•	•	•							L	L	268	L
Statistical clerks					•							•		L	L	-12	L
Stenographers				•	•	•	•							L	L	-96	L
Teacher aides	•	•			•	•	•	•					•	L	M	88	L
Telephone operators		•				•						•		L	M	89	L
Traffic, shipping, and receiving clerks			•	•	•									L	L	61	L

[1]Estimates not available.
[3]Vary, depending on job.

	Job requirements								Work environment			Occupational characteristics					
	1. Leadership/persuasion	2. Helping/instructing others	3. Problem solving/creativity	4. Initiative	5. Work as part of a team	6. Frequent public contact	7. Manual dexterity	8. Physical stamina	9. Hazardous	10. Outdoors	11. Confined	12. Geographically concentrated	13. Part-time	14. Earnings	15. Employment growth	16. Number of new jobs, 1984–95 (in thousands)	17. Entry requirements
Typists							•				•		•	L	L	11	L
Service Occupations																	
Protective Service Occupations																	
Correction officers	•	•		•			•	•			•			M	H	45	L
Firefighting occupations		•	•	•	•	•	•	•	•	•			•	M	M	48	L
Guards						•	•	•	•		•		•	L	H	188	L
Police and detectives	•	•	•	•	•	•	•		•					M	M	66	L
Food and Beverage Preparation and Service Occupations																	
Bartenders					•		•	•			•		•	L	H	112	M
Chefs and cooks, except short-order					•		•	•			•		•	L	H	210	M
Waiters and waitresses					•		•	•					•	L	H	424	L
Health Service Occupations																	
Dental assistants		•			•	•	•	•					•	L	H	48	L
Medical assistants		•			•	•	•		•					L	H	79	L
Nursing aides		•			•	•	•	•					•	L	H	348	L
Psychiatric aides		•			•		•	•						L	L	5	L
Cleaning Service Occupations																	
Janitors and cleaners							•						•	L	M	443	L
Personal Service Occupations																	
Barbers						•	•	•			•		•	L	L	4	M
Child-care workers	•	•		•		•		•					•	L	L	55	L
Cosmetologists and related workers						•	•	•			•		•	L	H	150	M
Flight attendants		•				•	•	•						M	H	13	L
Agricultural, Forestry, and Fishing Occupations																	
Farm operators and managers	•	•	•	•	•		•	•		•		•		M	L	-62	L
Mechanics and Repairers																	
Vehicle and Mobile Equipment Mechanics and Repairers																	
Aircraft mechanics and engine specialists			•		•		•	•	•			•		H	M	18	M
Automotive and motorcycle mechanics			•			•	•	•	•		•			M	H	185	M
Automotive body repairers			•				•	•	•		•			M	M	32	M

	Job requirements								Work environment			Occupational characteristics					
	1. Leadership/persuasion	2. Helping/instructing others	3. Problem solving/creativity	4. Initiative	5. Work as part of a team	6. Frequent public contact	7. Manual dexterity	8. Physical stamina	9. Hazardous	10. Outdoors	11. Confined	12. Geographically concentrated	13. Part-time	14. Earnings	15. Employment growth	16. Number of new jobs, 1984–95 (in thousands)	17. Entry requirements
Diesel mechanics			•			•	•	•	•		•			M	H	48	M
Farm equipment mechanics			•			•	•	•		•				M	L	2	M
Mobile heavy-equipment mechanics			•				•	•	•		•			M	M	12	M
Electrical and Electronic Equipment Repairers																	
Commercial and electronic equipment repairers			•	•		•	•							L	M	8	M
Communications equipment mechanics			•	•		•	•							M	L	3	M
Computer service technicians			•	•		•	•							M	H	28	M
Electronic home entertainment equipment repairers			•	•		•	•		•				•	M	M	7	M
Home appliance and power tool repairers			•	•		•	•							L	M	9	M
Line installers and cable splicers			•		•		•	•	•	•				M	M	24	L
Telephone installers and repairers			•		•	•	•	•	•					M	L	-19	L
Other Mechanics and Repairers																	
General maintenance mechanics			•				•		•					M	M	137	M
Heating, air-conditioning, and refrigeration mechanics			•				•		•					M	M	29	M
Industrial machinery repairers			•				•	•	•					M	L	34	M
Millwrights			•				•		•					H	L	6	M
Musical instrument repairers and tuners							•							L	L	1	M
Office machine and cash register servicers			•	•	•		•							M	H	16	M
Vending machine servicers and repairers			•	•			•							¹	M	5	M
Construction and Extractive Occupations																	
Construction Occupations																	
Bricklayers and stonemasons			•		•		•	•	•	•				M	M	15	M
Carpenters			•		•		•	•	•	•				M	M	101	M
Carpet installers			•		•	•	•	•						M	M	11	M
Concrete masons and terrazzo workers			•		•		•	•	•	•				M	M	17	M
Drywall workers and lathers			•		•		•	•						M	M	11	M

¹Estimates not available.

	Job requirements								Work environment			Occupational characteristics				
	1. Leadership/persuasion	2. Helping/instructing others	3. Problem solving/creativity	4. Initiative	5. Work as part of a team	6. Frequent public contact	7. Manual dexterity	8. Physical stamina	9. Hazardous	10. Outdoors	11. Confined	12. Geographically concentrated	13. Part-time	14. Earnings	15. Employment growth	16. Number of new jobs, 1984–95 (in thousands)	17. Entry requirements
Electricians			•		•		•	•	•	•				H	M	88	M
Glaziers			•		•		•	•	•					M	H	8	M
Insulation workers			•		•		•	•						M	M	7	M
Painters and paperhangers			•		•	•	•	•	•	•				M	L	17	M
Plasterers			•		•		•	•	•			•		M	L	1	M
Plumbers and pipefitters			•		•	•	•	•	•	•				H	M	61	M
Roofers			•		•		•	•	•	•				L	M	16	M
Sheet-metal workers			•		•		•	•	•					M	M	16	M
Structural and reinforcing metal workers			•		•		•	•	•	•				H	M	16	M
Tilesetters			•		•		•	•						M	M	3	M
Extractive Occupations																	
Roustabouts						•		•	•	•	•		•		M	L	2	L
Production Occupations																	
Blue-collar-worker supervisors	•	•	•	•	•		•		•					M	L	85	M
Precision Production Occupations																	
Boilermakers			•				•		•					M	L	4	M
Bookbinding workers		•			•		•	•	•		•			L	M	14	M
Butchers and meatcutters						•	•	•	•		•			L	L	-9	M
Compositors and typesetters							•	•	•		•			L	M	14	M
Dental laboratory technicians							•				•			L	M	10	M
Jewelers	•	•	•		•	•	•				•	•		L	L	3	M
Lithographic and photoengraving workers			•	•		•	•				•			H	M	13	M
Machinists			•				•	•	•		•	•		M	L	37	M
Photographic process workers							•				•			L	H	14	L
Shoe and leather workers and repairers			•		•	•	•							L	L	-8	M
Tool-and-die makers			•				•	•	•		•	•		H	L	16	M
Upholsterers							•	•			•			L	L	6	M
Plant and System Operators																	
Stationary engineers			•				•	•	•					M	L	4	M
Water and sewage treatment plant operators			•	•			•		•	•				L	M	10	M

[2]Less than 500.

	Job requirements								Work environment			Occupational characteristics				
	1. Leadership/persuasion	2. Helping/instructing others	3. Problem solving/creativity	4. Initiative	5. Work as part of a team	6. Frequent public contact	7. Manual dexterity	8. Physical stamina	9. Hazardous	10. Outdoors	11. Confined	12. Geographically concentrated	13. Part-time	14. Earnings	15. Employment growth	16. Number of new jobs, 1984–95 (in thousands)	17. Entry requirements
Machine Operators, Tenders, and Setup Workers																	
Metalworking and plastic-working machine operators							•	•	•		•	•			L	3	L
Numerical-control machine-tool operators			•				•	•	•		•			M	H	17	M
Printing press operators	•	•		•			•	•	•		•			M	M	26	M
Fabricators, Assemblers, and Handworking Occupations																	
Precision assemblers					•		•	•			•			L	M	66	L
Transportation equipment painters							•	•	•		•			M	M	9	M
Welders and cutters							•	•	•	•				M	M	41	M
Transportation and Material Moving Occupations																	
Aircraft pilots			•	•	•		•				•			H	H	18	M
Bus drivers			•		•	•	•				•	•		M	M	77	M
Construction machinery operators					•		•	•	•	•	•			M	M	32	M
Industrial truck and tractor operators			•				•	•			•			M	L	-46	M
Truck drivers			•				•	•			•			M	M	428	M
Handlers, Equipment Cleaners, Helpers, and Laborers																	
Construction trades helpers					•		•	•	•	•				L	L	27	L

Occupational Characteristics

(12) Geographically concentrated—50 percent or more of the jobs located in five states or fewer.

(13) Part-time—many workers employed for less than 35 hours a week.

(14) Earnings—three categories of earnings, based on 1985 averages, are shown:

L = lowest (10 percent or less); M = middle (11 to 19 percent); H = highest (20 percent or more)

Keep in mind that earnings within an occupation vary widely and that some workers earn more and some earn less than the average.

(15) Employment growth—three categories of projected growth from 1984 to 1995 are shown:

L = lowest; M = middle; H = highest

Job opportunities are usually favorable if employment is expected to increase at least as rapidly as for the economy as a whole (15 percent). But don't pick a job based solely on growth. Because of the need to replace workers who retire or leave the occupation for other reasons, slow-growing occupations may actually have more job opportunities than their growth rates indicates.

(16) Number of new jobs, 1984–95—the projected number of new jobs expected to become available. In most occupations, the number of job openings created by the need to replace workers who change occupations or leave the labor force will be much higher than the number of new jobs.

(17) Entry requirements—three categories of education and training requirements are shown:

L = high school or less education is sufficient, and the basics of the job can usually be learned in a few months of on-the-job training; M = post–high school training, such as apprenticeship or junior college, or many months or years of experience are required to be fully qualified; H = four or more years of college usually required.

Source: U.S. Department of Labor

c. Examine jobs with similar personality requirements and select those that are most interesting—As you'll recall from the discussion of John Holland's career model in Chapter 5, just as with personality, work environments can be organized by the RIASEC classifications: Realistic, Investigative, Artistic, Social, Enterprising, and Conventional. Your basic challenge is to match your personality to a work environment. For example, if you are a Realistic personality you should look for Realistic careers in order to find career satisfaction; if you're an Artistic personality, you should search for Artistic work environments, and so on.

The best way to find work environments that match your personality is for you to obtain a copy of the *Dictionary of Holland Occupational Codes: A Comprehensive Cross-Index of Holland's RIASEC Codes with 12,000 DOT Occupations* by John Holland and Gary D. Gottfredson (available at your local library or by calling Psychological Assessment Resources at 800-331-8378 [toll-free]). This dictionary does an absolutely marvelous job of classifying careers using the RIASEC method. By comparing your three-letter vocational personality code on the Vocational Identity Summary (assessed in Chapter 5) to jobs organized by Holland code, you'll find hundreds of potential *matches*. When exploring jobs, you should look at all six combinations of your three-letter code. In other words, if you are an RIC personality type, you should investigate RIC, RCI, CIR, CRI, ICR, and IRC jobs. In addition, you may find other interesting occupations by exploring any combination that begins with your first letter. In the RIC example just given, you would look at all jobs whose RIASEC code begins with an R regardless of the other two letters (RAE careers, for example).

Using the *Dictionary of Holland Occupational Codes,* simply review the jobs within the various six combinations of your personality type. Each time you encounter a job that sounds very interesting to you, list it on a sheet of paper. Don't worry about evaluating the jobs at this point; you'll get to that a little later in the process. After reviewing all the possible jobs matching your six RIASEC combinations and writing down the ones that sound interesting, review your list and circle the **five most interesting** jobs. After deciding which occupations hold the most interest for you, record these five jobs on the Career Exploration Worksheet.

As a way to whet your appetite for matching your personality to careers, I classified the nineteen job families you reviewed earlier using the RIASEC model. Take a look at Figure 15. Look for job families whose Holland type matches the *first* letter from your three-letter personality code (see the VIS). Each time you find a match, you should record the job family's number on the Career Exploration Worksheet. For example, if the first letter of your Holland code is an A, you would record number 9 (Writers, Artists, and Entertainers) on the worksheet. As you can see, different Holland types have different numbers of matching job families. In the case of the A example there is only one match. R, on the other hand, has six matches. Record only the matches on the worksheet.

d. Select the career/s you would like to explore further—Now, review all the job families and occupations listed in column 2. Of all

FIGURE 15
Career Job Families and Personality Type

	Career Job Families	Holland Type
1	Executive, Administrative, and Managerial Occupations	E
2	Engineers, Surveyors, and Architects	R
3	Natural Scientists and Mathematicians	I
4	Agricultural, Forestry, and Fishing Occupations	S
5	Teachers, Counselors, Librarians, and Archivists	S
6	Health Diagnosing and Treating Practitioners	S
7	Registered Nurses, Pharmacists, Dietitians, Therapists, and Physician Assistants	S
8	Health Technologists and Technicians	I
9	Writers, Artists, and Entertainers	A
10	Technologists and Technicians, Except Health	C
11	Marketing and Sales Occupations, Including Clerical	E
12	Administrative Support Occupations, Including Clerical	C
13	Service Occupations	S
14	Agricultural, Forestry, and Fishing Occupations	R
15	Mechanics and Repairers	R
16	Construction and Extractive Occupations	R
17	Production Occupations	R
18	Transportation and Material Moving Occupations	R
19	Handlers, Equipment Cleaners, Helpers, and Laborers	R

the possibilities listed in column 2, which do you most want to know more about? Make a list of a few careers you would like to explore further. Following is an example of a completed Career Exploration Worksheet.

A note about values

You've probably noticed that although *values* make up a significant part of your vocational identity, I did not include them on the Career Exploration Worksheet. This is not because they are unimportant. Certainly, finding a match between your values and your job choice is vitally important. It's this simple: If your job does not match your values, you'll be unhappy in your work. You will not find values on the Career Exploration Worksheet because, unlike personality and job skills, jobs cannot be organized by values. Specific occupations do differ

Career Exploration Worksheet

Exploration Questions	Possible Occupations to Explore
Your Heart	
1. Over the years, I've often wondered if I should consider _____ as a career for me.	
2. Regardless of my skills, or practicality, or whether I would even consider it as a career, for me the single most interesting job in the whole world is _____.	
Transferable Skills	
3. The two job families from Figure 13 that seem most interesting to me.	
4. The five jobs from Figure 14 that seem most interesting to me.	
Personality	
5. The five most interesting jobs from the *Dictionary of Holland Occupational Codes.*	
6. The job family/ies in Figure 15 whose Holland Type matches the first letter of my Holland code. NOTE: Different codes have different numbers of possible matches. R = 7, I = 2, A = 1, S = 5, E = 2, C = 2 Only record matches	

Example
Career Exploration Worksheet

Exploration Questions	Possible Occupations to Explore
Your Heart	
1. Over the years, I've often wondered if I should consider _____ as a career for me.	Psychologist
2. Regardless of my skills, or practicality, or whether I would even consider it as a career, for me the single most interesting job in the whole world is _____.	Physical therapist/counselor
Transferable Skills	
3. The two job families from Figure 13 that seem most interesting to me.	Number 4
	Number 6
4. The five jobs from Figure 14 that seem most interesting to me.	Psychologist
	Counselor
	Chiropractor
	Physical Therapist
	Veterinarian
Personality	
5. The five most interesting jobs from the *Dictionary of Holland Occupational Codes*	Psychologist
	Physical Therapist
	Speech Pathologist
	Podiatrist
	Veterinarian
6. The job family/ies in Figure 15 whose Holland Type matches the first letter of my Holland code. NOTE: Different codes have different numbers of possible matches. R = 7, I = 2, A = 1, S = 5, E = 2, C = 2 Only record matches	Number 4
	Number 5
	Number 6
	Number 7
	Number 13

Career(s) I'm Going to Explore

<u>Geriatric Physical Therapist</u>   <u>Veterinarian</u>   <u>Counselor</u>

somewhat in their values; for example, stockbrokers value income and status to a greater degree than forest rangers do. However, an organization's culture has much more to do with determining values than a job title does. For example, being a chef in the Nazi army during World War II is obviously and radically different from being a chef at Walt Disney World's EPCOT Center. While the culinary standards and actual work may be quite similar, the two organization's values are wildly different. This example, while far fetched, makes an important point. You must *absolutely, positively,* and *undoubtedly* do everything you can to determine the similarities between your values and those of the organization for which you will work. However, you can only do this during the job search, after you're in contact with a specific organization. I'll talk about how you can ensure a values match when you get to the job market research (Chapter 8) and networking (Chapter 9) parts of the book.

STEP 2: GATHER INFORMATION

From the thousands of possible jobs in the world, in Step 1 you identified one to three specific occupations that you'd like to know more about. As shown in Figure 8, you have three types of resources for gathering information about these occupations: publications, the Internet, and people. The best source of information regarding careers, by far, is people. While the other two sources add value to career decision making, only people can give you the in-depth kind of insight you'll need to choose a career objective.

Information source: Publications

You review publications to learn enough about an occupation to determine if it's worth *really* exploring. Publications can act as a screening device to help you either confirm or narrow your choices, but are not sufficient to launch a job search. If an occupation remains very interesting to you after you read about it, then you should further explore the career by talking to the best source of information: people. Libraries contain numerous published resources describing occupations. Figure 16 lists several of the best.

Take your list of occupations you'd like to know more about to the library, find one or more of the publications listed in Figure 16, and read about that occupation. After you know a little bit more about it, ask yourself, "Does this occupation seem to fit my vocational identity?" and "Do I still want to explore this career?" If the answers to these questions are yes, photocopy the information about your careers of interest. You'll need these photocopies when you prepare a career profile during Step 3.

Information source: The Internet

Like paper publications, the Internet offers a number of online resources to learn more about specific occupations. As with paper publications, electronic sources (Figure 17) provide you with information to determine if you want to continue exploring a specific occupation. Once again, after reviewing information about each career you listed in Step 1, ask yourself, "Does this occupation fit my vocational identity?" and "Do I still want to explore this career?" If the answer is yes to both questions,

FIGURE 16
Career exploration information source: publications

Publication	Source	Comments
The Guide for Occupational Exploration (GOE)	U.S. Department of Labor, Employment and Training Administration Available in most libraries	You can refer to Figure 10 in Chapter 5 to convert the GOE's twelve interest factors into your three-letter personality code. You can then explore the guide's hundreds of occupations.
Occupational Outlook Handbook	U.S. Department of Labor, Bureau of Labor Statistics Available in most libraries	Provides a wealth of information for specific occupations, including the nature of the work, working conditions, employment statistics, qualifications, job outlook, and earnings.
Occupational Outlook Quarterly	U.S. Department of Labor, Bureau of Labor Statistics Available in most libraries	Published four times a year, provides "how-to" information about today's jobs and those projected to be in demand in the future. Presents training opportunities and salary trends.
Dictionary of Occupational Titles	U.S. Department of Labor, Bureau of Labor Statistics Available in most libraries	Good news: lists over 20,000 jobs, provides detailed job descriptions, and organizes tasks using the data, people, and things model. Bad news: so unwieldy it's difficult for most job seekers to use.
Encyclopedia of Careers and Vocational Guidance	Available in most libraries	Presents career articles, history of particular jobs, typical career path, and resources for learning about training, internships, scholarships, and job placement.
Occupational Compensation Survey: Pay and Benefits	U.S. Department of Labor, Bureau of Labor Statistics Available in most libraries	Good news: the BLS reports the results of salary surveys in all Metropolitan Statistical Areas (MSA) in the U.S. Bad news: Not very accurate. *Remember:* The best source of information is from people actually doing the job in which you're interested and that is especially true regarding salaries.

download the information so you will have a hard copy to use when putting together career profiles in Step 3.

Information source: People

As I said earlier, this is where you will find the greatest wealth of information about careers. Your two primary tasks are first to identify and then to talk to people employed in the career(s) in which you are interested. That is, you need to locate people actually doing the kind of work you're interested in doing, and then set up informational meetings.

During discussion of networking strategies in Chapter 9, I will talk about another kind of meeting I call an advice-and-information meeting. The informational meeting during career exploration is different from the advice and information networking meeting. I provide a great deal of detail about the advice and informational networking meeting in Chapter 9. I mention it here only to distinguish the two types of meetings.

For some careers, you'll find it quite simple to locate people actually doing the work you're interested in doing. If you want to locate a rabbi, you can call a synagogue; to find a nurse, you can get in touch with the local hospital; to find an elementary teacher, contact the neighborhood school. In some cases, however, finding people employed in the occupations you'd like to explore is more difficult. For example, where would you look to learn more about a biochemistry career?

Here are a couple of tips for locating contacts for your informational meetings. If the occupation of interest requires a degree, telephone a college or university that offers that

FIGURE 17
Career exploration information source: The Internet

Publication	Source & Internet Address	Comments
Occupational Outlook Handbook	U.S. Department of Labor, Bureau of Labor Statistics http://stats.bls.gov/oco/oco1000.htm	Fully searchable—describes nature of the work, working conditions, employment statistics, qualifications, job outlook, and earnings.
Occupational Outlook Quarterly	U.S. Department of Labor, Bureau of Labor Statistics http://stats.bls.gov/empooq0.htm	You can order reprints and view topics but the publication cannot be read online.
JobSmart	http://jobsmart.org/tools/salary/index.htm	Terrific site offering salary information about a number of jobs as well as other career related information.

kind of degree and ask to speak to professors who teach in that discipline. You'll find that most of these professors enjoy talking about their field. You can set up an informational meeting with one of the professors, or ask where you might contact recent graduates to learn about the career. Here's another option. The *Occupational Outlook Handbook* lists the settings where particular careers are found. Try contacting companies in your area that have businesses like those mentioned in the handbook. Also, don't forget your existing network. Contact your neighbors, friends, religious leaders, or members of organizations to which you belong. Ask those in your network where you can find people employed in the careers you'd like to explore. The bottom line is this: If you ask enough people, someone will give you a company name or a person's name that will turn into an opportunity to set up an informational meeting.

Your informational meeting agenda

As you will learn after conducting a couple of them, these meetings are a great way to learn about careers. Once you've located someone who actually does the kind of work you're interested in exploring, contact him or her by phone. Say that you are in the midst of a career transition and explain how you got his or her name. If someone referred you, be sure to use that person's name in your introduction. Quickly explain the reason for your desire to have this meeting. Say that the "meeting's purpose is to learn more about the _____ career field so that I can make an informed decision about my career direction." *Let the contact know that the meeting will take no more than 15 to 30 minutes.* Finally, assure the contact

that you will not ask him or her for a job: *"I promise you that I will not ask you for a job; I am only seeking information about your career field."*

During the meeting, you should absolutely *not* ask for an interview or a job. Asking for an interview or job during an informational meeting can backfire, ruining potential job opportunities with the contact's company and with others the contact may tell. People do not appreciate being deceived. If you say the meeting is about gathering information, make sure the meeting is about gathering information. Obviously, if the *contact* offers you an interview (and he or she probably will not), you certainly can agree to it if you would like. Because one of these informational meetings does occasionally lead to an offer of an interview, I suggest that you do not begin setting up informational interviews until you've prepared your résumé (Chapter 7) and you are ready to perform well in a job interview (Chapter 10).

Go to the informational meeting prepared to find out about the contact's career field and hold it to 30 minutes maximum. It's best if you begin to close the meeting after about 25 minutes. If the contact indicates that he or she would like to continue, then spend no more than 10 more minutes, thank the person for his or her time, and leave. You should send a thank-you note the *next* morning.

Remember, the goal of the informational meeting is to find out more about a particular career in order to determine how well it matches your vocational identity. Be sure to take along a notebook to jot down as many detailed notes as possible during your dialogue. You will find the following questions useful.

- What do you enjoy most about this career?
- What do you least enjoy about this career?
- What are the basic qualifications required in this career?
- What is a typical advancement path in this career?
- What do you think it takes to be successful in this career?
- What kind of person would find it difficult to succeed in this career?
- What is the typical salary range for people in this career?
- Who else do you know that works in this career field who would be willing to talk to me? (This is the *most* important question—try to get at least three names of other contacts.)

One caveat: Remember that the majority of people are unhappy in their careers. What does this fact have to do with informational meetings? Maybe a lot. If your contact happens to be part of the majority, then he or she may provide pretty skewed answers to your questions. Actually, the meeting can be helpful either way. Your contact may be unhappy about matters that would delight you. If you determine your contact is unhappy in this career, take his or her attitude into consideration as you evaluate the meeting.

STEP 3: ORGANIZE THE INFORMATION

In Step 1 you chose one to three careers to explore. In Step 2 you gathered information about those careers from paper and electronic publications and from people. In Step 3 it's time to organize your information. Gather your photocopies, downloaded files, and notes from your informational meetings. For each career you explored, prepare a career profile using the following example.

Example
Career Profile

Job Title/s: Physical Therapist

The Reasons I Chose to Explore This Career: I've always thought this was an interesting career. Also, it was one of the jobs I selected from the World of Work table and it seems to fit my vocational personality.

Job Description: Physical therapists work in a variety of settings, relieving pain and improving mobility for patients suffering from injuries and disease. They evaluate medical histories and test and measure strength and flexibility, range of motion, and ability to function.

Educational Requirements: Must pass a state licensor exam after graduating from an accredited physical therapy program (four-year program).

Transferable Skill Requirements: Among others, administering activities and programs, analyzing information, asking questions of people, building rapport with people, dealing with difficult people, developing plans to reach objectives, interpersonal skills, listening, motivating/inspiring others, verbalizing ideas, and writing reports.

Outlook for Future: While there is not as high a demand as in the past, the outlook is still very bright, with most graduates receiving multiple job offers.

Typical Career Path: Most begin as a staff physical therapist and after two to four years can become a department manager. Some move on to rehabilitation director with responsibility over several areas, including physical therapy and occupational therapy.

Salary: The average salary for staff therapists is $37,596, with the top 10 percent earning about $60,000.

STEP 4: EVALUATE THE INFORMATION

You are now at a point where you can compare all the information you gathered about your vocational identity with the data collected while exploring various careers. By now you know the basic question: "Does a particular career fit my vocational identity?" As you review each career profile, ask yourself the questions in Figure 18.

    I know a 38-year-old man who was faced with a significant career choice. He had to decide between two very different career options. He committed himself to making a quality decision. After self-assessment, he asked all of the questions below in relation to each of the two options. In fact, I've never seen a more thorough job of evaluating career options. He listed each vocational identity element on a sheet of paper. First, he rated the degree to which each option fulfilled his most important values. Similarly, he evaluated how well each position matched all the other aspects of his vocational identity. He then weighted each element of his vocational identity in terms of its importance and created a somewhat complex

FIGURE 18
Questions to Evaluate Career Options

- Will this career allow me to exercise my treasure-yielding skills? If yes, how?
- Does this career seem to fit my personality (RIASEC Code)? If yes, in what way(s)?
- From what I know so far, is this career a good match with my values? If yes, how?
- Is this career consistent with my life's purpose? If yes, how?
- Overall, does this career seem to fit my vocational identity? If yes, why do I think so?
- Am I genuinely excited about pursuing this career option? If yes, why?

mathematical equation. When he solved the equation, one option beat out the other by a very narrow margin. Being a rational person, he telephoned the employer holding the winning career option and informed them of his decision to accept their offer. He then promptly resigned from his job, leaving the promotion that represented the second option. Unfortunately, within three days of starting his new career, he was painfully miserable and confused. When I asked him why he left his job he said, "I was always happy there, but the data indicated that this career option was better. I never really felt comfortable with the decision, but the process was so thorough." Whatever you do, *don't* do as this fellow did. He disregarded his intuition—his heart. Here is one of my favorite quotes:

"Not everything that can be counted counts;

not everything that counts can be counted."

Albert Einstein

I cannot say this too strongly: When making career decisions, LISTEN TO YOUR HEART. Obviously, I believe in gathering and evaluating information; both about you and about career options. But at the end of the day, if you want to find your ideal destination you must listen for your calling. Believe me, it's out there. If your heart, your gut, your sixth sense, that small inner voice, or whatever you call it does not get you excited about a career choice, and if you don't *feel* comfortable—don't do it.

Ah . . . but if your answers to all the vocational identity questions in Figure 18 are yes, and you do feel a genuine excitement and a quiet confidence in a particular career direction—take it! You'll be moving toward your ideal destination, moving toward career satisfaction, and taking the first step toward reaping career treasure. Congratulations!

If the answer to any of the questions in Figure 18 is no, or you feel uncomfortable with a career choice, go back to Step 1 and go through the process again, exploring different careers until you know one is right for you.

STEP 5: WRITE YOUR CAREER OBJECTIVE

The career statement's chief purpose is to identify a job and industry target at which to aim your job search efforts. The statement will help focus and guide your job search. Obviously, to serve as a legitimate employment opportunity, the position and industry identified in your career objective must be available in the marketplace. However, because you will not begin to evaluate the job market until Chapter 8, think of your career objective as "a work in progress." You may modify your career objective as you learn more about the job market. The objective statement is defined as a one-sentence statement that conveys the position and industry you are seeking.

Examples
Objective Statements

- I am seeking a sales management position within the mainframe computer industry.
- I am seeking a position as a director of compensation and benefits within the retail clothing industry.
- I am seeking a project manager position within an international manufacturing organization.

EXERCISE 9
Write Your Career Objective

On a sheet of paper, write a draft of your career objective. Remember, this statement reflects your vocational identity and aims at finding your ideal destination.

After writing your career objective, ask yourself these five questions:

- Is this objective consistent with my personal mission statement?
- Do my past work accomplishments (from Exercise 7, page 49) support this objective?
- Do my knowledge, skills, and values lend themselves to this objective?
- Do my vocational interests and personality match this objective?
- Does my educational background support this objective?

If the answer to any of the first four questions is no, modify your objective until you can answer yes. After responding yes to all four, answer the fifth question regarding educational qualification. If you can answer yes to the fifth question as well, turn to Appendix A and write your career objective at the top of the front page of the Vocational Identity Summary. If the answer to the educational question is no, read the following section.

What if I need more/different education?

During your exploration, you may find a career that matches every aspect of your vocational identity, but requires education that you don't have. A significant life decision now faces you. The decision is not as simple as whether or not to go to school, however. Fundamentally, it's an issue of whether or not you will pursue your ideal destination. Please understand that I am not saying you should seek an education that you do not wish to pursue. What I am saying is that you should base your decision on your life's purpose, and not just make a school/no school decision. As much as any other career choice, this one requires that you carefully evaluate your values and purpose. If you are an adult, returning to school will almost certainly require financial sacrifice—at least short-term. You will have to ask yourself "How important is money to me?" and "How will the changes in social and economic status impact me and others in my family?" Returning to school may or may not be consistent with your life's purpose and with other values important to you. Only you can decide if it makes sense for your life. Look once again at the values you listed on the VIS. I also urge you to reread your life's mission statement and review the statements that you hope others will make about you toward the end of your life. After this review, then make your choice about whether or not to return to school.

"I'm too old to go back to school."

I've heard this complaint numerous times; it just does not hold water. If you believe that you are too old to return to school, you should complete the following activity.

My age today _____

My age in five years if I pursue an education _____

My age in five years if I do not pursue an education _____

I'm sure you get the point. Your choice of whether or not to pursue additional formal education does not impact your age in any way. The school/no school debate is simply a question of how you will choose to spend your time.

By the way, you may find JobTrak's Internet listing of about 450 college majors at four-year and two-year institutions of interest. Their Web site address is: http://www.jobtrak.com/docs/collegelist.html.

ONE LAST ASSESSMENT: YOUR FINANCES

Reality calling: You can only spend as much time exploring career options and searching for the ideal job as your bank account will allow. If you are currently employed and considering a change of careers, you can probably explore options for quite some time. However, what if you lost your job several months ago, and the power company just sent you a notice to pay by next Tuesday or learn to enjoy reading by candlelight? Given this situation, you need to move along pretty quickly in finding gainful employment. Searching for your ideal destination may have to wait. I present several options for what to do when you don't find your perfect career in Chapter 13. Regardless of your current situation, it is important that you evaluate your current financial needs prior to launching a job search campaign. Following is an exercise to help you do this. Part A provides a list of potential sources of income, while Part B summarizes your expenses and allows you to estimate these for the next six months. Simply complete both Part A and Part B to get a snapshot of your finances. This exercise is obviously not a comprehensive financial plan, but it does provide you and your family with rough financial estimates that will allow for meaningful discussion about your job search realities.

EXERCISE 10
Financial Assessment

· ·

Part A—Possible Sources of Income

Average Monthly Amount

☐ Severance pay _____

☐ Alimony/child support _____

☐ Consulting fee, contract services(s), and part-time work _____

☐ Dividends (stocks) _____

☐ Spouse's income _____

☐ Interest income _____

☐ Rental income _____

☐ Unemployment compensation _____

☐ Other income _____

TOTAL MONTHLY INCOME _____

Part B—Monthly Expenses

Expenses	1	2	3	4	5	6
HOUSING						
Rent or mortgage payment						
Maintenance and repairs						
Home insurance						
Property taxes						
UTILITIES						
Electricity						
Heating fuel						
Telephone (local and long distance)						
Water, sewer, trash collection						
GROCERIES						
Cigarettes, beverages						
Food						
Other						

Expenses	1	2	3	4	5	6

TRANSPORTATION
Bus/carpooling/parking/
  taxi
Car payment
Gasoline/oil
Car repairs, tires,
  maintenance
Insurance
Commuter expenses						

EDUCATION
  Tuition, books, special fees
  Professional dues and
    continuing education
  Subscriptions to
    publications						

PERSONAL CARE
  Drugs/prescriptions
  Hospitalization
  Life insurance
  Doctors, dentists
  Hair/Beauty
  Health club						

ENTERTAINMENT
  Cable television
  Dining out
  Vacations
  Concerts and shows
  Hobbies						

HOUSEHOLD
EXPENDITURES
  Furniture/appliances
  Supplies (cleaning and
    maintenance)						

CLOTHING
  Adults
  Children
  Laundry/cleaners						

LOANS/INSTALLMENTS/
BILLS/TAXES
  Income (federal, state)
  Other						

Expenses	1	2	3	4	5	6
MISCELLANEOUS EXPENSES						
Alimony/child support payments						
Baby-sitting/child care						
Dues/subscriptions (newspapers, books)						
Gifts/birthdays/holidays						
Religious and other contributions						
TOTAL MONTHLY EXPENSES						
TOTAL MONTHLY INCOME From Part A: Sources of Income						

ONCE UPON A TIME AGAIN

While I was picking up some letterhead from the print shop recently, I ran into an acquaintance whom I'll call Jim. Jim asked me what I'd been up to, and I told him that, among other things, I was writing this book. In the course of that discussion, I shared my ideas about discovering one's vocational identity and matching it to a career. I told him that I believe the best question anyone can ask when making a career choice is "What is it that I really *want* to do?" Jim paused, then looked at me and said, "Paul, what do you think would happen to our society, to our country, to this economy, if everyone just went off and did what they wanted to do?" I asked Jim what he thought the answer to his question was. He replied, "Well, it would go down—I mean, the

> "Your work is to discover your work and then with all your heart to give yourself to it."
>
> Buddha

standard of living, the economy—everything." I said, "Jim, I think the GNP would increase, poverty would decrease, stress-related health-care costs would decline, and people would be much happier."

You should know that Jim is in the process of making his fourth voluntary career change in the last five years. From seminary to sales jobs, Jim's career has been full of dissatisfaction. He continues to try to do the *right* thing; but has never considered that the right thing might be what his heart desires most. I asked him, "If you could do anything, regardless of practicality, what is it that you really *want* to do?" He quickly replied, "I've always *wanted* to be in landscaping, but I've got to feed my family." "Jim," I inquired, "don't you think that many people involved in landscaping make a decent living?" It was clear that this one stumped him. For some reason it just never occurred to him that he could choose a career based on what he wanted. Strangely, he seems to feel that if he wants to do it, and he doesn't wear a suit, it's probably not a legitimate career choice. Throughout his entire adult life he has disregarded the very thing he should have attended to: his ideal destination is calling.

I am hopeful that Jim will think about our conversation and decide to consider career options that he deeply desires. I am confident that is what you will do, and frankly, that gets me pretty excited. You now know much more about yourself than most people do. Not only that, but you've set out in search of an extraordinarily worthy goal: career treasure. Now that you know the destination for which you're aiming, turn to Part II and let's get going on equipping you for the job search campaign.

PART

2

EQUIPPING YOURSELF FOR THE JOB SEARCH

7

WRITE A WINNING RÉSUMÉ AND COVER LETTER

∙∙∙

"How forcible are right words!"
Job 5:13

RÉSUMÉ REALITY

Twenty to 30 seconds. Not much time to present your life story—but a résumé screener will typically invest no more time than this in an initial review. Résumé screeners are not insensitive; they're faced with incredible challenges. In small companies, those with 100 or fewer employees, the résumé screener is often the owner or president. In larger companies, the decision maker (or hiring manager) will usually delegate initial résumé screening to the personnel department. In either case, productivity demands, multiple competing business priorities, and pressure from others all contribute to the résumé screener's need to fill job openings as quickly as possible.

For just a minute, put yourself in the position of a human resource (HR) professional charged by a hiring manager to identify three qualified job candidates. You learn that the hiring manager is anxious to fill the position and expects you to present quality job candidates to interview—"right now!" First, you must become familiar enough with the job's requirements that you can effectively screen résumés. You decide to talk in depth with the hiring manager, maybe someone in the company doing the same type of job, and study the job's description (usually safely hidden in the file cabinet). On the basis of what you learn, you write a newspaper advertisement that highlights the job's most important requirements and run the ad in Sunday's employment section.

Now, imagine receiving several hundred résumés in Tuesday's and Wednesday's mail in response to Sunday's advertisement. (Although this is a hypothetical example, it is not at all unusual to receive this many responses to one advertisement in a major newspaper.) Now, imagine the hiring manager calling Wednesday afternoon and saying something like this: "Well, how is it going? Do you have anyone yet? You know we really need someone in here as soon as possible!" How would you respond to this manager? My guess is that you would do what most of the HR people I know do: identify three to five *obviously* qualified candidates as quickly as you can. Here is an example of a typical screening process:

Phase 1: Review the giant stack of résumés, spending about half a minute on each, and create two piles:

> *Pile 1: I'll look at this one again later.*
> *Pile 2: No, thanks.*

Phase 2: Send rejection letters to all the folks in pile two above. Return to pile one and spend another ninety seconds reviewing the résumés. Once again, create two piles:

> *Pile 1: These ten people look obviously qualified. We should interview some of them.*
> *Pile 2: No, thanks.*

Phase 3: Send rejection letters to the folks in pile two above. Decide how to best manage the *obviously* qualified candidates.

> *From Pile 1 in Phase 2: I'll pick my top three candidates, bring them in for interviews, and I'll hold the others in reserve*

in case the hiring manager doesn't like any of my top three candidates.

So what if you screen out fifty or sixty others who are reasonably qualified for the position? You've met your obligation; you've delivered three obviously qualified job candidates. You can now deal with the six additional stacks of résumés you received in response to the company's other Sunday job advertisements.

A résumé's purpose

Many people mistakenly believe that a résumé's purpose is to get a job. It's not. Think about your own purchasing strategies. Would you buy a car based solely upon a brochure? Of course not. Yet most cars cost less than the annual salary you're asking an employer to invest in you. Think of the job search campaign as an introduction of a new product. You represent the product, and your résumé plays a vital role in the advertising strategy. You have a 20-second visual ad that must grab a potential employer's attention. Like the automobile company with a new model, you want the potential buyer to take you for a test drive. The purpose of a résumé is to gain job interview opportunities. In 20 to 30 seconds, your résumé should convey that you obviously are a person who is worth learning more about—a person who is worth interviewing.

Multiple pathways to job interviews

Fortunately, responding to newspaper advertisements is not the only way to gain job interviews. In Chapter 9 you will learn five strategies to get face-to-face meetings with decision makers. Regardless of the strategy, your résumé will almost certainly play an important role. Here are three other pathways where your résumé may lead to an opportunity for a job interview with a decision maker.

- **Employment agencies**—As Chapter 9 will discuss, you may wish to register with an employment agency or a recruiting firm. Although these agencies typically reformat résumés to standardize their presentations of candidates, you will need to supply a quality résumé.

- **References**—You can use your résumé to ensure that your references are familiar with all of your job strengths, work history, and accomplishments.

- **Network contacts**—You will enhance your networking activities (Chapter 9) by providing contacts, particularly those you do not know, with your work history and accomplishments. For those contacts you already know, your résumé can provide an update about your current situation and career objective. Also, when you leave a copy behind, you never know to whom your contact may hand your résumé at a later time.

One last point about your résumé's purpose: it often serves as the structure for a job interview. This is nothing but good news. Interviewers appreciate the guidance, and you will encounter fewer surprises. Because you're the résumé's author, you are able to highlight areas that you would particularly like to discuss.

THE FOUR STYLES OF RÉSUMÉS

If you're like most people, you've seen a number of résumés. While stylistically you may have found these résumés quite diverse, they all fell into one of three categories: chronological, functional, or combination. These three categories used to be the end of the story when describing the types or styles of résumés. Recently, however, because of the increased usage of computers in the hiring process, a fourth type of résumé has emerged: the scannable résumé. All four types of résumés aim for the same goal: a job interview with a decision maker. (Refer to Appendix B for additional résumé examples.)

The chronological résumé

This type of résumé is the most traditional, listing work experiences chronologically from the most recent position backward. You should highlight your accomplishments for each of your previous positions. This format's strength rests in its ability to present you and your experiences in a very organized, straightforward manner. Its disadvantage lies in the fact that its orientation is historical rather than future-oriented. For many people, the chronological format is the format of choice. However, if your employment history has breaks in it, or if you are attempting to change careers, this type of résumé is not for you.

The functional résumé

This format's primary difference resides in the way it presents work experiences. While the chronological format focuses on sequential work history, the functional format focuses on job skills and professional expertise and work accomplishments. This format groups accomplishments around specific functional headings; it presents work history in only a brief outline toward the end of the résumé.

Example
Chronological Résumé

John Hunt
1234 Some Boulevard
My Town, My State 33333
444-555-9876

Career Objective
Seeking an entry level human resource position that allows me to make important contributions using my organizational, interpersonal, business, and educational skills.

Summary Statement
A highly motivated, dedicated individual with six years management experience and one year human resources experience.

- Excellent interpersonal/communication skills
- Ability to lead and work within a team environment
- Strong coaching and leadership skills
- Ability to manage multiple projects

Education
A.A.—Valencia Community College, Orlando, Florida—June 1990
B.A.—Organizational Behavior, Rollins College, Winter Park, Florida—Anticipated next May

Work Experience

Walt Disney World Corporation, *Lake Buena Vista, Florida*   1993—Present

Human Resources Intern—Responsible for coordinating and implementing training initiatives, recognition programs, and employee celebration events.
- Designed and implemented a new hire orientation program that increased employee effectiveness
- Participated in the development and implementation of a career development program that decreased turnover, increased the number of promotable employees, and increased employee job satisfaction.

Merchandise Mail Order Clerk—Responsible for answering incoming customer calls, taking merchandise orders, and tracing lost packages.
- Increased speed and accuracy of package tracing by initiating a process where the operators contacted the shipping company directly, resulting in decreased wait times for the customers.

Merchandise Sales Hostess—Responsible for upholding the Disney standards by providing excellent customer service.

Example
Functional Résumé

JOHN HUNT
1234 Some Boulevard
My Town, My State 33333
444-555-9876

OBJECTIVE

A position in business development and finance where I will utilize my experience and expertise to contribute to the overall success of my employer.

SUMMARY

A results-oriented professional who has high standards and a sense of team. Over twenty years of consumer credit and sales experience. Major strengths in the areas of business development, customer relations, training, credit evaluation, risk control, and leading people.

SELECTED ACCOMPLISHMENTS

Business Development and Finance

- Provided leasing and credit expertise that resulted in the sign-up and development of over 80 automotive dealer customers that produced in excess of $2 million per month in lease originations.
- Created training sessions for new accounts which reduced the start-up time to generate business and convinced these customers that my organization would meet their financial and customer service needs.
- Developed new finance strategies that helped to increase sales volume by 8%.
- Increased finance income by over 17% during a period of 14 months.
- Increased finance office outstanding loan portfolio from $890,000 to over $2.1 million while reducing the delinquency rate from 1.7% to .75%.

Risk Control

- Collected $750,000 of uncashed finance contracts in 60 days which helped reduce a $2 million backlog of account receivables.
- Designed administrative procedures that reduced turnaround time for contracts in transit by 43%, thereby reducing variable expenses.

Leadership

- Lead 16 full-time and 3 part-time employees in the Consumer Banking Account Maintenance section that posted entries to the general ledger, corrected consumer accounts, and tracked Division income.
- Administered the budgets for three cost centers with $290 million in outstanding loan balances in the Consumer Banking Division.
- Managed 7 full-time and 10 part-time collectors who controlled and reduced the delinquency rate by 1.63% for $21 million of MasterCard outstandings.

Functonal Résumé (continued)

JOHN HUNT
Page 2

EMPLOYMENT

REX HOWARD AUTOMOTIVE GROUP, *Spokane, Washington* **1994–199x**
 Finance Manager

MARK WILLIAMS AUTOMOTIVE GROUP, *Spokane, Washington* **1991–1994**
 Finance Manager

TRUST LIFE INSURANCE COMPANY, *Spokane, Washington* **1990–1991**
 Insurance Agent

ABC VEHICLE LEASING, INC., *Boston, Massachusetts* **1987–1990**
 Regional Sales Manager

COMMERCE NATIONAL BANK, *Baltmore, Maryland* **1980–1987**
 Senior Leasing/Office Manager

ASSOCIATES FINANCE CORPORATION, *Virginia Beach, Virginia* **1978–1980**
 Branch Manager

EDUCATION
A.A. Liberal Arts, Essex Community College, Baltimore, Maryland—June, 1978

Example
Combination Résumé

John Hunt
1234 Some Boulevard
My Town, My State 33333
444-555-9876

OBJECTIVE
Position as an administrator for a large medical practice, MSO, or IPA.

SUMMARY
A well-organized manager and administrator with experience in managing a multi-location medical practice and eight years of hospital experience within multi-hospital systems. Solid accomplishments in the following areas:

- Managed-care strategy
- Contract negotiation
- Cost control
- Marketing and Sales

- Finance
- Budget preparation
- Hospital contracting
- Staff management

MAJOR ACCOMPLISHMENTS

Finance and General Management
- Managed the account receivable balance to an average of 50 days in account receivable.
- Saved $250,000 in premiums by changing physician life insurance policies.

Health-Care Management
- Negotiated contracts with 25 HMOs.
- Recruited three new physicians and two nurse practitioners.
- Conducted review of all grants received by major hospital and its affiliated hospitals and identified $1.2 million in uncharged expenses.

CAREER EXPERIENCE

MEDICAL ASSOCIATES OF THE MIDWEST   1993–Present
Chicago, Illinois

Administrator—Manage and direct all nonclinical aspects of eight-physician, three-office group practice with special emphasis on strategic planning, managed-care negotiations, marketing, and financial oversight.

Combination Résumé (continued)

John Hunt
Page 2

MEDICAL ASSOCIATES OF THE MIDWEST   1993–Present
Chicago, Illinois

Administrator—Manage and direct all nonclinical aspects of eight-physician, three-office group practice with special emphasis on strategic planning, managed-care negotiations, marketing, and financial oversight.

MEDCARE, INC. (An HMO)   1993
Detroit, Michigan

Hospital Contracts Administrator—Planned, negotiated, and maintained all contracts with hospitals, hospital-based physicians, and skilled nursing facilities for this commercial and Medicare HMO. Responsible for negotiations with physician-hospital organizations.

HEALTH CARE SOLUTIONS   1992–1993
Ann Arbor, Michigan

Consultant—Performed market assessment studies, developed provider networks, revenue recovery projects, and other consulting engagements in the managed-care field.

DOCTORS GENERAL HOSPITAL   1989–1992
Saginaw, Michigan

Special Projects Coordinator—Researched new product lines and services and conducted surveys, focus groups, and other marketing projects to determine feasibility and viability.

EDUCATION

Master of Business Administration—The University of Michigan, Ann Arbor, Michigan—May, 1985

Master of Health Science, Health and Hospital Administration— The University of Michigan, Ann Arbor, Michigan—May, 1985

B.A., Chemistry—University of Central Michigan, Mt. Pleasant, Michigan—June, 1979

The primary advantage to this format is that it downplays any unusual or erratic work history, and can direct attention away from positions you do not wish to highlight because they do not directly relate to the position for which you wish to apply. This format is particularly useful when you change career fields. The format has the disadvantage of being less well organized than the chronological résumé. Thus, the functional résumé is more difficult to review than the chronological format. Also, for some seasoned résumé reviewers the functional format serves as a clue to ask, "Is this applicant trying to hide something?"

The combination résumé

As you probably suspect, this format combines aspects of both the chronological and functional résumé styles. I particularly like this format for executives with $75,000+ salary aspirations. As you will see in the examples, this type of résumé quickly highlights and markets executives' major accomplishments and skills.

The scannable résumé

Along with changing virtually every other aspect of our lives, computers are also changing résumé writing. Human resource departments are increasingly relying upon OCR (optical character recognition) software to read, evaluate, and store résumés. The computer scans the résumé, rather than typing it, allowing it to capture important information very quickly. Along with storing information such as the applicant's name, address, phone number, job titles, years of experience, and objective, the computer also looks for *key words*. Key words are nouns that describe skill sets, talents, and experience. Each time a search for a job candidate begins, the company can query the computer, asking it to look for "hits," or résumés with certain skill, education, and experience profiles. To maximize "hits" during these computer searches, a well-prepared scannable résumé includes many specific key words. Here's an example of a summary from a scannable résumé:

An administrator with an M.B.A. and eight years of medical practice experience in MSO and IPA with skills in managed care strategy, finance, contract negotiation, budget preparation, and hospital contracting.

While this approach might not make for great reading for a person, the computer will like it a lot.

When you prepare a résumé for a computer, you must make sure the computer can read it. You can use a chronological, functional, or combination format; but several rules change. For example, while you should stay away from jargon and acronyms in traditional résumés, you should include them in preparing a scannable résumé. The reason is that organizations often use the jargon as part of the computer search criteria. Here are a number of other things to keep in mind when preparing a computer friendly résumé:

- The copy you send to the organization must be of laser printer quality and very clean. It's best to send an original and not a copy.
- All headings should use standard language, e.g., Experience, Summary, Objective, or Accomplishments.
- Use standard spacing; do not compress letters.
- To ensure the computer can read your résumé, use orthodox typefaces such as

Courier, Futura, Helvetica, Palatino, Optima, New Century, or Universe. Do not use shadowing or reverse print.

- While standard résumés should be limited to a maximum of two pages, multiple pages are of much less concern because computers can easily scan multiple pages. Do not staple or fold pages.

- The first thing on the page should be your name and address, and you should use a standard address format.

- If you provide more than one phone number, list each number on its own separate line.

- As with all résumés, use *only* white, 8½ x 11-inch paper and print on only one side.

- Do not use columns or vertical or horizontal lines. This will confuse the computer.

- Avoid the use of bold, italic, and underlining as these elements can also confuse the computer.

- In general, keep the format as simple and straightforward as possible.

Joyce Lain Kennedy, author of *The Electronic Job Search Revolution*, provides some very valuable tips on electronic résumé writing on the Internet (http://www.espan.com/docs/jlkresu.html).

If you would like to actually create your résumé online, try Resumix Résumé Builder (http://www.resumix.com/resume/resume-form.html).

GUIDELINES FOR PREPARING YOUR RÉSUMÉ

When preparing your résumé remember the maxim: **less is more**. Generally, résumés should be one or two pages and *no* longer. And one page is often better than two. On one occasion a professional presented me with a 42-page résumé. Forty-two pages! This professional apparently did not know that a résumé reader spends most of his or her attention on the top half of the first page. He or she will spend less time examining the bottom of the first page; less still on the second. It's doubtful that a résumé reader will look beyond the second page.

Your résumé should have plenty of white space, be flawless in terms of spelling and accuracy, and demonstrate your benefit to future employers. I am often asked "What colors of paper are best?" Here's the answer: white and white. A white, 25 percent cotton-bond paper conveys a very professional image and runs zero risk of offending a reader. Please don't even think about using a typewriter or a non-letter-quality printer to prepare your résumé. Today, résumé readers expect letter-quality laser printing—period. If you do not own a personal computer with a high-quality laser printer, many of the national chain copy shops rent them by the hour. If you don't know how to use a computer, find someone who does and ask, beg, or pay them to prepare your résumé. Here are several other important things to keep in mind when preparing your résumé:

- Choose only common fonts such as Courier, Helvetica, or Times Roman

- While some bolding can add visual appeal, use it judiciously and stay away from outlining and shadowing

- Use only one font throughout the résumé

- Include your name at the top of every page of the résumé (see examples)

While you may need to seek typing assistance, you should never have someone else prepare your résumé's content. The process of accumulating your skills and accomplishments and thinking through the issues will greatly increase your confidence and ability to perform in job interviews. During the descriptions of the four résumé styles, I gave you some idea about which format is most useful in what kind of circumstance. However, there are no absolutely pat answers about which résumé style you should use; your comfort with the résumé is the most important factor.

The features versus benefits distinction

As any salesperson knows, the buyer (the potential employer) does not purchase features, but instead buys benefits. Put another way, people do not care about *features*; only *benefits* motivate buying behavior. Understanding this distinction is vital to understanding how people make purchasing decisions. A product's features (such as a toothpaste's new formula) only matter when customers believe they will receive benefits (like whiter teeth and more sex appeal).

As you prepare your résumé, constantly keep the features vs. benefits distinction in mind. After you put together each part of your résumé, ask yourself, "What is the benefit to the potential employer?" If you cannot determine a benefit, rework that section of the résumé until you can.

What you should always include in your résumé

Regardless of the format—chronological, functional, combination, or scannable—every résumé should always contain these elements:

- Contact information
- An objective and/or summary statement
- Work history
- Accomplishments
- Educational background

Contact information

Include your name, complete mailing address, and home phone number. Increasingly, contact information includes e-mail addresses, particularly for high-tech jobs.

Objective or summary statement

While you may wish to include both, you should include one of these; either an objective statement or summary.

Objective statement—As you read in Chapter 6, the career objective is a one-sentence statement that conveys the position and industry you are seeking. If you decide to include your objective statement on your résumé, it will help résumé reviewers quickly determine the kind of position you're seeking. However, this presents two problems. Your objective may appear either too narrow or too broad to a résumé screener. If you feel this is a concern, include your career objective in the body of a cover letter instead of on the résumé. By doing this you can avoid the hassle of rewriting your résumé every time you need to modify your career objective.

The summary statement—The summary statement is like the opening sentence of a novel: it should compel the audience to want to read further. The statement elaborates upon the career objective and *very quickly* provides the résumé reviewer with a lot of key information. This statement should showcase you at your highest level of competence. The summary statement identifies your job strengths and the benefits the organization will realize by hiring you. The summary statement is broad enough to apply to a number of different positions; remember, your career objective will address the specific positions for which you apply. Figure 19 contains summary statements corresponding to the examples of career objectives in Chapter 6.

Work history

This is the meat of the résumé. To achieve an opportunity for a job interview, your work history must show how you can add value to a potential employer's current situation. Work history includes five essentials:

- Current and past job titles
- The names of employers and their locations
- Dates of employment
- Responsibilities
- *Most importantly*, accomplishments

You may also wish to include the level of the person to whom you reported, who and how many people reported to you, and the size of your budget. What you did in 1968 is not especially relevant to your current career objective. You should include only about the last ten years of your work experience or your last three jobs.

Most rules have exceptions; and here's one for the ten-year rule just mentioned. I've worked with a number of people who decided to make significant career changes. In some of these cases, their most recent work experiences do not relate to their new career objective as well as earlier experiences do. If you find yourself in this situation, where experiences beyond ten years old relate best your current career objective, you should strongly consider a func-

FIGURE 19
Career Objectives and Corresponding Summary Statements

Career Objective	Summary Statement
I am seeking a sales management position within the mainframe computer industry.	An energetic, results-oriented sales professional with more than fifteen years of experience in the computer industry. A solid list of sales management accomplishments demonstrates an ability to deliver sales through leading and developing others.
I am seeking a position as a director of compensation and benefits in a high-tech business.	Nine years of experience in Human Resources. Six of those years were spent as department head of compensation and benefits for a medium-sized research and development firm in the defense industry. Demonstrated ability to work in a team environment and as a business partner with line management.
I am seeking a project manager position within an international manufacturing organization.	A technically competent, well-organized individual. Major strengths include SPC, ISO 9000, and proven ability to lead diverse task forces and project teams to innovative accomplishments.

tional résumé. With a functional résumé you can include older experiences that highlight your accomplishments, but downplay when they occurred.

Job title—You should provide job titles that are generic enough that any employer can understand what you did. Many organizations assign job titles that make little sense outside that organization. If this is true in your case, your job title will not communicate meaningful information to potential employers. For example, if your last job title was Client Liaison Consultant, but in essence you were a salesperson, use a more common general title such as marketing representative, salesperson, or client relations professional. I am *not* suggesting that you exaggerate your responsibilities or that you mislead anyone. To the contrary, by using a more common yet more accurate job title, your résumé will more accurately depict what you actually did. If you held a number of different jobs for one company, you should list each of them and their locations; this is especially true if the titles demonstrate increasing job breadth or responsibility.

Company name and location—Include the company's complete name and location. All that is necessary in terms of location is city and state. If you were located in several different locations with several different job titles, you should usually include all of the locations.

Dates of employment—As with everything else in your résumé, these dates must be absolutely accurate. Of course, representing yourself accurately is a matter of integrity. However, there is another reason you should make sure of the accuracy of your employment dates. Potential employers usually verify your work history with past employers. For a variety of legal reasons, few companies will officially provide information about a person's past employment history—with one exception. They almost always will give your dates of employment. If you make an error, even unintentionally, your potential employer will probably find out and you may appear to be dishonest. This could put your candidacy in great jeopardy, even if a potential employer likes everything else about you.

Second, you should have no gaps in employment. Many, if not most, résumé screeners will not consider résumés with employment gaps. Avoid them if at all possible. You can eliminate the specific employment dates and show only the years as one strategy for removing employment history gaps.

Example

Specific Dates

Acme Widget Company	March 14, 1995 to Present
A Big Shoe Company	January 15, 1990 to November 1, 1994

Years Only

Acme Widget Company	1995 to Present
A Big Shoe Company	1990 to 1994

This strategy usually removes undue attention to short employment gaps. Nevertheless, though an employer will probably never question you about exact dates, be prepared to respond with specific dates in case they do ask. If your work history is very erratic, a functional résumé will help focus attention on your talents and skills while placing less emphasis on your work history.

Example
Bulleted Responsibilities are Still Just Responsibilities

BILL'S WORK HISTORY: FROM FIRST DRAFT

Finance Manager, A Big Car Dealer   **1995–1997**

Responsible for the overall management and reporting of the store's credit purchases, leases, and retail financing. Responsibilities included: generating income through the sale of bank rates, extended service agreement accident/health insurance coverage, gap insurance, and aftermarket accessories; obtaining consumer credit purchases, leases, or retail financing, placing credit with proper retail/lease sources, selling the placement of the paper, and tracking these placements by number and value of finance/lease source; and maintaining relationships with lenders and ensuring proper documentation is prepared for immediate funding by the retail/lease dealers.

FROM SECOND DRAFT

Finance Manager, A Big Car Dealer   **1995–1997**

Responsible for the overall management and reporting of the store's credit purchases, leases, and retail financing. Responsibilities included:

- generating income through the sale of bank rates, extended service agreement accident/health insurance coverage, gap insurance, and aftermarket accessories
- obtaining consumer credit purchases, leases, or retail financing, placing credit with proper retail/lease sources, selling the placement of the paper, and tracking these placements by number and value of finance/lease source
- maintaining relationships with lenders and ensuring proper documentation is prepared for immediate funding by the retail/lease dealers

---

One last point: You should be consistent with any abbreviations throughout your résumé. If you abbreviate months in one place, for example, abbreviate them throughout the résumé.

Responsibilities—Most résumés spend a lot of time and space attempting to demonstrate the author's value by detailing the scope of responsibilities. I commonly see résumés where the person's description of responsibilities for each job takes up a quarter of the page. This is simply not effective. Why? Because potential employers care relatively little about applicants' responsibilities and a great deal about their contributions. You can best prove the benefit you'll provide to future employers by listing your work accomplishments. Most résumés don't do this. Compared to the typical résumé, great résumés spend relatively little space expanding upon responsibilities and more on demonstrating potential benefit by showing past accomplishments.

Accomplishments—*This is the most important ink on the résumé.* If your résumé evidences that you benefited employers in the past, potential employers will assume that you will provide them benefits in the future. Once again, most résumés present lengthy narratives describing responsibilities with little demonstration of any benefit received by the employer.

Make your past benefits obvious, and you'll separate yourself from others in the job market. The OAR statements you developed in Exercise 7 accomplish this quite effectively. The three elements that make up these single-sentence statements succinctly describe your past accomplishments. Because you used the OAR format along with the action verbs listed in Chapter 4, these statements will dynamically demonstrate your potential to contribute to your next employer.

The three elements in the OAR statements

- *Opportunities* you seized to make improvements or to solve problems
- *Actions* you took to make improvements or to solve these problems
- *Results* or benefits the employer received, in quantitative terms

In the chronological format, list two to four accomplishments that support your career objective below each brief job description. With the functional and combination résumés, select seven to twelve of your best OAR statements supporting your career objective. As you can see in the sample functional and combination résumés, you can simply list these statements under a "Selected Accomplishments" heading or group them under functional themes, e.g., finance, people management, etc.

If for some reason you did not create accomplishment statements by completing Exercise 7, please do so now. As I said in Chapter 4, this exercise is one of the most useful in the book. The exercise's results form the heart of

the winning résumé and will give you powerful ammunition for the job interview.

Form does not equal substance

A gentleman I will call Bill recently lost his job and called me to ask for assistance in preparing his résumé. I agreed to meet with him, and I asked him to bring a copy of his current résumé to our meeting. As I looked at his résumé in that first meeting, it was clear that, like most people, Bill had simply written long, uninteresting narratives describing each of the positions he had held. I gave him the OAR exercise and a number of sample résumés, asked him to create a second draft, and set up a second meeting.

At the second meeting, I once again reviewed his résumé. By looking at his second draft, I could tell that Bill had reviewed the example résumés I supplied him during our initial meeting. In fact, his résumé now looked a lot like the examples. Although the second draft of his résumé looked different, it still didn't contain the substance required by the OAR method. The example above contains excerpts from Bill's original résumé and the second draft.

In terms of generating interviews, Bill's second draft was no better than the first. Here is the reason: *Placing bullets in front of responsibilities does not magically turn them into accomplishment statements.* For a résumé to be a maximally effective marketing tool, it must dynamically demonstrate the writer's work accomplishments. To best demonstrate your accomplishments, you should:

- Provide one-sentence accomplishment statements that contain all three OAR elements
- Make sure the accomplishment statements contain action verbs from Chapter 4

Example

BILL'S WORK HISTORY: FROM FINAL RÉSUMÉ

Finance Manager, A Big Car Dealer   1995–1997

Responsible for generating income through the sale of aftermarket products and insurance, qualifying consumer applications for credit purchases, maintaining relationships with lenders, providing executive reports of revenue generated by all departments, and training and motivating salespeople.

- Designed administrative procedures that reduced turnaround time for contracts in transit by 43% thereby reducing variable expenses.

- Collected $750,000 of uncashed finance contracts in sixty days, which helped reduce a $2-million backlog of account receivables.

- Write the R portion of the accomplishment in quantitative terms whenever possible

After another round of discussion, Bill went back to the résumé drawing board and produced the accomplishments shown in the next example. As compared to the first and second drafts, the final version of his résumé is easier to read, more interesting, and does a much better job of demonstrating Bill's value to his past and future employers.

Educational background

A brief description of your educational background should follow your work history and accomplishments and fall toward the end of your résumé. Begin with your highest degree and include the institution bestowing the degree, the date you received the degree, and any special academic awards. Also include continuing education, seminars, and so forth in this section. You should always list college degrees regardless of whether or not the degree specifically relates to your career objective. Employers will see any degree as an indication of your abilities to set and reach long-term goals and to stay motivated for extended periods of time.

There are three reasons you may wish to place your educational information at the beginning of your résumé, rather than at the end. First, if you are a new college graduate, your work history is probably limited. Thus, your new degree is one of your strongest assets. Second, if you are applying for a position within an academic environment, your résumé should list your educational information first. Third, you should place your education at the beginning of the résumé if it gives you a competitive advantage over most in the field. For example, if you are seeking a human resources position and you have an M.B.A. degree, you should list it at the beginning of your résumé. An M.B.A. would put you ahead of much of your job-searching competition because many employers would view it as a real plus, but few in the HR field have such a degree.

What you may wish to include in your résumé

Skills profile

A skills profile placed just below the summary can quickly highlight many of the writer's most marketable skills. Several of the résumé examples in Appendix B include a skills profile. While typically used with a combination résumé, other résumé formats can also make use of a skills profile. Because it is very possible that an interviewer will ask, make sure that you can describe solid accomplishments (OAR) to support any skills listed in your profile. An example of a summary with a skills profile appears below.

Foreign language expertise

With business becoming more and more global, foreign language expertise is also in high demand. If you decide to include this on your résumé, be sure to indicate the language type, e.g., Spanish, whether you speak and/or read the language, and your degree of fluency, e.g., fluent, knowledgeable, or some knowledge.

Professional affiliations and licenses

If these affiliations or licenses support your career objective, be sure to include them.

Miscellaneous achievements

Include any other achievements that directly support your career objective or demonstrate your excellence.

Things to avoid putting in your résumé

Résumé titles

Do not include Résumé, Vita, Life History, or any other title at the top of the page. It's obvious what it is, it takes up valuable space, and it's out of fashion.

Photographs

Once a common practice, this is no longer done.

References

Do not include references in your résumé. Also, do not include the statement *References furnished upon request*. This is understood. The hiring organization will let you know when and if they wish to speak with any references.

Race, age, religion, gender, or national origin

Title VII of the 1964 Civil Rights Amendment and the Age Discrimination in Employment

---

Example
Summary statement example with a skills profile included

Summary—Nine years of experience in human resources. Six of those years were spent as department head of compensation and benefits for a medium-sized research and development firm in the defense industry. Demonstrated ability to work in a team environment and as a business partner with line management. Particular strengths include:

- Skill-based pay expertise
- 401(k) plan design and administration
- Variable compensation plan design, administration, and evaluation
- Supervisory pay increases linked to people management performance

Act (ADEA) guarantee equal employment opportunities regardless of age, race, religion, gender, or national origin. Companies may ask you to indicate some of this information on an application blank for tracking purposes only. Do not, however, include reference to any of these factors in your résumé.

Letters of recommendation

Once again, reviewers have little time to read the résumé itself, let alone additional materials. Unless the hiring organization requests it (a common practice in academics), or unless the president of the United States is willing to write a letter on your behalf (be sure he uses the fancy stationery with the big seal), do not include these with your résumé.

Salary requirements

Do not include salary requirements or other demands. Chapter 12 describes the timing and suggests strategies for negotiating your best deal—for sure, the best time to begin salary negotiation is *not* in your résumé.

Military service

If your military experience does not specifically pertain to your career objective, there is no strong reason to include it.

Why you left your last job

It is important for you to have a solid, straightforward answer about why you left previous jobs. The time for these answers is during the interview, however, not in your résumé. I will discuss how to answer this question in Chapter 10 and in Appendix D.

GETTING DOWN TO BUSINESS

To prepare your résumé (assuming you already completed Exercise 7), follow these seven basic steps.

Step 1—Select one of the three primary styles (chronological, functional, combination). You will find additional résumé examples in Appendix B to assist you in creating your résumé.

Step 2—Complete the résumé worksheet associated with the style you selected. The worksheets appear in Appendix A.

Step 3—Type your résumé on a computer and print it on a laser printer.

Step 4—Proofread the résumé.

Step 5—Proofread it again.

Step 6—Have three people you respect proofread the résumé.

Step 7—Go through the résumé checklist as shown in Figure 20 until you can check every item.

If you select a functional format, you will most likely want to group your accomplishment statements (OAR) by function as in the example below. This example groups six accomplishments under two headings.

Example

Major Accomplishments

Finance and General Management

- Managed the accounts receivable balance to an average of forty days in accounts receivable.
- Saved $250,000 in premiums by changing physician life insurance policies.

- Achieved a reduction of twenty full-time employees and increased revenues and outside business by 150 percent.

Health-Care Management

- Negotiated contracts with twenty-five HMOs.
- Recruited three new physicians and two nurse practitioners.
- Conducted review of all grants received by major hospital and its affiliated hospitals and identified $1.2 million in uncharged expenses.

Also, while it is an option for the other two formats, you will need to create a skills profile if you choose to use the combination résumé.

THE VERBAL ADVERTISEMENT

As I said earlier, your résumé serves as a visual advertisement for your job market product: you. However, along with your résumé, you also need to prepare a verbal advertisement, lasting about 30 seconds. Jim Niemus, a consultant and friend of mine, calls this the 30-second elevator speech. Whether it's on an elevator, in the grocery store, over the telephone, or at a party, you will have an opportunity to give this speech numerous times. In one of these settings someone will ask, "So, what are you up to now?" or "Can you tell me a little about yourself?" These are golden opportunities. When done well, the 30-second verbal advertisement can create a lasting and positive impression. It is not at all unusual that in the days and weeks that follow the presentation of your 30-second verbal ad, your contact will

hear of an opportunity that sounds as if it might match your needs. A positive impression left during your 30-second ad can lead to a meeting with a contact or to a job interview with a decision maker that may never have occurred otherwise.

When creating your verbal advertisement, I suggest that you identify three themes, or messages, that you'd like to convey. Think of a three-legged stool; each leg representing one of the themes. For the first leg of the stool, modify your summary statement so that it works well in a conversation. Select an accomplishment or two to serve as the second leg. Your career objective is the third. The ad should be upbeat, compelling, and true. It should represent you in a good light and separate you from others in the job market. Here is an example:

Leg 1 (From the summary statement)

I am a very fortunate person. During my nine years of experience in Human Resources, I've had the privilege of working with a number of very talented and dedicated people. Through those experiences, I've learned how to work in, and help create, a team environment and to operate as a business partner to help reach corporate objectives.

Leg 2 (Sample accomplishments—OAR)

For example, I created a succession planning system that reduced the need for outside recruiting by 80 percent and saved more than $250,000 in fees.

Leg 3 (From the objective statement)

I'm currently seeking an opportunity to use my experiences in a position as a director of human resources in a high-tech business.

FIGURE 20
Résumé Checklist

√	
	GENERAL
	Limited the résumé to two pages Absolutely NO mistakes: spelling, grammar, and historical accuracy
	High-quality overall appearance: format, layout, neat, clean, plenty of white space on page
	25 percent cotton bond paper with matching paper for cover letter
	Had at least two people whom I respect review the résumé before wide distribution
	DID NOT INCLUDE
	Did not include title such as résumé, vita, etc.
	Did not include photograph
	Did not include salary information
	Did not include information that might lead to discrimination: age, race, marital status, religion, national origin, gender
	Did not include references or the phase "References available upon request"
	Did not include reason for leaving earlier positions
	CAREER OBJECTIVE
	One sentence that describes the position and the industry where I would like to find employment
	Demonstrates the level of responsibility I can handle
	Everything on the résumé clearly supports my career objective
	SUMMARY
	Summary is compelling and will cause the reader to want to explore my résumé further
	WORK HISTORY AND ACHIEVEMENTS
	Work history is in reverse chronological order
	No unexplained gaps in my employment history
	Included last ten years or last three jobs
	Included company name, location, job title, dates of employment
	All achievements listed in the résumé support my career objective
	Each achievement begins with an action word
	Achievements are written in OAR format and show benefit received by employer
	Confident that my greatest strengths are shown: knowledge, skills, and abilities
	EDUCATION
	Education is presented toward the end of the résumé with highest degree first; includes institution, degree, and year of graduation

After you create the verbal advertisement, practice it until it feels comfortable and natural. You don't need to memorize it word for word, but you do need to remember all three parts, or "legs," of the verbal advertisement. Time the ad to make sure that it's between 25 and 30 seconds. Get ready to use it! Most people engaged in a job search have an opportunity to give their 30-second speech within a day or two after its preparation.

PREPARING REFERENCES

I said you should not include references in your résumé. However, when you become a serious candidate, your next employer will probably ask you to supply references—usually about three. Most organizations do check references, and although few personal references provide negative input, they may not "sell" you as well as they could. Although rare, a personal reference will occasionally supply negative information, and this can be deadly for your job prospects. You need to check your references to determine whether or not they will convey the message that you would want to supply to prospective employers.

Although not included in your résumé, you need to build your reference list in advance of beginning your job search campaign. In general, do not include religious references, personal friends, or anyone who is a poor communicator. Consider past bosses, customers, college professors and administrators, high-level company executives, or peers who are familiar with your work. Whenever possible, meet with a reference in person and describe your current situation and career objective, and

ask if he or she is willing to serve as a personal reference by telephone *and* by writing a one-page letter of reference. Target only individuals who are enthusiastic about you and will provide an outstanding reference. Although a potential employer will likely only ask you to supply three references for any given position, you may want to compile a reference list with a few additional names (six or seven) so that you can select the three most appropriate names for each specific job situation.

After identifying your references, ask if you could supply them with a draft of a one-page reference letter. Most individuals appreciate this because it makes their task easier and ensures that they cover the issues you want them to cover. If a reference wishes to make changes to your draft, reach agreement about what these changes would include, and ask if you can get a copy of the final draft.

Figure 21 lists several issues those providing reference should include in their letter. One last item to keep in mind: remember to inform your references when you secure a new position.

COVER LETTERS

Along with your résumé and verbal advertisement, you will need one more communication tool: terrific cover letters. These letters play a terribly important role in representing you to others. I have seen many people work long hours preparing a résumé, only to blow a potential interview by sending an inferior letter. Please pay as much attention to this part of your marketing package as you do to your résumé.

There are five basic types of cover letters:

FIGURE 21
Reference Letter Guidelines

1. Describe the nature of the relationship between the reference and you. Also, include the length of the relationship.

2. Your two or three greatest strengths, such as technical skills, interpersonal skills, and personal characteristics.*

3. A concrete example of a time you overcame a difficult situation and added value to the organization.

4. Explanation about why you left the organization, e.g., restructuring, philosophical differences, better opportunity, desire for more responsibility, and so on.

5. A positive statement conveying your ability to work well with others such as former bosses, subordinates, peers, and customers.

6. A strong summary statement of recommendation, e.g., "I highly recommend Mr. Doe for the Director of Engineering position with your firm. He is a talented, technically competent, hard-working individual and a terrific team player who is marked by integrity and compassion toward others."

7. If the reference is from a former employer, a statement that indicates that the organization would readily hire you again.

8. Indicate whether the reference may be contacted for additional information and if so, where and when the reference can be reached.

*__Note:__ Strengths should relate specifically to your current career objective; that is, to the job you are seeking.

- Letters that accompany the résumé
- Letters as follow-up to interviews
- Thank-you notes
- Requests for advice and information meetings
- Job acceptance and rejection letters

Appendix C contains several example cover letters from all five of these categories. This chapter gives you a basic outline for two formats of letters to accompany your résumé. I will provide a basic format for letters to request advice and information interviews and thank-you notes in Chapter 9, follow-up after job interviews in Chapter 10, and job acceptance and rejection letters in Chapter 12.

General guidelines and a basic format

As with résumés, *simple* and *professional* are two words you should keep in mind when writing business letters. Cover letters should be no more than one page in length. Prepare your letters on a laser printer using 8½ x 11-inch white paper that matches your résumé. Whenever possible, address each letter to a person's

Cover Letter to Accompany Your Résumé: Basic Format

Your Street Address
City, State, ZIP Code

Today's Date

Addressee's Name
Position
Company Name
Street or P.O. Box
City, State, ZIP Code

Dear Dr./Mr./Ms. Name:

Paragraph 1: Purpose—In two or three brief sentences, explain your purpose for writing the letter.

Paragraph 2: Background and Interest—In three to four sentences, explain your background and demonstrate how you have contributed in the past. You should use several action words from the action word list in Chapter 4. Also, tactfully demonstrate any company or industry knowledge you gained during your research (Chapter 8) and networking (Chapter 9).

- **Bullets—Demonstrate your past achievements**——Show one or two OAR statements or use the Requirements/Qualifications comparison (see page 131).

- Once again, your OAR statements will prove to set you apart from the typical applicant.

Paragraph 3: Actions—In one or two sentences, explain what actions you would like the addressee to take, or what actions you will take to move the hiring process forward.

Paragraph 4: Appreciation/thank-you—In one sentence, thank the addressee.

Sincerely,

Your Name Typed
Phone number

Enc. résumé

name, not "To Whom it May Concern," "Dear Sirs or Madam," etc. You should always include your return address and phone number. Place the date two lines below your address, and type the closing ("Sincerely") two lines below the last sentence. Always type your name and sign the letter in blue or black ink. You should also apply steps 4 and 5 from the résumé guidelines: proofread and then proofread again. A typographical or grammatical error may make the difference between your dream job and a continued job search. The basic cover letter format to accompany your résumé appears on the previous page.

Your needs/my qualifications cover letter

A second format for a cover letter to accompany your résumé is what I call a *Your Needs/My Qualifications* letter. Use this style of letter to respond to advertisements or after you review a job description. Recruiters and outplacement firms commonly use this format with great success.

In this type of format, you create two columns between the second and third paragraph: "Your Needs" and "My Qualifications." In the first column, list the job's requirements as spelled out in an advertisement or job description. In the second column, address each of these requirements by demonstrating how your background, skills, and achievements meet these requirements. This is the only cover letter format where it is acceptable to go to two pages in length.

This approach saves the reviewer a tremendous amount of time and can quickly build an incredibly compelling case for interviewing you. However, there is one caveat. If you do not

FIGURE 22
Cover Letter Checklist

✓	GENERAL
	Limit the letter to one page (except for Your Needs/My Qualifications format)
	Absolutely NO mistakes: spelling, grammar, and historical accuracy
	High-quality overall appearance: format, layout, neat, clean, plenty of white space on page
	25 percent cotton bond paper with matching paper for résumé
	Signed letter
	Included all necessary enclosures; e.g., résumé
	Included your return address and phone number
✓	DID NOT INCLUDE
	Did not include salary information
	Did not include information that might lead to discrimination: age, race, marital status, religion, national origin, gender
	Did not include reason for leaving earlier positions

meet all of the company's needs, this approach will point that out very quickly. Only select the *Your Needs/My Qualifications* letter when you match every requirement referred to in an advertisement or job description. When you do, this is an absolutely terrific style of cover letter—one that often yields results!

KEEP YOUR EYES ON THE PRIZE

This chapter has given you a number of very practical tools and some proven advice that will

Your Needs/My Qualifications Format

Your Street Address
City, State, ZIP Code

Today's Date

Addressee's Name
Position
Company Name
Street or P.O. Box
City, State, ZIP Code

Dear Dr./Mr./Ms. Name:

Paragraph 1: Purpose—In two or three brief sentences, explain your purpose for writing the letter.

Paragraph 2: Background and Interest—In three to four sentences, explain your background and demonstrate how you have contributed in the past. You should use several action words from Table X. Also, tactfully demonstrate any company or industry knowledge you gained during your research (Chapter 8) and networking (Chapter 11).

Your Needs	*My Qualifications*
1.	1.
2.	2.
3.	3.
4.	4.

Paragraph 3: Actions—In one or two sentences, explain what actions you would like your addressee to take or what actions you will take to move the hiring process forward.

Paragraph 4: Appreciation/thank-you—In one sentence, thank the addressee.

Sincerely,

Your Name Typed
Phone number

Enc. résumé

assist you in getting a job. However, getting a job could be the worst thing that ever happens to your career—that is, if it's the wrong job. Please do not lose sight of the goal: to find the best job. Your efforts in earlier chapters prepared you to begin the job search campaign focused on your career objective, not on getting a job. This distinction is vital in the search for career treasure. The ideas, techniques, and strategies in Parts II and III will work regardless of your job target, as long as your skills meet the job's qualifications. Every day, thousands of people use at least some of these strategies to find jobs that produce the special kind of unhappiness called *job dissatisfaction*. At the end of the job search, your weeks, perhaps many months, of job searching should produce the best job; the one most like your vocational identity.

Before sending any cover letter, be sure to complete the Cover Letter Checklist as shown in Figure 22.

You now know the kinds of things you would like to do, and you have your basic tools in place (résumé, verbal ad, cover letters). Now it's time for you to locate the best job prospects. It's time to conduct job market research.

8

Conduct Market Research: From Shoe Leather to Cyberspace

*"Attempt the end, and never stand to doubt;
nothing's so hard but search will find it out."*
Robert Herrick

BOY SCOUT WISDOM: "BE PREPARED"

"All right, class, settle down. Please put away your books. We're going to have a little pop quiz covering last night's assignment." These infamous words can often strike fear in the hearts of students. The class clown may turn suddenly serious, the usually serious student may begin to tell awful jokes, and throughout the class, squirming becomes more prevalent than breathing. Most students inevitably begin to protest about the unfairness of such a quiz. In every class, however, one or two students do not engage in arguments about fairness. Instead, these few students sit quietly—confident, ready, and even eager to move ahead. What separates the few ready to perform from the mass shuddering in fear? They did their homework! Not only did they read the assignment but they also outlined the material, memorized prominent information, and in other ways prepared themselves to excel.

Most students do not live by the Boy Scout motto "Be prepared." Instead, they often wait until the last day, sometimes the last few hours, and then cram for a scheduled exam. Because of their lack of preparation, they usually underperform. An unscheduled exam is even worse. A pop quiz hits these students right where it hurts, targeting their lack of readiness. Because they're unprepared, they somehow feel that the teacher is unfair. The most valuable lesson taught by pop quizzes is never about chemistry, history, or the like, but about the fact that, unfortunately, life is very unpredictable.

Like the rest of life, the job search is full of both scheduled and unscheduled exams. Job search exams are opportunities to discover a job lead or to demonstrate your benefits to a potential employer. These opportunities may occur in wildly disparate environments—in the grocery store, in an elevator, on the golf course, or during a job interview. And guess what? Just like the majority of students, most people don't do their homework when it comes to job hunting. Sadly, when opportunities pass by the unprepared, rather than analyzing how they could ready themselves to perform better, they often blame others for failing job search exams.

Hey, come back here

You've written your career objective and prepared your résumé, verbal ad, and cover letters. You may now feel a strong urge to immediately go looking for a job. If you've just found yourself out of work because of some circumstance such as corporate restructuring, this urge will be particularly strong. If you enter the marketplace without doing all of your homework, however, there is a very good chance that you will quickly become disillusioned. Disillusionment occurs when initial job-hunting efforts result in failure. However, disillusionment is not the only problem with beginning the job search campaign without adequate preparation.

After encountering the frustration associated with being unprepared, many in the job race decide to return to the starting line and begin again. Unfortunately, they'll find this impossible for two reasons. First, earlier interactions with contacts in their network already

created lasting impressions. While unprepared job hunters can indeed restart the race, they cannot begin at the original starting line. Instead, they must restart the job search race with whatever impressions their lack of preparation created. Sometimes this means that not only will they restart the race behind the original line, but they also may even have to begin on a fairly steep incline. Second, many opportunities knock but once. Jobs get filled. If a job seeker is unprepared at the time an opportunity presents itself, there may be no time for recovery.

JOB SEARCH HOMEWORK

Obviously, reaching your career objective is considerably more important than any school exam. Remember the ultimate job search goal: to locate a job that resonates with your vocational identity and rewards you with career treasure. Here are several practical outcomes of doing *all* of your homework:

- You will gain significant competitive advantage over the vast majority of job seekers who do relatively little homework.
- You will find more potential jobs from which to choose.
- You increase the likelihood that you will find a job you really love.
- You shorten the length of time you will look for work.
- You will be able to present yourself as one of the quietly confident, ready to demonstrate your benefits. In short, you will be prepared to excel when opportunity knocks.

Figure 23 shows six types of homework required to prepare thoroughly for the job search. In Part 1 you became very knowledge-

FIGURE 23
Job Search Homework

Homework	Benefits
Part 1: Choosing Your Perfect Career	
Chapters 3, 4, and 5 Assessment of You (Values and Purpose, Transferable Skills, and Vocational Personality)	Clear understanding of your vocational identity. You can evaluate jobs in terms of their ability to deliver career satisfaction. Also, you know the job search product (you) far better than the majority of job hunters.
Chapter 6 Career Exploration	Knowledge of the kinds of careers that will deliver career satisfaction because they match your vocational identity.
Part 2: Equipping Yourself for the Job Search	
Chapter 7 Prepare Advertisements (Résumé and Verbal Ad)	Presentation of your vocational identity and background that demonstrates your *benefit* to a potential employer in a compelling way.
Chapter 8 Job Market Research	You know which industries and organizations to initially target for jobs. Because of your superior knowledge, you will increase your attractiveness as a future employee.
Chapter 9 Development of a Job Campaign Strategy	You will spend your efforts in the most productive manner, ensuring that you will maximize your job offer opportunities.
Chapter 10 Interview Preparation	Prepares you to present yourself in the best light; to demonstrate your benefits to the employer. Equally important, you're prepared to evaluate the job's ability to meet your vocational identity needs.

able about the job search product—you. By preparing both visual and verbal advertisements (your résumé and 30-second verbal ad) in Chapter 7, you equipped yourself to market this product. It's now time to turn your attention toward methods and resources for learning more about your customers—potential employers. The table also shows the benefits of carefully preparing for the job interview and building a job campaign strategy.

CONDUCTING COMPANY AND INDUSTRY RESEARCH

The research process I will give you in this chapter is *not* designed to discover job leads. WAIT—don't turn the page! You'll find that conducting this research is worth your time. Trust me. Keep reading, and you'll discover the important benefits of doing this type of research. I recognize the importance of finding good job leads, and we'll get to that issue in Chapter 9. Now, let's get back to the how-tos of conducting company and industry research.

Some career books are written as if the job search's goal is to find job openings. Of course, finding jobs is a very important part of the job search. However, the most important part of job hunting is securing a job, not just finding jobs. I'm interested not only in helping you locate opportunities, but also in providing you with the skills necessary to capture the job opportunity once you locate it. Knowing how to research companies and industries is one of those skills. So, the research methods and resources provided in this chapter prepare you to make good decisions and to excel at several points during the job hunt. The benefits of conducting company and industry research are as follows:

- Lays the groundwork for developing your job search's strategic plan
- Serves as a significant part of your dialogue during your networking advice and information meetings
- Provides a wealth of information that prepares you for the job interview
- Gives you valuable information useful during the negotiating phase

Two primary goals of company and industry research

There are two basic goals to achieve through company and industry research. Selecting specific industries and organizations to target with your initial job search efforts represents the first goal. Obviously, more companies exist in the world than you could ever personally contact. Also, not all organizations or industry segments represent equally attractive opportunities. You need to focus your efforts on the targets most likely to deliver opportunities that meet your specific needs. Second, possessing industry and company-specific knowledge will separate you from other job hunters and demonstrate to potential employers that you're one smart cookie.

This is the job search race's starting line. You should go through this chapter's four-step research process *prior* to entering the job marketplace. This is essential for conducting a high-quality job search campaign. By learning about industry trends, specific companies, salaries, and key industry and company executives, you will effectively prepare yourself to enter the marketplace.

THE STARTING LINE: A FOUR-STEP COMPANY AND MARKET RESEARCH PROCESS

This process readies you to begin the job search much more prepared than most of your competition. Along with more knowledge, the process will generate two tangible end products: a list of companies to target initially with your job-hunting efforts and company profiles that summarize some key information about specific companies.

While this process represents the official beginning of the job hunt, research doesn't end after you enter the marketplace. When you contact companies using the strategies you will develop in Chapter 9, you'll begin to locate a number of companies of interest and uncover fresh job leads. Each time you have an interest in a new company or job lead, you should prepare another company profile as described in Step 4 of the process. This research will prepare you very well to make contact with an organization through networking or correspondence or in a job interview.

Step 1—Create an initial company/ industry list

You already possess the knowledge needed to complete Step 1. Simply sit down in your favorite chair with a few pieces of paper and a pen. Now, based upon your previous work experiences, your career objective, what you learned during career exploration in Chapter 6, your intuition, and any other knowledge of the world of work, list any industries and specific companies you'd like to know more about. Don't weed out any industry or company that comes to mind without a good reason.

If you're new to an area, or if you have interest in various geographical locations, you'll need to increase your knowledge of these local job markets. Contact the local Chamber of Commerce and request a list of its members and information about the area's largest companies, e.g., company size, revenues, etc. Area phone books, available from the local phone company or public libraries, contain names of

many organizations under headings such as consultants, health care, and so on. Also, you may wish to contact the Commerce Department's Bureau of Economic Analysis, Regional Economic Measurement Division at 202-606-5360 (or online at http://www.bea.doc.gov) for local income and statistical information and growth rates.

If you would like to generate more initial companies to research, but don't know where to find them, refer to the resources provided in Appendix E.

Step 2—Organize the initial list into manageable groups

The task in Step 2 is to organize the job market into five to eight segments, or manageable groups of employers. This segmenting will allow you to organize market research results. Here are several classifications you could use to group organizations:

- Standard Fortune 500 classifications
- Standard Industrial Classification (SIC) codes
- Size
- Type of organization; e.g., service, manufacturing, telecommunications, high tech, etc.
- Geographic location
- Type of corporate cultures; e.g., fast-paced, democratic, etc.

You should develop your own scheme, one that makes the most sense to you. Your own comfort level is the main thing to keep in mind as you think about how to create these five to eight groups. As your job search moves along, you will learn of opportunities and organizations that you currently do not know. You can then organize these new leads within these groups.

Step 3—Select specific companies to research

You will need to decide which companies to research. Select at least five to ten organizations from the list that you think you would like to contact, to learn more about, and perhaps work for. These organizations are your initial *target companies*. List these companies on a new sheet of paper. For each target, include the company's name, address, phone number, and the industry group (if known). As mentioned, you'll add and subtract names to this list as you learn more about the job market.

Step 4—Conduct research and prepare company profiles

This is where the research work really begins. For target companies, you should acquire as much information as is reasonably possible. Remember, these are the companies you would like to contact. As you prepare to contact these companies, try to learn something about each company's history, position within its industry, key management, and corporate culture. Of course, keeping the information organized is vital to the success of your research efforts.

For each target company, create a short, one- to one-and-a-half page company profile that summarizes your research. The following example displays a completed company profile on a hypothetical company. Figure 24 (page 140) shows seven questions with answers that allow you to create the company profiles as you prepare for contacting target companies.

RESEARCH SOURCES

In order to answer the seven questions in Figure 24, you'll need to spend time at the local library or on the computer, or both. I've tried to make your job a lot easier by giving you two lists of good research sources in Appendix E. First, you'll find an alphabetical list of published sources. Second, I've distilled some of the most useful computer sources from the vast online possibilities available and listed them. Third, you'll find a table that matches both paper and online research sources to the seven research questions.

Note: The corporations' annual reports and the references provided in Appendix E will give you the information you need to prepare the research summary.

Paper research sources

The computer is certainly a valuable tool. However, as Nicholas Negroponte observed in his book *Being Digital*, "Right now it is hard, but not impossible, to compete with the qualities of a printed book. A book has a high-contrast display, is lightweight, easy to thumb through, and not very expensive." In short, books still represent a great technology. Appendix E lists a number of publications with brief descriptions of each. I've also given you the Library of Congress classification or ISBN numbers for most of the works, to help you locate the publications once you get to the library. These numbers are fairly consistent across all U.S. libraries. As you research organizations and industries you'll find that the publications in Appendix E contain lots of useful information.

Example

Company Profile

Company: Heartland Training & Development, Inc.
Market Segment: Training Organizations

Summary:

Located in Dallas, Texas, Heartland designs and delivers comprehensive training and development programs aimed at improving employee performance. Their services include needs assessment, pilot testing, training presentations, and formal scientific program evaluation. Areas of specialty: Team Building, Management Development, and Managing Change.

Customers:

Serves approximately 30 percent of Fortune 500; 50 percent of Fortune's top 20
Total customer base includes 2,000 companies ranging in size from 20 to 140,000 employees.

Profile:

Second-largest training and development company in the U.S.
Employee-owned since 1991
Sales growth has averaged 15 percent per year over last five years
Committed to becoming the largest training and development company by the year 2000
Corporate culture based upon "freedom to act" and trust of the individual

History:

Founded by J. Smith, Ph.D., in 1972. A longtime training and development expert, Smith left a large Northeastern computer manufacturing company to move to the Southwest in order to create a "different kind of company." Smith quickly brought his former employer on as a major client and used that base to build a thriving company. Empowerment and company ownership have played important roles in building Heartland's culture. Smith sold his interest to employees and retired in 1991.

Miscellaneous:

Current CEO: D. Wiggins, former CFO with 14 years tenure at Heartland

Online research sources

Tom Brokaw now signs off his newscasts by asking you to e-mail him through NBC's Web site at www.nbc.com to let him know what you thought of the broadcast. You can tour real estate properties thousands of miles away, make an offer, and apply for a loan and never leave your current home. Computing buzzwords and acronyms abound—WWW, URLs, FAQs, search engines, HTTP, virtual libraries, online resource guides, and hot links. Whew! How the world has changed in the last couple of years.

As a trip to the career section of your favorite bookstore will show, along with every other aspect of our lives, the electronic revolution is dramatically affecting job searching. The

FIGURE 24
The Seven Company and Industry Research Questions

1. What organizations/industries are most likely to want my skills?
2. What industries/organizations are growing that need my skills?
3. Which organizations have locations in which I'm interested?
4. What salary ranges are present for my job objective within particular industries/organizations?
5. What do recent business trends look like and what is the future likely to hold for this industry/organization?
6. What is the history and size of this industry/organization?
7. Who are the key leaders/personnel associated with this industry/organization?

computer (CD-ROM and the Internet) can serve two primary purposes in the job hunt: conducting company and industry research and locating job openings. It's this second purpose—finding job openings—that gets most people excited about electronic job hunting. In my view, however, the computer is great for conducting research, and much less valuable for finding a job. Appendix E provides online resources to assist in conducting company and industry research. In Chapter 9, I'll say more about the value of electronic job hunting and give you a number of resources that list job openings.

Computers, particularly the Internet, offer two great advantages over any other means of conducting research. First, unlike libraries, government agencies, and the like, you can access electronic resources 24 hours a day, seven days a week. Second, your geographic reach is unlimited. You can research sources in San Francisco and New York within seconds of each other, even if you live in Colby, Kansas. Additionally, almost all of the information on the Internet is FREE (at least at this time).

You'll find about fifty URLs (Uniform Resource Locators) listed in the Online Research Resources in Appendix E. To access a particular resource once you're on the Internet, type the URL exactly as shown, with no spaces.

If you're already familiar with the Net, you know that it is a very dynamic place. Sites come and sites go daily, by the hundreds. I'm certain that by the time you review Appendix E, some sites will have changed addresses, while others will have merged with other sites or disappeared altogether. This ever-changing landscape makes *virtual libraries* and *search engines* absolutely invaluable. With these two tools, even if specific URLs move or disappear, you can find another URL to access for a source of information.

Virtual libraries contain information collected and housed by broad topics. In most, you can look through their catalogs much as you would in your local library, click on a category of interest, and review pertinent information. Search engines, on the other hand, use key words, such as *career, jobs,* and *employment,* to search the vast information contained on the entire Internet. Some search engines (e.g., AltaVista) attempt to search every inch of the World Wide Web. Others (e.g., Yahoo) search only the most common or useful sites. In any event, after locating documents containing the key words you specified, the search engine then links you with the original source. For most of us (certainly for me), the distinction between virtual libraries and search engines is not very important, however. Both virtual libraries and search engines are great ways to sort easily through the morass of Internet information to find the stuff you're really interested in seeing. For practical purposes, therefore, I'll use the term *search engines* to refer to both virtual libraries and search engines. While the URLs of specific sites are handy, familiarity with the search engines is essential for getting around the Net. All search engines do not work the same; they look for information in different places and in different ways. As a result, you will need to try different search engines at different times to find the information you want. I've provided you with eight different search engines and a site that will link you to a number of others.

If you are unfamiliar with the Internet, I suggest you begin your online experience by reviewing The Riley Guide (http://www.dbm. com/jobguide/). In my view, this is one of the most useful job search sites on the Web. The guide describes Internet etiquette, newsgroups, virtual libraries, and search engines as they relate to job hunting. Next, you may want to take a quick look at The Free Online Dictionary of Computing. It contains most of the terms you're likely to encounter as you enter cyberspace. You can get there by visiting the LDOL CareerNet Reference site and then clicking on the link to the dictionary (or at http://www.ldol. state.la.us/career1/HP_REFER.HTM).

Here are some general company and industry research guidelines. When you first come to a new site, read the FAQs (frequently asked questions). For any target company, try to find a home page by typing the company's name plus .com or through one of the search engines (try Hoovers.com—great site!). Once you get the company's home page, read as much about the organization as you can, e.g., mission statement, financials, corporate officers, etc. By no means is my list of online sources all-encompassing. In Appendix E, I've simply tried to give you some of the most valuable Web sites for gathering research information.

SEEK AND YE SHALL FIND

This chapter gave you a process for conducting company and industry research, an outline for summarizing this research, and oodles of sources for information. Obviously, doing research requires effort—sometimes quite a bit. Many job hunters do not know how to learn about potential employers' businesses. The relatively few that do know, for one reason or another, often don't put out the effort demanded by research. It's the extra effort that separates fair from good, and good from great, in job hunters' effectiveness in the marketplace. If you do your research homework, unlike most of your job searching competition, you will know your customers' (potential employers) business needs and interests—and it will show. You'll enter the marketplace prepared to excel.

## 9

THE BEST JOB-FINDING METHODS

"Order and simplification are the first steps toward the mastery of a subject—the actual enemy is the unknown."
Thomas Mann

THE RIGHT GAME PLAN

Over the years, I've had the wonderful privilege of assisting graduating students, out-of-work adults, and many who are simply unhappy in their jobs as they begin to look for a new career. One of the first things I do as I begin to work with job hunters is to ask them these three questions. How will you go about finding a job? What things will you do? How much time will you spend doing those things? The reason I ask them, and you, these questions is because I want to know two things: Do they have a plan? If so, does the plan make sense?

I've observed that most people, whether they're already in the midst of job hunting or just beginning to consider the prospects of a search, answer these questions with a fair amount of hesitancy in their voice. The hesi-

tancy indicates a lack of confidence with their job search plan. Here's a promise. If you build a strategic job search campaign around the ideas presented in this chapter, you'll know you have a great plan and you will be able to answer these three questions confidently.

Here is a sampling of typical responses to these questions:

- I guess I'll look in the paper at the classifieds.
- I'll call all of my contacts and see if they know about any jobs.
- I don't know.
- I'll send out a lot of résumés to hundreds of companies; I'm very persistent.
- I hear job fairs are a great way to get connected with employers.
- I'm going to focus my time on the Internet; there are thousands of jobs listed there!

- It doesn't really matter, it's just a question of luck.
- I'll dedicate at least 10 to 20 hours a week to job searching.
- I'll spend most of my time responding to ads and sending letters and résumés because it's a numbers game.

Take a moment to compare your answers to the ones above. While these answers are common, you should know that some are dead wrong and others are "close but no cigar." None of these answers reflects a strong job search campaign based upon marketplace reality.

If I could put time in a bottle, the first thing that I'd like to do . . .

Unlike your family vacation or a Sunday drive, when it comes to finding a job, I assume you're not interested in the scenic route. You want a job—and you want it now. As you've evidenced by reading this chapter, you're willing to learn how to become proficient with a number of job-finding strategies. However, just doing a lot of things and doing them well will not help you find a job quickly.

Looking for work is a full-time job

You'll probably recall from reading Chapter 1 that job search effort given is often strongly connected to results received. By treating your job-hunting campaign as a full-time job, you dramatically improve two things: the length of the job search and your attitude during the campaign.

Think about this example. Suppose that the amount of time required to secure your next job is fixed. In other words, regardless of the amount of time you spend each week looking for work, you will not find a job until you expend a certain amount of effort. Now suppose your job search will require a total of ninety working days of effort. Each week presents you with 168 total hours. If you decide to spend 25 hours per week looking for a job (or 15 percent of your total time), your search would take about twenty-nine calendar weeks to reach ninety working days. That's more than seven months of job hunting. If, on the other hand, you choose to job search 40 hours per week (or just slightly less than 25 percent of your total time), you will reach ninety working days in eighteen calendar weeks. That's only about four and a half months. The point is simple: more looking = quicker results.

And then there is that second advantage I mentioned earlier. The more rapidly you find a job, the less likely you will become discouraged. Discouragement leads to lack of confidence. A lack of confidence can make you a less attractive job candidate. If you, and potential employers, see yourself as a marginally attractive candidate, you may become willing to settle for a lesser job. If you work at the job search as a full-time, 40-hour-a-week job, you will find it much easier to maintain enthusiasm and self-confidence throughout the campaign.

Spend your time wisely

Working hard, even if you are very good at executing your strategy, may not be enough, however. After you decide how much time to dedicate to the job search, you should respond to the three questions in the first paragraph only after you answer this additional question: *Of all the job search strategies available, which ones are most likely to result in finding a job?* Once you know the answer to this question, you can begin designing an effective job search strategy.

In the last decade or so, many businesses have faced a similar situation. One of the central ideas in much of modern management thinking is the concept of *continuous improvement.* Basically, proponents of this notion assume that product quality, and ultimately increased profitability, will result from working very diligently at getting better and better at doing things. There's one problem with this thinking. If organizations get better and better at doing the wrong things, they're actually getting worse and worse. Here is the point. You should build a campaign that focuses your efforts on job-finding activities that get results. Just like the advertising manager who must decide how to distribute the advertising budget among various possibilities such as radio, television, newspaper, billboards, and salespeople, you must decide how you will disburse your job search efforts. To find a good job quickly, first do the right things—then learn to do them well.

So, when it comes to job finding, what are the right things? As you can see in Figure 25, two job-hunting approaches yield about 85 percent of all of the results: networking and responses to advertisements. All other approaches taken together, such as employment agencies and search firms, targeted and broadcast mailings, computer databases, and job fairs account for the remaining 15 percent.

Obviously, not all approaches to the job market are equal. In fact, a number of strategies, such as broadcast mailings and job fairs, are so unlikely to result in a job that I believe you should not waste a minute of your limited

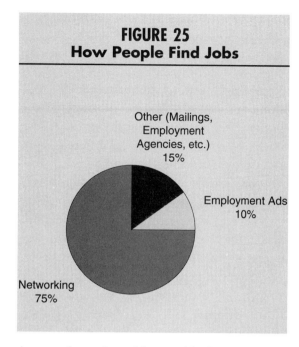

FIGURE 25
How People Find Jobs

Other (Mailings, Employment Agencies, etc.) 15%

Employment Ads 10%

Networking 75%

time on them. Sure, it's possible that you might find a job with one of these really ineffective methods, but it's extremely unlikely. Remember, you have only 168 hours per week. Time spent on less effective strategies is time away from more effective means of securing interviews and ultimately the right job.

The most effective job-hunting methods

The bulk of this chapter's pages contains the how-tos of five job-hunting methods. As I'm sure you already noticed in Figure 25, even among effective job-finding methods, great variation in success rates exists. You'll find these five methods presented in descending order, from the most effective to the least effective:

- Networking
- Responding to published advertisements

- Employment agencies and search firms
- Targeted mailings
- Online job hunting

A solid job search campaign should incorporate several, perhaps all, of these market approaches. Of course, it just makes sense to allocate your time among these different methods in proportion to their likelihood of delivering your career objective. In other words, emphasize those job search strategies most likely to yield results. For example, because networking accounts for 75 to 85 percent of job-finding success, you should spend at least 75 percent of your efforts in networking activities.

I *highly* recommend that you take the time to write a formal job search campaign strategy for two primary reasons. First, the job search's strategic plan plays a major role in networking activities. Second, a solid plan will give you a great deal of confidence. Toward the end of this chapter, after you've learned the ins and outs of the five methods listed above, I'll give you a strategic plan outline. Basically, your strategic marketing plan will answer the three questions I asked you in the first paragraph: How will you go about finding a job? What things will you do? How much time will you spend doing those things? After reading this chapter and writing your job-hunting strategy, you'll know you have a great plan that makes a lot of sense with regard to the demands of the marketplace.

NETWORKING: THE BEST WAY TO FIND WORK

Most job hunters do not spend the majority of their time networking. There are three common reasons why. First, many do not know what a truly effective job-finding method networking is. You're already ahead of the game because you now realize that 75 to 85 percent of all the people who find jobs do so through networking. A second reason most job hunters don't expend the majority of their job search effort in networking is that they really don't know how to do it very well. Third, for many, just thinking about networking generates a fair amount of discomfort. Their thinking goes something like this: "I hate rejection. I particularly hate rejection in areas that are important to me. My career is very important to me. I will receive the most face-to-face rejection during networking. I believe I'll answer ads in the classifieds."

These three concerns are quite legitimate. Nevertheless, your job-hunting efforts should include a healthy dose of networking because it is the *best* way to find a great job! However, I want you to feel very comfortable with the idea of including networking as a major part of your job search campaign. So, I'll explain why networking is so successful in finding work and then give you the details of a networking process that will reduce rejection by about 99.5 percent.

The hidden job market

Only 10 to 15 percent of job hunters find work through published sources. The many *unadvertised* jobs of the hidden job market exist for a variety of reasons:

- Introduction of new products or services
- Too few workers to meet production demands

- Someone just resigned (maybe only 30 minutes before you arrive!)
- Restructuring (yes, it creates jobs as well as eliminates them)
- Jobs to be advertised in *next* week's newspaper
- Company growth
- Unrecognized need (that is, until you showed up)

More jobs exist in the hidden job market than workers to fill them. Think about this. Every Sunday, thousands of people looking for work walk down to the end of their driveway or the convenience store, pick up the paper, and pore over the hundreds of jobs. They sort through the morass and begin preparing cover letters and résumés to send on Monday morning. The key: thousands of people—hundreds of jobs.

Every Monday, thousands of unadvertised job opportunities go unnoticed by most job hunters. A few people who know the secrets of effective networking explore the vast hidden job market, eventually finding work. The key: a few people—thousands of jobs.

Most available jobs—certainly the best jobs—reside in the hidden job market. Most of your job-hunting competition is not in the hidden job market. Obviously, you should look for jobs in the hidden job market. And here is the bottom line: networking is the *only* way to get to the unadvertised positions held in the hidden job market.

What networking is and how you do it

Networking is a process by which you learn about the job market and increase your number of contacts. Networking both extends earlier company and industry research and represents your entry into the job marketplace. As you'll soon see, networking is not calling all the people you know and asking them if they know about any job openings. The many benefits of networking include:

- Increasing your number of contacts
- Acquainting people with your marketable job skills
- Discovering leads to unadvertised jobs in the hidden job market
- Extending your market research by gaining additional information about specific industries and companies
- Allowing you to practice your communication and interviewing skills
- Causing others to remember you when a future position becomes available in their organization or elsewhere
- Establishing a business network that you can draw upon for support and information after you secure a position

Building an initial contact list

Each of us possesses a circle of contacts—individuals whom we know. Each of those individuals has his or her own contacts. The exponential nature of networking is astounding! If you contact one individual and that individual provides you with three contacts and you follow up with those three contacts and repeat this process through five stages, you will have 122 contacts working on your job search; in six stages it's 488 people!

To begin the networking process, you need to identify potential contacts. To construct a potential contact list, begin by reviewing Figure 26. This table describes various types of relationships. Each type of relationship has the potential to provide you with networking contacts. Create a contact list on a sheet of paper with these five columns:

industry. And they can refer you to other B contacts as well as to C contacts.

Of course, finding, meeting, and eventually interviewing with C contacts represents networking's most desired outcome. Once you complete your initial contact list, it's time to

Contact Name	Nature of the Relationship	Address	Phone	A/B/C Classification

Each time someone comes to mind, write his or her name on your contact list. Next, categorize the relationship of each person you listed. In Figure 27, you will find a scheme for classifying three levels of networking contacts as either A, B, or C.

Most of us can identify 20 to 25 individuals whom we know well enough that we would feel comfortable contacting them (A contacts). This is a good place to start. In advice and information meetings with A contacts, you can practice your presentation in a safe environment. Most important, A contacts will refer you to B contacts—sometimes even to C contacts.

In addition to A contacts, try to identify another 5 to 15 additional people you do not know, or don't know very well, but who could provide useful information as you continue your market research (B contacts). These B contacts are an *extremely* important part of the networking process. B contacts are those people who are well established in the industries you targeted during your research and who have their own large circle of contacts. They know what's going on. They know who's hiring, who's growing, and the latest industry trends, and they know others who are key players in the

begin conducting advice and information meetings.

Say, can I ask you a couple of questions?

Some people feel reluctant to begin networking because they do not wish to impose upon others or to ask for "favors." Still others resist making networking a major part of their job search because they believe that if contacts know they're looking for work, they will not agree to a meeting. In most cases, both of these concerns are true. If you call people in your network, tell them that you're looking for work, and then ask for a meeting, most people will NOT meet with you. It's not that they don't care about you. They simply do not want to be in a position to disappoint you. They often begin a refusal to meet by saying something like, "Gee, I'd like to help if I could, but . . ." Most network contacts feel that since they can't hire you, they have nothing to offer. None of us wants to be in the uncomfortable position of looking across the desk at someone seeking employment and saying, "Sorry, we're not hiring," or "I'm not the one who makes hiring decisions around here."

FIGURE 26
Potential Contacts

FRIENDS AND FAMILY	SOCIAL
Neighbors Brothers/Sisters/Parents Other Relatives Personal Friends	Fraternities/Sororities Sports Club Members Country Club Members Social Club Members Other Clubs (e.g., Lions, Rotary, Kiwanis)

COMMUNITY	PROFESSIONAL
PTA Members Community Business People School Board Members Civic Leaders Journalists	Consultants Current and Former Bosses Current and Former Coworkers Human Resources and Personnel Company Directors and Other Executives Lawyers Politicians and Other Public Figures Recently Retired Company Executives Chamber of Commerce Staff and Members

FINANCIAL	RELIGIOUS
Banker Financial Planner Accountant/CPA Insurance Agent	Pastor/Rabbi/Priest Religious Congregation Members

HEALTH CARE	OTHER
Dentist Doctor Psychologist/Psychiatrists Other Health-Care Professionals	Authors People Mentioned in the Newspaper or Magazine Articles Salespeople or Company Representatives Former Classmates Public Relations People Teachers/College Professors

FIGURE 27
The Three Levels of Networking Contacts

A— People in your existing network you know fairly well and would feel comfortable contacting

B— Individuals you may or may not have met who can provide important information about an industry segment or company and who could refer you to decision makers in the hiring process

C— A decision maker in the hiring process

I have some very good news for you. There is a much better way to go about making contact with people in your network. The first and foremost thing for you to keep in mind as you begin to network is this: **These are advice and information meetings, not interviews, and you will *not* ask anyone for a job during these meetings.** During the networking meeting, you will ask for *information* and receive *advice* and these activities represent your purpose.

What kind of advice and information? Good question. You will ask about two issues during the meeting. First, you will describe the formal job-finding strategy you will put together at the end of this chapter. Then ask the contact to comment on this marketing strategy given what he or she knows about the job market, this industry, your career objective, and you. In essence, your question is this: "What do you think about my marketing plan, and what advice do you have?" As you can imagine, you're likely to learn a lot from the contact's answers. Although it is not typical, don't be surprised if you get a direct lead for a hot job prospect as part of the advice.

The second kind of information you're after pertains to company and industry knowledge. Networking gives you an opportunity to extend greatly the market research you began in the last chapter. This "field" research often yields the kind of information that you just can't gather through any other means. You will find this information and these insights extraordinarily useful as your campaign progresses.

When you approach contacts about gaining advice and information rather than asking about a job, you remove any of your contact's concern about not being able to meet your job-finding need. You'll find that most people feel quite flattered when asked for advice and counsel. Once they know your purpose—advice and information—almost everyone you contact will be willing to meet with you.

Setting up advice meetings with A contacts

If you think this approach makes sense (and believe me, it works), you're probably asking how to set up these advice meetings. Begin by telephoning those people with whom you have the greatest level of comfort, your A contacts. Although A contacts are people with whom you feel fairly comfortable, you should still do your homework. Jot down a note that lists the main points you plan to make. After your initial greeting, you'll need to supply a context for your conversation. Let the contact know that you are evaluating your career. You might say something like this: "*(Contact's name), I'm at an important place in my career, and I'm looking at all my options.*" Next, state the central purpose of the call. "*I've put together a strategy to market myself, and I'd very much appreciate a chance to meet with you for a few minutes and get your feedback and advice about what I've put together."* Always remember that you will ask for advice and information, not for a job. *"I promise I will not ask you for a job or even if you know of any current job openings. I'm simply seeking your feedback and advice."* Finally, let the contact know how much time you're requesting. *"I'm sure that the meeting will take no longer than half an hour."*

You don't need to use the exact words I've given you. Indeed, you'll feel and sound much more natural if you write your own script. Just make sure that what you plan to say informs the A contact of the following:

- That you are at an important place in your career and that you are surveying your options
- That you are seeking feedback on your marketing strategy
- That you're looking for information about the business environment (industry and company information)
- That you will not ask for a job nor do you even expect the contact to know of any current job openings.

After you outline, or write down in some detail, what you intend to say, I suggest that you practice at least the opening sentence or two in front of a mirror or on a tape recorder.

Each time you set up a networking meeting, enter the contact's name on a copy of the Networking Contact Sheet. Make as many copies as you need of the Networking Contact Sheet found in Appendix A. Keep the Contact Sheets filed alphabetically by the contact's name. Be sure to take this sheet with you to the meeting and then use the sheet to record and analyze the information and advice you receive from your contact.

Setting up advice meetings with a referral

Receiving two to four referrals represents one of the primary goals of the advice meeting with an A contact. These referrals are names of other people you can contact for additional advice and information. Strategically, it's very important that you move as quickly as possible from meetings with A contacts to interactions with B and C contacts. This is when you will gain the most insider information about the hidden job market.

Because you don't know the B and C referrals as you do the A contacts, you may be more comfortable if you send an introductory letter prior to calling them. You should not include a résumé with the letter. A résumé will quickly change your contact's opinion about your intent. Remember, these information and advice meetings are not job interviews. A sample introductory letter for a referral contact is shown on the next page.

As stated in the letter, follow up the next week with a telephone call. The phone call should be very similar to an A contact call with these two exceptions: You will need to refer to the letter, and you may need to summarize the contents of the letter. After your greeting, immediately mention the name of the person who referred you; for example, *"I was referred to you by (say the first and last name of the person who referred you)."* Quickly let the referral know you have an interest in a particular field or industry. *"I am very interested in (your career field—e.g., finance, maintenance—or the referral's industry—e.g., chemical manufacturing) and (say the first name of the person who referred you) said you would be a good person for me to talk to."* Next, restate your purpose as described in the letter.

Example
Request for networking meeting to a referral

1234 Some Boulevard
My Town, My State 33333

October 3, 199x

Linda Powell
(Job Title)
Next Employer, Inc.
105 Treasure Street
Ideal Destination, FL 54321

Dear Ms. Powell:

Our mutual friend (person's name who referred you) suggested that I contact you. I am seeking advice about my career interest in (your career field) and about the (the contact's industry).

I have worked as a real estate broker for two years and I am looking for new challenges in the field. I have designed a plan for marketing myself and I would very much like to meet with you to get your feedback about my plan. I am only seeking advice and feedback about my marketing plan and information about the real estate field and commercial real estate industry.

Andy convinced me that your advice would be invaluable to me as I gather information about my career transition. I would like to meet with you personally. The meeting should take no more than 30 minutes.

I will call you early next week to find the best time on your schedule for us to get together.

Sincerely,

John Hunt
444-555-9876

"As you know from my letter, I've put together a strategy to market myself, and I'd very much appreciate a chance to meet with you for a few minutes and get your advice about what I've put together. I would also very much like to learn more about the (the referral's industry) industry." Again, defuse the situation by saying *"I promise I will not ask you for a job or even if you know of any current job openings. I'm simply seeking your feedback and advice."* Finally, be very specific about the amount of time you're requesting. *"I'm sure that the meeting will take no longer than half an hour."*

If you're going to be authentic, you must develop your own words. Work on it until it feels natural. For some this means hours of practice; for others it's six bulleted points and you're off! Either way, make sure your approach informs the referral of these issues:

- The name of the person who referred you to him or her
- That you have an interest in a particular career field and/or industry
- That you're looking for information about the business environment (industry and company information)
- That you are seeking feedback on your marketing strategy
- That you will not ask for a job nor do you expect the referral to know of any current job openings
- That the requested meeting will take no more than half an hour

As with the A contact calls, I suggest that you practice at least the opening sentence or two in front of a mirror or on a tape recorder. If it would make you feel more prepared, ask a friend or your spouse to take the part of the contact and then role-play the phone call.

The advice meeting's agenda

You should carefully prepare the meeting agenda to ensure that you do not waste the contact's time or your own. This preparation also indicates that you are a professional who knows how to handle information and meetings. Please carefully review the detailed advice and information agenda provided. As you can see, the outline includes sections for an introduction, the main presentation, and a closing. You will find this carefully constructed advice meeting agenda very effective.

DWYSYD

A very good friend is a top executive of a major corporation. The first time I met him, I noticed a rather unattractive 10" by 30" sign on his office wall. The sign's capital letters DWYSYD were fire-engine red and the background was taxicab yellow. Shortly after that first meeting began, I asked him what the sign was all about. He smiled and explained that the letters were an acronym that stood for *Do What You Say You'll Do.*

Over the years, I've come to learn that a good deal of this executive's considerable success and outstanding reputation in his local community and in business rests upon his commitment to DWYSYD. Nowhere is this attitude more important than in the networking process.

I cannot overemphasize the importance of maintaining authenticity and integrity throughout your networking. When you call to set up the meeting you will say that you're seeking advice and information and that you promise not to ask for a job. If you violate this promise you will seriously undermine your credibility. Networking is powerful. It can turn its power against you as much as it can provide benefit. If you fake it when building rapport, if you say you'll only need 30 minutes and stay an hour, or if you promise not to ask for a job but do, several things will happen. You will not receive referrals or important insider information, if a job does exist in the organization it won't be yours, and your reputation for misleading will travel. This last point is particularly harmful for your career prospects. In order for your networking to succeed, you must DWYSYD.

Example
Suggested Advice Meeting Agenda

INTRODUCTION

Build a relationship

Begin to build a rapport by emphasizing your relationship with the referral source. Comment on any genuine mutual interests you observe in the office (e.g., pictures of children, fishing, awards, etc.), and/or compliment the office appearance or the demeanor of the secretary. **CAUTION:** Above all, *be authentic.*

Put the contact at ease

Again, state that you are not going to ask for a job or even ask if the contact knows of any job openings. Instead, you are going to ask for *advice* and *information* about your job search strategy and about the business/industry.

PRESENTATION

Purpose of the meeting

Now state specifically what you would like to accomplish at this meeting. For example, "The purpose of this meeting is to share my career objective and my current strategic plan to market myself, to ask you for information about several companies I plan to target, and to get your advice and feedback regarding these plans."

Your career objective

Simply state your 30-second verbal commercial from Chapter 7 and include your career objective statement.

Current strategies

Briefly share your marketing strategies from your formal job search strategy. In other words, explain what you plan to do to reach your career objective.

Feedback about your job search strategies

Early in your networking campaign with A contacts only—Ask the following questions: (1) Does my career objective make sense to you? (2) Do my strategies to address the job market seem like a good approach? (3) Do you perceive any obstacles to my career objective or current strategy? (4)

What industry segments are likely to represent the best opportunity given what you know about me and my skills? **OPTION:** You may wish to share an early draft of your résumé with the first few contacts for feedback and advice. Do not leave a draft behind, however. If the contact wants a résumé, promise to mail it when it is complete. Also, if the contact offers to share your résumé with one of his/her contacts, persuade the contact to allow you to send your own résumé so that you can follow up appropriately.

    Later on in the job search campaign—Simply ask for a reaction to your objective and current strategies. Also ask, "In addition to the strategies I discussed, are there any other strategies that you can think of that I should engage in as I begin my job search?"

Market research questions

    Industry segment questions—Ask the contact about his/her industry. What strengths, weaknesses, and trends currently exist? What threats may hinder the industry in the future? What are the best ways for me to stay up to date with what is happening to this industry?

    Target company questions—Ask the contact if she or he knows of any particular companies you should contact as you begin your job search. If the contact has difficulty generating company names, show your Target Company List (Chapter 8) and ask if these companies appear to be reasonable targets given what the contact knows about you and the particular companies. Ask if he/she would suggest any other companies.

    Research summary questions—If you need information to complete one or more of your company profiles (Chapter 8) and your contact has knowledge about one of these companies, ask the appropriate questions to complete the summaries.

Ask for referrals

    This is the most important part of your meeting. Often, C contacts are four or five links away from initial contacts; remember, C contacts are the decision makers. Ask the contact if he/she would please provide three names of individuals that you could contact to continue your market research. Although most will, don't become discouraged if the contact does not provide you with referrals. Do not take it personally, and remember that persistence is the name of the job search game. You may find that asking your contact for names of individuals at specific companies on your Target Company List will serve as a reminder to your contact of his or her own network.

CLOSING

Summary

    Briefly, in 1 to 2 minutes, summarize the meeting.

Plans for follow-up

    Describe your plans for follow-up as outlined in the next section.

Thank-You

    Thank the contact for his or her time and the invaluable information and advice you received.

In addition to carefully planning the advice meeting agenda, a few additional issues warrant attention.

- Take the Networking Contact Sheet that you completed at the time you set up the meeting, a nice pen, paper for note-taking, a copy of a near final draft of your résumé, and business cards (if appropriate). A good portfolio or briefcase is the best way to carry these materials to your meetings.

- Be sensitive to contacts' time and do **not** take more time than you have promised. Begin to close the meeting after about 25 to 30 minutes. However, if the contact indicates that spending a few more minutes is acceptable and you feel the meeting is going well, take another 15 to 20 minutes and then close the meeting.

- Follow-up is vitally important to the success of any networking campaign. First, during the closing of the meeting, let the contact know that you will telephone in two to three weeks to update him or her. Second, you should mail a written thank-you note within two days. The note should include (see Appendix C for a sample follow-up letter):
  — Gratitude for the person who referred you to this contact because the information was very valuable
  — A thank-you for the time the contact spent with you
  — A reminder that you will call with an update within two or three weeks as promised in the meeting
  — A comment that you will send a final copy of your résumé when it is completed

- After you secure employment, be sure to send a letter and a new business card to all people with whom you networked.

Getting to interviews with C contacts

While it is true that networking activities aim at gathering advice and information, the marketing campaign's ultimate goal is to secure an interview with a decision maker; that is, *the person who can make the hiring decision.* If you do not talk to the person with the power to hire you, you will not get the job. Through networking, you'll learn of job opportunities in the hidden job market that you can pursue. Perhaps a contact will invite you to apply for a position in his or her company. Some of these opportunities will turn into interviews with decision makers. Occasionally, when you meet with a C contact, a networking meeting will turn into a job interview. DWYSYD does not mean that you can't respond if *they* ask. I'll say this just one last time: there is no better way to get an interview with a decision maker than through networking.

Networking is time-consuming and demands a good deal of tenacity and occasionally a thick skin. However, if you do all of your homework, as described in the next chapter on interviewing, you will ensure that you will talk to people who want to talk to you. Why? Because, through your marketing research and networking activities you are seeking a match between your vocational identity and the needs of the marketplace. Finding this match is at least as important to employers as it is to you.

Dealing with secretaries

Many people, particularly decision makers, are inundated daily with phone calls. It would be *impossible* to deal with every telephone call. Most of the calls are unimportant in terms of the decision maker's immediate tasks. Screening calls is one of the secretary's primary job responsibilities. By making sure that only those calls that are important to the decision maker get through, the secretary greatly increases the decision maker's productivity. While you should not take this screening personally, you will encounter it and you need strategies to overcome it. Remember, however, if you do not talk directly with the decision maker, you will not find employment with that firm. Here are several tips for dealing with the secretary:

- Be extremely courteous and respectful. Not only is this person an important part of the target organization, but the secretary also represents a vital link between you and the contact.

- Learn the secretary's name and use it several times during the initial call and list it on the Networking Contact Sheet so you can address the secretary by name during subsequent calls.

- Introduce yourself and spell your name. Remember to speak slowly enough for the secretary to write down the information. If the secretary asks you to repeat it, you are probably speaking too quickly.

- Tell the secretary that you recently corresponded with the decision maker and that he or she is expecting you to call.

- If you were referred, mention the name of the person who referred you.

- If the secretary asks if you are looking for a job, explain that you are merely seeking advice and information at this time and will not ask the contact for a job.

- Avoid letting the secretary redirect your call to the personnel department; this is often the end of your search with this company. State that you will not be asking (contact's name) for a job and that you really wish to meet with him or her personally.

- Whenever possible, avoid letting the responsibility for telephoning shift from you to the targeted contact. "I'll ask Mr. or Ms. Contact to call you," can be deadly. If you fail to reach the contact, *always* state that you will call again.

- The secretary can't screen you out if he or she is not there. Try calling a few minutes before or after normal working hours or during lunch.

- If you continue to have difficulty, contact the main switchboard, tell them that you corresponded with (the contact's name) and that he or she is expecting your call. Then ask for the contact's direct line. Surprisingly, sometimes this is all it takes to get through to the contact. (Again, you may have more success with the contact's direct line before or after normal working hours, or during the lunch hour.)

RESPONDING TO EMPLOYMENT ADVERTISEMENTS

This is where most job hunters spend most of their time. That's unfortunate. Compared to networking, job searchers find very few jobs by responding to employment advertisements. When I teach job-hunting techniques in group settings, I like to ask participants at the beginning of the workshop how they are currently looking for work. Of course, most respond that they are diligently sending out lots of paper in response to advertisements and in broadcast mailings.

While this marketing approach is not nearly as effective as networking, sometimes job hunters do find jobs, even very good jobs, by responding to published advertisements. Because responding to ads is the second most effective marketing approach, and because none of us can possibly resist it, you should include it as a *part* of your job search campaign. However, think of this part of the campaign as good work for *non–prime time*, when most networking cannot be done. Respond to published job ads early in the morning, or late at night, or on weekends. Save the majority of *prime time*, 8 a.m. to 5 p.m., Monday through Friday, for networking.

Two kinds of advertisements

Advertisements come in two flavors: blind ads or open ads. You'll find both types of ads in a variety of different published sources. A sampling of sources is presented in Figure 28.

Blind advertisements

Many employment advertisements appear as blind ads. These ads do not indicate the hiring company's name or location. The ad asks you to respond to either a newspaper box or a post office box. Hiring companies run these sorts of ads for a variety of reasons:

- They do not want to write a response to every applicant
- They do not want their competition or personnel within their own organization to know of upcoming personnel changes

FIGURE 28
Possible Sources for Advertised Job Opportunities

- Local Newspaper
- Professional/Technical Journals
- Industry and Trade Magazines
- Society and Trade Newsletters
- University Publications and Newsletters
- State and Federal Employment Bulletins
- Weekly Publications
  The National Business Employment Weekly
- Online Job Search Services (See this chapter's section: Online Job Hunting)
- Local Business Publications

- The personnel department does not wish to be flooded with calls from applicants following up on mailed materials
- They may simply be conducting research to determine market conditions

Employment agencies and executive search firms also run blind ads. In many of these cases, no actual job opening exists; the firms run the ads merely to ensure that their files contain a pool of potential candidates in a variety of fields.

Open advertisements

In the case of open advertisements, the company prints its location, name, and the rules for responding to the ad. Typically, the personnel department places these ads and requests that applicants send résumés and cover letters to that department.

Tips for responding to published job leads

Your response to the ads should include a cover letter and résumé. It's always much better to write to an individual rather than a department, post office box, or "to whom it may concern." With blind ads, of course, it's often impossible to know to whom you're sending your materials. If the ad contains a U.S. Post Office Box rather than a newspaper box, you can contact the post office, however, and ask for the name of the company renting that box. By law, the Postmaster must give you the company's name if the company indicated when they rented the box that they "do business with the public."

FIGURE 29
Job Advertisement

POSITIONS AVAILABLE:

**CITY OF DELTONA
PERSONNEL MANAGER**

Full-time salaried position reporting to Finance Director. Resp. for admin of City's Personnel Policies including the areas of recruitment & selection of new employees, maintenance of employee personnel files, benefit packages and retirement plans, and administration of union contracts and Personnel Policies. MIN REQUIREMENTS: Bachelor's Degree in Personnel, Public or Business Administration or closely related field. Three years min. exp. in a resp. supervisory position in personnel/human resources field. Exp. in personal computer applications and labor/contract negotiations. Knowledge of current labor law, ADA legislation/rules, personnel practices, and related compliance issues. BEGINNING SALARY: $30,000 annually.

However, with open ads, just a little research on your part can help your materials stand above others'. If you call the company's main telephone number and ask for the correct spelling of the name, the job title, and the mailing address of the person who is in charge of a particular function (e.g., sales and marketing, finance, etc.) the operator will very often give this information to you. This person undoubtedly is a decision maker. Whether or not this person will make the final hiring decision for the job for which you are applying, he or she is an important influencer in the process. Even if this individual will not conduct the job interview, it's much better to have a senior executive forward your materials to someone else in the organization than to have them stuck in the human resources or personnel department. If the switchboard operator asks you why you need this information, simply reply that "I'm putting together some important personal correspondence and want to make sure that everything is just right."

If you come across an advertisement that is appealing, but it's several days or weeks old, don't panic. Most jobs take several weeks, sometimes months, to fill. In fact, while I don't recommend it as a strategy of choice, responding a few days after the ad first runs can work to your advantage. Because employers receive the bulk of ad responses immediately after the ad runs, your materials may experience a less severe screening by arriving a few days or weeks later than most.

A caveat

I've actually heard of an occasion where a job hunter responded to a blind classified ad on Sunday, only to get a call from his own personnel department the same week. You see, he inadvertently applied for another position in his own organization. Pretty embarrassing, right? In Chapter 11, I'll talk to you more about managing a job search when you're currently employed. For now, let me simply advise that if you are concerned about confidentiality, avoid blind ads.

Save time and grief—make sure you fit

Because time is one of your most valuable job search assets, only spend time responding to ads for which you have a sincere interest and are qualified. If the ad details the job's requirements, preparing a *Your Needs/My Qualifications* cover letter represents one of the best ways to determine how well your skills match the job. Chapter 7 presented the basic outline for the *Your Needs/My Qualifications* cover letter format. Figure 29 on the previous page is an actual classified advertisement from the *Orlando Sentinel.* On the next page you'll see *Your Needs/My Qualifications* letter written in response. If your skills match the company's needs, this letter format will dramatically increase your chances of obtaining a job interview. However, if your skills do not match the organization's published requirements, you'll discover this fact pretty quickly using this format. If your skills don't match, you'll do yourself and the organization a favor by redirecting your efforts to other advertisements and other job-finding methods.

EMPLOYMENT AGENCIES AND SEARCH FIRMS

When it comes to employment agencies and search firms, myths abound. First, these folks do not work for you. They work for employers and for themselves. Second, they do not have an inexhaustible pool of great employment opportunities just waiting for you. Keep in mind that very few people find new jobs through employment agencies and search firms.

Nevertheless, you should still consider registering with a few of them as a *part* of your overall campaign strategy. However, build realistic expectations given the few jobs actually acquired in this fashion. Never forget that these firms work for the employer, not for you, and prepare to be selective when choosing firms with which you'll work.

Employment agencies

Employment agencies typically fill positions with salaries of $45,000 or less. These agencies fill both permanent and temporary positions. Some operate as an unspecialized agency handling a wide variety of positions. Most agencies, however, specialize within particular industries, such as high-tech manufacturing or hospitality, or within certain functions, such as finance, human resources, or accounting.

While employment agencies' fees are often employer paid, the agency may sometimes ask **you** to pay the fee (usually about 5 to 15 percent of your annual starting salary). Before you sign *any* employment agency document, read the fine print; you may be signing a contract that entitles the agency to extract a fee from you even if you find a job on your own! I *strongly* suggest that you consider only employer-paid agencies. If you do decide to work with an agency where you will pay the fee, have an attorney familiar with employment agencies review any documents you're asked to sign.

Example
Your Needs/My Qualifications
Response to Classified Ad

105 Some Street
My Town, Mystate 55555

February 28, 199x

Ms. J. Hunt
Finance Director
City Government
520 Easy Street
Anytown, USA 33333

Dear Ms. Hunt:

I read your October 19 advertisement in the *Orlando Sentinel* with great interest. I believe my skills and experience closely match the requirements for the Personnel Manager position.

I have eight years of personnel experience with a solid track record of accomplishments. I would like to highlight my qualifications in response to the job's requirements.

Your Needs	My Qualifications
1. Bachelor's degree in personnel, public, or business administration	1. Bachelor's degree in business administration. Currently pursuing master's degree in industrial relations. Anticipated next spring.
2. Three years of supervisory experience in a personnel position	2. Three years as compensation manager supervising two analysts and support staff.
3. Experience in personal computer applications	3. Familiar with Lotus, Excel, Word, Word Perfect, and PC-based HRIS software.
4. Labor contract negotiations and knowledge of current labor law such as ADA	4. Played support role in Acme's successful 1995 negotiations with the IBEW union. Master's degree course work has included instruction in Title VII, ADEA, and ADA.

I would like to learn more about the position and have an opportunity to meet with you face-to-face to give you a better idea of my abilities. I look forward to hearing from you soon.

Thank you for your consideration.

Sincerely,

Your Name Typed
407-555-1234

Enc. Résumé

Remember that these agencies are in the business of filling assignments or jobs, not finding you employment. They may distribute or "shop" your résumé widely. This uncontrolled distribution could potentially lead to an embarrassing situation if you are unaware of which firms have seen your résumé. If you decide to include employment agencies as part of your overall job search campaign, I suggest the following:

- Use only a few high-quality agencies.
- Ask for referrals from other individuals who have recently worked with this agency; then call the referrals and ask what it was like to work with this agency.
- Negotiate how and to which organizations your résumé will be distributed. Make sure you can eliminate any organizations from the agency's list that you wish to contact on your own.
- Meet face-to-face with the particular agent with whom you will be working. Make sure you are comfortable with this person. In many cases, the individual agent is much more important than the agency.

Search firms

These firms go by many names, including search firms, executive recruiters, and headhunters. They specialize in positions with salaries starting at about $50,000 and in rare cases exceeding $1,000,000. Their primary job is to find *employed* executives and convince them to leave their current position for another one. They generally operate in one of two ways. If they operate on *retainer*, the firm has an exclusive arrangement with an organization for a particular job and will collect a fee based on about 30 percent

of the first year's salary. (Yes, I know that's a lot of money. That's why so few jobs are available through these firms; employers simply don't want to pay this much to locate someone unless they really have to do so.) If the recruiter works on a *contingency* basis, the employer will only pay the firm after they match an individual to a job and the person begins work. In this case, the fee is typically much less. In the case of a contingency arrangement, a number of search firms may be working on the same "search."

Most search firms have a "replacement" clause in their contract with the employer. If the new employee leaves the firm too quickly, usually within the first three to six months, the search firm must find a replacement for no additional charge. This is one of the main reasons recruiters may call with words of encouragement several times within the first few weeks after they place someone in a new position.

In addition to following my suggestions for working with employment agencies, you should investigate these issues:

- Learn a bit about the search firm's history and size and the background of the owners or principles.
- Learn whether the search firm is operating on a contingency or retainer basis.
- Ask the types of positions or industries with which they typically work.

If at all possible, you should ask for references from other clients they have recently placed. Please do your homework and call these references; you may learn some very important things.

Although in many cases the recruiter will not divulge the name of the firm for which he or she is working, if you ask questions about the size, location, and industry, you often will be able to make a pretty good guess.

In some fields, such as high technology, or some occupations, such as physical therapy, recruiters can find you work almost immediately. The reason is that the demand for workers in these situations is incredibly high. Think about this: if the demand is this high, do you really need an employment agency or search firm to assist you in locating employment?

SEND TARGETED MAILINGS

The word "broadcast" originated as an agricultural term. To sow seeds using the broadcast method, a farmer would reach into a bag of seeds, grab large handfuls of seed, and then throw, or cast, these handfuls of seed upon the ground. The farmer hoped that enough crops would grow from his effort to sustain the farm and the farmer's family. Needless to say, broadcasting seed is not the most efficient method of planting and farmers seldom use it today.

A broadcast letter approach consists of writing a cover letter that fits all companies (basically a form letter), generating a large list of companies, changing the company name and address for each of the companies on the list, tossing in your résumé, and mailing the form letter and the résumé to all these companies. This approach is so ineffective that I believe it is largely a waste of your time.

On the other hand, if during your market research you discover companies you might like to work for, but you have no networking contact within these companies, you should contact these organizations through a targeted-mail approach. The primary differences between the targeted-mailing approach and the broadcast approach are as follows:

- Contact only those companies that your market research indicates are potential matches between your vocational identity (interests, skills, and abilities, and values and purpose) and the organization's needs
- Each letter is somewhat unique (specific to the particular company you are approaching), incorporates information from your research, and describes the *benefits* that your skills, abilities, and experience can bring to this company
- Most important, address the letter to a decision maker in the organization, *not* to the human resources or personnel department
- Mail a maximum of ten to fifteen letters per week, and follow up every letter with a phone call to the decision maker to whom you mailed the letter
- As discussed in the résumé section, be sure not to include potentially discriminatory information such as age, gender, race, religion, marital status, or personal information (e.g., hobbies, number of children, or salary information)
- The letter should be one page (absolutely no more than two pages) and include:
  — a **powerful** opening statement describing one of your strongest *accomplishments* or how your *market research* indicates the potentially good fit between you and the organization
  — a description of your career objective and latest work experience with several additional accomplishments

— a conclusion stating that you will follow up the next week by telephone to set up a meeting

The following sample letter incorporates these suggestions and uses one of the examples of career objectives first seen in Chapter 6.

ONLINE JOB HUNTING

This is not a very good way to find a job. Perhaps I should be a little more specific. This is not a very good way to secure employment; you'll find thousands of jobs. While the Internet is a great way to conduct research, as discussed in the last chapter, for most it's pretty much a waste of time in locating a job—a lot of time. There are exceptions. For those in high-tech fields or with very specific job skills, the Internet is a much more valuable tool than for most job hunters.

You're probably asking, "If it doesn't work, why include it in the list of the most effective ways to search for jobs?" Even though it's fairly ineffective, I believe there are two reasons why you should consider using the Internet in your job search.

First, you can jump on the Internet at any time of the day or night. You can job search after Jay Leno finishes his monologue. And you should only job search on the Internet at times when you cannot do anything else. After working hard at networking activities during prime time (8 a.m. to 5 p.m.). After you've contacted the three search firms you're going to use. After you've mailed this week's last set of materials to target companies or in response to published ads. When you're just too darn tired to do

anything else. Beware—nothing will gobble time, some of it in pretty entertaining ways, as quickly as the Internet. However, if you job search on line during times you would otherwise do nothing, it can add value.

The second reason you should consider including the computer in your marketing strategy relates to the Internet's incredibly rapid growth. While its current effectiveness in job hunting is only minimal, no one can predict its value even six months from today. I would not be at all surprised to see online job hunting surpass classified advertising's effectiveness within the next couple of years. You might as well learn now what will soon be a much more important part of all of our lives.

To job search on line you'll need to know about networking on the Net, consider posting your résumé online, and learn how to locate the most valuable job posting sites.

Networking on the Net

On the Internet, you can really reach out and touch someone. Whether they're in Paris, Texas, or Paris, France, you can find people with similar interests. Along with conducting research, this is one of the most useful job search tools offered through the Internet. Just like face-to-face networking, online contacts can provide valuable information regarding industry trends, referrals, or even job leads.

To find networking contacts online, you'll need to become familiar with Usenet newsgroups. As I did in the last chapter, I suggest that you take a look at The Riley Guide (http://www.dbm. com/jobguide/) as an introduction. If you're new to the Internet, you'll find the guide's discussion of *The Fine Art of Correct Behavior*

Example
Targeted Mailing Letter

J. Doe
1515 Some Street
Smallville, USA 55555

July 4, 199x
S. Smith
President
Unico, Inc.
55 Big Street
Anytown, USA 45454

Dear Ms. Smith:

As the head of the compensation and benefits department at Techo, Inc., I designed and implemented a company-wide variable compensation plan that saved Techo $2.5 million over five years and increased employees' satisfaction with their pay.

I am relocating to Anytown, and I am seeking a position as a director of compensation and benefits in a high-tech business. Last year, I designed a compensation package that linked supervisors' people management skills to annual pay increases. This compensation package resulted in more than 10 percent improvement in employee satisfaction scores while no increase in company costs was incurred. I also recently implemented a managed care program that reduced Techo's health-care cost by 5 percent. The enclosed résumé details my work history and outlines a number of additional work accomplishments.

I will call you next week in order to set up a face-to-face meeting with you. If you would like to talk to me sooner than next week, please call me at 407-555-1212.

Sincerely,

J. Doe

Enc. Résumé

---

on the Internet quite valuable. The guide also suggests that you read the information provided at *Newsgroup FAQ's* (http://www.cis.ohio-state.edu/hypertext/faq/usenet/top.html), hosted by Ohio State University, before you actively participate in a newsgroup discussion.

Liszt (http://www.Liszt.com) is perhaps the best source for locating others with similar interests on the Net. Liszt provides access to literally thousands of mailing lists. These mailing lists are simply groups of people who share information and ideas about topics of common interest. However, I strongly suggest that you read Liszt's *Tips for Newcomers*, especially the *Any warnings before I get started?* section, before you attempt to engage in any newsgroup discussion.

Posting your résumé on the Net

Of all the ideas in this book, this is the one most likely **not** to result in adding value to your career. There are simply not enough employers searching through the tens of thousands of résumés. Nevertheless, the Internet has experienced an explosion of services that will assist in writing an electronic résumé and in posting that résumé for employers to see. Again, for those in high-tech jobs, the probability of finding employment through electronic résumé posting is much greater than for most. Rather than give you a long list of services and Internet addresses, let me give you one that will be more than enough. If you decide to post your résumé on line, try Yahoo (http://www.yahoo.com/ Business_and_Economy/Employment/ Résumés/). At the time of this writing, Yahoo listed 105 résumé services; most of them will post your résumé.

Job postings on the Net

This is the reason many job hunters' pulses start racing at mention of the Internet. Just imagine it. Thousands of local, national, even international jobs at your fingertips. Just enter the kind of job you're interested in finding in the little box next to the gray search button on the screen, push the "Enter" key, wait about 5 seconds, pick your job, and live happily ever after—right? Wrong!

Again, by pursuing the Internet's job data banks, you will find a large number of jobs. Here are two factors, however, that make job finding difficult in these data banks. First, a lot more people are looking online than there are jobs available (similar to looking through newspaper ads). Second, it's difficult to find the right kind of job. You may look through hundreds of jobs and not find any job that appears worth pursuing. Chances are extremely low that you'll be able to find a job this way, unless you're in a high-tech field such as computer programming or engineering. If you decide to include online job searching as part of your strategic plan, you'll find some of the best sites to consider in Appendix E.

BUILD YOUR STRATEGIC MARKETING PLAN

As I said earlier in the chapter, I highly recommend that you take the time to write a formal job search campaign strategy. You will probably find that you need to update, or perhaps substantially modify, the original plan as you learn more about the marketplace. By no means do you need to create a complex, multiple-page document. The strategic plan does not need to be elaborate, just straightforward and effective. Your responses to the three questions from the first paragraph, given what you now know about the job market, will form the core of the plan: How will you go about finding a job?

What things will you do? How much time will you spend doing those things?

Refer to the completed example of a Strategic Plan Worksheet that follows as you decide about the three questions and prepare to write your plan. Note that the total hours at the top of the worksheet should match the total hours at the bottom.

After you complete the worksheet, you are ready to write a formal job search marketing plan. There is no magic for determining the length of the written plan. You may decide to make it one or two pages, or twenty. You are the judge. Just complete the Strategic Plan Worksheet and then review the outline shown in Figure 30.

When you complete your marketing plan, you can confidently enter the job marketplace, secure in knowing that you have a plan that makes a lot of sense. The techniques described in this chapter, especially networking, will lead to job leads and ultimately to interviews. That's the good news. The bad news is that if you perform poorly in the interview, all of your work will mean nothing—you won't get that particular job. That's why I recommend that before you launch your marketing efforts in full force you begin to prepare for the main event—the job interview.

Example
Strategic Plan Worksheet

Total hours I will commit to spend each week working on my job search **40**

Market approach	Yes/No	Percentage of total time each week	Hours per week for this approach
Networking	Yes	75%	30 hours
Answering Ads	Yes	10%	4 hours
Employment Agencies/ Recruiters	No	N/A	N/A
Targeted Mailings	Yes	5%	2 hours
Internet	Yes	10%	4 hours
TOTAL HOURS			40 hours

FIGURE 30
Job Search Marketing Campaign Strategy

Summary—Summarize your overall plan in one or two paragraphs. Include your career objective and a brief overview of each of the next three sections.

Career Treasure and Success—Review your Vocational Identity Summary page. In one or two paragraphs, describe what represents your personal career treasure, what you value, and what needs to occur during your job search for you to consider it a real success. Be sure to note the most significant benefits you feel you bring to potential employers.

Target Industry Segments and Companies—Based upon your market research from Chapter 8, identify those market segments, industries, and companies you intend to approach.

Job Market Approaches—Review your completed Strategic Plan Worksheet. Describe the total amount of time you will dedicate to job searching, which job-finding methods you will use to approach the marketplace, and the percentage of time you will spend on each.

CHAPTER

10

PREPARE FOR THE JOB INTERVIEW

· ·

"So, why did you leave your last position?"
"What did you like least about your last job?"
"What is it that annoys you in others?"
"What would you say is your biggest career mistake?"
Perhaps your next interviewer

IT'S SHOW TIME!

As you sit in the lobby waiting for the interview to begin, you feel confident. This is the moment you've been waiting for! Because of your hard work in earlier chapters, you know a lot about yourself, about the job market, and about this company. Finally your diligence is ready to pay off. Just as you hoped, the marketing plan you prepared in the last chapter delivered a job interview with a decision maker. Your best business suit has never looked better on you. At last you will have an opportunity to show your stuff, let an employer know what you're made of—to shine.

The interviewer greets you with a firm handshake and asks you to come back to his office. You exchange a few pleasantries, and then it begins. "So, tell me a little about yourself."

Your mind races and your heart begins to beat a little faster. "That's it? My life, or at least my career, hangs in the balance, and the interviewer asked this question? What does he want to know? How long should my answer be? How can I demonstrate my value to the company through this question? Why is he smiling?"

For years, personnel research has shown that interviews do a pretty poor job of predicting a job candidate's future success on the job. In fact, when done properly, psychological tests, assessment centers, application blanks, and even reviews of certain kinds of historical data are all better predictors of future job performance.

While the research evidence demonstrating interviews' weak ability to predict future job performance is quite clear, another fact is even clearer: *you will have to go through an interview to get a job.* While your performance during the interview may reveal almost nothing about how well you will perform on the job, it is a *terrific* predictor of whether or not you'll receive an offer.

Begin preparing now!

Readying yourself to excel during job interviews represents the *most critical* part of your job search preparation for two reasons. First, regardless of how well you do everything else, performing well during the job interview will almost certainly play a major, perhaps *the major*, role in determining whether a company offers you a position. Second, the job interview affords you an excellent opportunity to evaluate the organization as you decide whether it meets your career needs.

The previous chapter's job search strategies furnished information about how to secure a job interview with a decision maker. Chapter 10 gives you the knowledge necessary to perform well during the actual job interview. If you follow the entire process laid out in the book, you will practice a considerable amount of interviewing before you get to the job interview. In Chapter 6, you learned to conduct exploration interviews with people actually doing the kind of work you'd like to do. The advice and information interviews discussed in Chapter 9 also serve as practice for your communication and interview skills.

However, you need to know much more about job interviewing in order to ensure success—that is, to get a terrific job! Over the course of this chapter, I will tell you about the various types of interviews you're likely to encounter, tips and strategies for answering tough interview questions, proper dress, how to evaluate your performance, and how to follow up effectively after the interview. People often ask me when they should prepare for job interviews. I strongly suggest that you start preparing immediately for the job interview that will lead to your next job. Why? Because once you begin job hunting, it is impossible to predict exactly when an interview opportunity will emerge. By starting now, you will be able to capitalize on any interview opportunity; whether it occurs the first week of the campaign or six months after you launch your job search.

Remember both interview objectives

In his excellent book *Outplace Yourself,* C. H. Logue defines interviewing as "a two-way communication process where you (interviewee) and the company (interviewer) gather information from one another to determine if there is a potential match." I like this definition particularly well because it nicely captures the two-way nature of an ideal job interview. In my view, for you to excel during a job interview you must pay close attention to both aspects of this definition. While it is true that you must sell yourself to the company to receive an offer, you should also use the interview to determine if a job opportunity matches your vocational identity.

Play the right game

Sometimes a job interview feels like a contest—and we all like to win. You may have heard the interview advice, "Get the offer, then decide if you want the job." This advice emphasizes the selling side of interviewing. Of course, being prepared to answer difficult interview questions, dressing correctly, following up, and so forth are very important parts of job hunting. However, mastering the techniques aimed at getting a job offer is only part of the interview picture. Focusing only on getting an offer is a mistake; maybe a *really big* mistake. Winning is important, but make sure you're playing the right game.

I'm assuming, of course, that your ultimate goal is not just to get a job, but to get a job that matches your vocational identity. I'm also assuming you're diligently searching for career treasure. If so, then please do not attempt to *appear* to be the right person for the job. Instead, seek to *discover* and then *demonstrate* that you're the right person for the job. The difference between trying to appear to be the right person and discovering the appropriateness of the position is subtle, but important. Let me explain.

When presenting yourself to others, you possess a fairly wide range of behaviors from which you can choose. However, the range of behaviors that you enjoy using, that truly reflect who you are, are much narrower than all the possible choices available. If your goal is to find career treasure, then you must present yourself using this narrower set of behaviors; the ones that represent the real you. When seeking career treasure, authenticity and genuineness must be your sales approach. You must also sincerely evaluate the organization's fit with all aspects of your vocational identity. Why? Because if you must *act* in a way that is unnatural or uncomfortable during the interview in order to get a job offer, doesn't it stand to reason that the job and organization probably will not deliver career

satisfaction? Sure, you might get the offer based upon your interview performance, but the job offer resulted from a facade. You'll soon tire of using the false persona and long for a chance to find joy in your work. If your interview performance doesn't represent your vocational identity, even if you get the offer, you lose.

On the other hand, if your interview performance is effective from a sales perspective *and* genuinely reflects who you are, you cannot lose. If your interview performance effectively represents your values, personality, and skills, and the interviewer doesn't offer you the job, you win. If the fit is wrong, the fit is wrong—so be it. There will be another—a better— opportunity down the job search road. Like many things in life, the right position is well worth waiting for. I absolutely want you to win the contest; but I want you to win the career treasure game, not just the get-a-job game.

VOCATIONAL IDENTITY MEETS THE MARKETPLACE

Please find the Vocational Identity Summary (VIS) you completed in Part I and the results from Exercise 7 in Chapter 3. Spend a few minutes reviewing the VIS and the entire list of OAR statements created in Exercise 7.

Taken together, the VIS and OAR statements represent a snapshot of you as a worker. These two tools will help you showcase yourself as a person who can add benefit to an employer.

Career Treasure = Employer's Treasure

This is an amazing thing! When a job and an organization match your skills, values, and personalty, and further your life's purpose, you'll find mounds of career treasure. In addition to feeling satisfied with your career, you will be maximally creative, productive, and committed to your work. Voila, every employer's dream come true!

In essence, you and the potential employer have an opportunity in the interview to explore whether you and the job match; whether you both will discover treasure. Of course, unless the interviewer has read this book, he or she has never heard of the term "career treasure." Not only that, but the interviewer will focus much more on the company's needs than on yours. Regardless, the equation is still true. When you accurately and effectively share information that represents your vocational identity, you will sell yourself to the *right* buyer. You both win!

A number of career books provide job interview tips, with several giving you answers to difficult interview questions. I've done this, too. You'll soon see that I give you a lot of tips throughout the rest of the chapter and Appendix D contains answers to many difficult interview questions. I think you will find the tips and answers to tough interview questions helpful. However, I believe the best interview preparation is much more fundamental.

The job interview challenges you to articulate sharply the kind of person you are, to identify your work-related strengths, and to demonstrate how you will make valuable contributions in the future. My most fundamental (and I believe valuable) interview advice is this: You should commit the VIS and all of Exercise 7's OAR statements to memory. I don't mean you that you need to memorize every element verbatim. However, you should know the information well enough to verbalize the essence of

all of the elements. You'll find that effectively communicating the information from the VIS and *especially* the OAR statements will sell you very well to interviewers. At the same time, you will feel confident about responding to tough interview questions with information and examples from the real you, instead of memorizing someone else's answers from a book.

The two types of interviews

As you launch your job search, it is important for you to be aware of the two types of interviews you may encounter. This awareness will help you determine how far along you are in the employer's hiring process, and protect you from surprises. From the company's perspective, an interview's purpose is either to reduce the size of the applicant pool (screening interview) or to make a hiring decision (the job interview).

THE SCREENING INTERVIEW

The human resource (a.k.a. personnel) department or perhaps a search firm conducts this sort of interview to help reduce the total number of potential candidates to a manageable number. The company brings back for a second interview those candidates who survive the screen. Usually the managers making the final hiring decisions do not become involved in the interview process until this second interview. The screening interview is sometimes conducted by phone and typically does not last very long.

Your goal in a screening interview is to demonstrate that your skills and abilities deserve further review by those who will make the hiring decision. Remember: the person conducting the screening interview may not make the final decision about hiring you, but he or she can certainly decide that you will not go farther in the hiring process.

Is that the phone I hear?

More and more often, employers conduct screening interviews by telephone. The telephone dramatically reduces the costs associated with interviewing and allows the organization to screen several candidates very quickly. From an employer's perspective, this is good news. From your perspective, it can be a little harrowing. Here is a story to illustrate this point.

Imagine going on a brisk walk on a hot but lovely summer day. The birds are singing, the sun is shinning, and fortunately the fresh air is clearing your head. Four hours on the Internet did nothing for your job prospects, but it did deliver a dull headache. However, the idea to get a little exercise was clearly a good one. Returning home, you're a changed person; a little sweaty, but ready to take on the job-hunting world again. A quick shower, and then it's back to setting up advice meetings.

Your singing is interrupted by the ring of the telephone. It must be your brother returning your call from earlier this morning. You turn off the shower, quickly wrap a towel around yourself, and race to pick up the phone. The caller's greeting makes it clear that this is not your brother. "Hello, I'm Barbara Hill from the Acme company. We've been reviewing the résumé you sent us, and I'd like to ask you a few questions." Just as she finishes her opening lines, you hear the door to the garage open. "Honey, I'm home. Don't be alarmed, we're not being invaded. Susie is sick, so we decided

to move the Girl Scout meeting over here—honey—HONEY, ARE YOU HERE?"

The point of this little story is pretty obvious: you absolutely cannot predict when an employer may call to conduct a screening interview. You can do a number of things to prepare yourself to excel during a phone screening interview, which I'll tell you about in a minute. However, no amount of preparation can overcome the Girl Scout troop from the story above, or a crying baby, the neighbor's chain saw, or a host of other things outside of your direct control. Many times, the interviewer's only purpose is to establish an appointment for a phone interview. Other times, however, an interviewer will plunge ahead with interview questions. If you determine that the timing of an interview call will not allow you to perform well, reschedule it. Even if the interviewer shows understanding ("I have kids myself, don't worry about it."), if you cannot concentrate because of disruptions, find a better time. Virtually all interviewers will allow you to do this.

The phone interview kit

You should put together a phone interview kit. Just like a first aid kit, the materials in your phone interview kit will help you respond appropriately at the time of need. Because you can't see the interviewer's body language or facial expressions, phone interviews make interpreting the interviewer's response to your answers difficult. This is certainly a disadvantage as compared to face-to-face meetings. Also, because the phone interviewer is often taking notes, you may experience some awkward moments of silence. Be patient. Realize that along with the disadvantages, phone interviews provide a distinct advantage as well: cheat sheets. Can you imagine a teacher giving an important exam and letting you have all the materials needed to answer the questions right in front of you? That's what it's like with the phone interview kit. The kit contains the following materials:

- Your finalized résumé
- Your Vocational Identity Summary
- A list of your accomplishment statements (OAR)
- A notepad
- A pen
- Access to the company profiles prepared during research
- A phone interview form (Appendix A)

After pulling these materials together, keep them by the telephone at all times. Choose a phone located in the quietest room that will allow you to sit comfortably and take notes. Each time the telephone rings, be sure to answer this phone. That way you won't need to ask the caller to wait while you move to another room. If you have children, you may find that having family discussions and building in boundaries at the beginning of your job search will prepare everyone for the day the first screening call occurs.

After the caller identifies himself or herself, make sure to ask for the correct spelling of the caller's name. Write the name on the Phone Interview Form. Refer to the caller as Mr. or Ms., and use his or her last name several times during the conversation. One of the primary things the interviewer wishes to learn from the interview is your level of motivation. Interviewers want to know if you have that *can-do* attitude. To demonstrate *can do*, sound enthusiastic and upbeat, and act excited about this

interview opportunity. As simple as it sounds, smiling while talking on the phone greatly increases your appeal. Try it. Begin practicing it on your next phone call. You may look a little goofy, but you'll sound fantastic.

Toward the end of the interview, most interviewers will ask if you have any questions. Of course, you should certainly ask any questions that came to mind during the interview. In addition, consider asking the three questions shown on the Phone Interview Form:

- How would you describe this position's ideal candidate?
- Where would I be able to make the most immediate and valuable contributions?
- What are the department's/organization's biggest current challenges?

When you ask these three questions you accomplish two things. First, you show that you're a thoughtful candidate with a *can-do* attitude who cares about the organization's needs. Second, you learn information invaluable for any future job interviews with a decision maker. In essence, these questions ask the interviewer to explain the organization's most pressing needs. Now, in all future interactions with the company, you can respond directly to the organization's need to fill this position, and explain clearly the benefits of hiring you.

As with all parts of the job search process, confidence is key. The company already has some interest in you based upon your résumé. The screening interviewer's primary tasks are to determine if you behave in a professional manner; seem bright, energetic, and positive; appear to be a good fit with the company's culture; and if your résumé is an accurate representation of your skills and abilities. Listen carefully to the interviewer's questions, rephrase and repeat back to the interviewer any question if you're unsure of its intent, and then provide direct and succinct answers.

As the interview comes to its conclusion, you will have an opportunity to leave a strong last impression. Typically, the interviewer will say something like, "Well, are there any other questions?" or "Is there anything else I can tell you?" You need to let the interviewer know that you're interested in the position and a motivated person. You can convey your interest by saying something such as "No, this is a quite an interesting sounding position, and I'd very much welcome an opportunity to meet face-to-face to learn more about how I can make a contribution to (say the organization's name)." Even if you passed the screen, the caller may or may not invite you for a job interview at this time, but you'll end on a good note either way.

Finally, ask if you can contact the interviewer in the event that you have additional questions. They will almost always say yes. Ask for the interviewer's direct phone number and record this on the Phone Interview Form. This way you can bypass switchboards and most phone screens. Be careful not to abuse this privilege. A call, maybe two, is a good way to stay in touch and to show your continued interest. However, too many calls and you move from "can do" to "no can do." I've known of job candidates who moved from the strongly considered category to the rejection pile simply because they became a nuisance.

THE JOB INTERVIEW

If you are going to work for someone else, this is the gateway through which you must pass to collect career treasure. But what are you likely to encounter? It's very hard to say because job interviews can vary widely in style, content, sophistication, and length. Interviews may be highly structured, with the interviewer asking specific questions of each candidate, to highly unstructured, where you and the interviewer seem to just chat. Some organizations, particularly for higher-level jobs, use a series of interviews conducted by a number of people throughout the day. Additionally, depending upon the company and the position, the organization may use the first job interview as an additional screen of candidates, and may ask you to return for yet another series of interviews. In short, no one can predict with any kind of certainty the exact conditions of your next job interview. However, you can easily learn enough about the most likely scenarios and prepare broadly enough for various kinds of questions and interviewers that you can enter the job interview event with a great deal of confidence. The remainder of this chapter covers four topics to prepare you to give a confident performance.

- Four common interview styles
- The preparation necessary to excel during the job interview
- Tips for performing well during the job interview
- Tough interview questions

FOUR COMMON STYLES OF JOB INTERVIEWS

During a job interview, the interviewer has only two primary tasks: to gather information about you and to evaluate that information and decide whether or not to offer you a position. However, you may encounter a variety of *styles* of job interviews for three reasons. First, different situations call for different interviewing techniques. Second, different interviewers possess different levels of interviewing knowledge and expertise. Third, even among those most knowledgeable, much disagreement exists regarding the best way to conduct an interview. The four styles of interviews and combinations of the four styles presented here do not exhaust all the possible ways companies conduct interviews, but they cover about 95 percent of the cases.

Situational interviews

In a situational interview, the interviewer will present a hypothetical situation to the job candidate. The interviewer describes a hypothetical situation that calls for some sort of decision and action. The interviewer then asks how the candidate would respond to the situation. First and foremost, do not respond to the question too quickly. Take a few moments to consider carefully the situation. Ask yourself if you have ever encountered a similar situation during your work history. Perhaps one of your accomplishments addresses a very similar situation. As I will emphasize later in the chapter, your accomplishment statements are a great way to respond to interview questions clearly, succinctly, and with specifics. Believe me, you will

impress the interviewer. After reflecting for a moment, answer the question as directly as possible.

Behavioral interviews

As stated earlier in the book, psychologists know that the best predictor of future behavior is past behavior. This fact drives the use of the behavioral interview technique. During the questioning, the interviewer will ask you about real situations you faced in the past and about how you responded to these situations. The basic assumption: If your past actions were effective and added benefit to your employer, your future actions are likely to do the same. Once again, your accomplishment statements will prove invaluable.

Panel (team or group) interview

As the name suggests, several people will attend this interview, all of whom may ask questions. They may present hypothetical situations, ask about real situations faced in the past, or ask other questions about a candidate's background or future expectations. If you encounter this style of interview, be sure to address your answers to all members of the panel and do not become too focused on the most dominant personality. Remember that all members of the panel will have input in evaluating your interview performance. Sometimes the quietest member carries the most weight in terms of your evaluation.

Stress interview

Once popular, companies use the stress interview much less often today. By changing directions and asking rapid-fire, difficult questions, in a somewhat confrontational style, the interviewer attempts to "stress" the candidate and determine how the candidate performs in such a situation. Frankly, I believe the stress interview is a bad idea and that organizations should not use it. Unfortunately, a few still do. If you encounter this sort of interview, do not take it personally, remain calm, and reflect a few moments before you respond. Remember to smile, and respond to the content of the questions, rather than to the interviewer's theatrics.

Regardless of the kind of job interview you encounter, come prepared to share your accomplishment statements (OAR) at appropriate times and keep the features vs. benefits distinction in mind. Before you attend any interview, be sure to complete the pre-interview checklist shown on page 183.

PREPARE TO EXCEL

Most people do *not* do adequate prework prior to the interview; if you do, you will gain competitive advantage over the vast majority of job applicants. Three areas of interview prework deserve your attention:

- Yourself
- The company
- Practice

Prework about yourself: Self-Assessment

If you worked through the self-assessments and wrote your career objective in Part I, and prepared your 30-second verbal ad in Chapter 7, you have completed almost all of this part of the interview homework. If you haven't filled out the exercises in Part I or the verbal advertisement in Chapter 7, I strongly suggest that you

do so now. These exercises will lay a foundation for outstanding performance during the job interview.

Understanding your vocational identity, creating your career objective, and preparing your list of accomplishments all prepare you for three aspects of peak interview performance. First, you will be able to present yourself as a person who clearly understands him or herself. Thoroughly knowing the product is key to all successful marketing. Second, selling yourself will be much easier when you can draw upon your work accomplishments to demonstrate your future benefits and value to the company. The OAR statements from Exercise 7 do this magnificently. Third, and most important, in the event the company extends a job offer, you will be able to evaluate how well the offer matches your vocational identity and career objective.

After completing the exercises, committing the results to memory is the only remaining prework about yourself. You should be able to state quickly your three greatest strengths, your career objective, and your top ten marketable job skills, and draw upon all of your accomplishment statements (from Exercise 7) from memory. I say more about the best way to communicate your weaknesses when I discuss tough interview questions in Appendix D. Also, the day before the interview, review your résumé and be prepared to support your career objective and summary statement with examples from your accomplishment list.

Prework about the company: Research

By creating the company profiles in Chapter 8 and adding to this knowledge as you conducted advice and informational meetings, you did a great deal of this portion of the interview prework. Your knowledge about the interviewing company and its industry will serve you well during the interview. However, if you schedule an interview with a company for which you do not have a research summary, you will need to do as much homework as time allows. Here are several additional ideas for quickly gaining company knowledge, or supplementing your earlier research:

- Obtain an annual report and any company or product brochures and read them in some detail prior to the interview.

- Locate a knowledgeable customer who does business with the company. Briefly interview the customer and find out why the customer does business with this company rather than the competition. Also ask what the customer likes best and least about this organization.

- Through your network or a search firm or by asking questions directly of the company attempt to locate and then contact former incumbents who held the job for which you are interviewing. If you cannot locate someone who held the identical job, locate someone who worked in the same department or division. Prepare a list of questions to ask these former incumbents and listen carefully to their responses. Although people seldom "burn their bridges," often what they don't say, or how they say it, is the most valuable information you will receive prior to the interview.

- Through your network, find out as much as you can about the interviewer.

- Important: Prepare a list of questions to ask the company. *Be sure to ask questions that will help you understand the fit between your financial needs, your vocational identity, your career objective, and this job and organization.* As a starting point, here are several examples:
  — Why is this position open?
  — How much overnight travel is involved?
  — To whom will I report?
  — What is the career path?
  — May I meet those with whom I would be working?
  — How do the responsibilities of this position fit into the company's overall strategy?
  — What are the biggest challenges facing this organization over the next three years?
  — How could I best make an immediate contribution?
  — How is employee performance measured?
  — What are the biggest pluses of working for this organization? Are there any minuses?
  — What is the company's employee turnover record?
  — How does this company compare to the competition?

Here's one last bit of advice: find out *exactly* where the interview will occur. You might be surprised to learn that people sometimes get lost on the way to the interview. They think they know where they're going, but somehow that building they confidently anticipated seeing at the corner of Smith and Jones Streets is not there; or they arrive 10 minutes early at the wrong office. Either way, they show up a few minutes late, flustered, and searching for enough confidence to introduce themselves. Occasionally, they completely miss their interview and call to reschedule. Needless to say, these folks seldom receive job offers. Please get exact directions to the interview location. If you are even slightly unsure of the location, drive to it a day or two before the interview date, or leave with an enormous amount of extra time to make up for any difficulties you might encounter.

Prework about the interview event: Practice

Although both career exploration interviews and networking advice meetings provided you with an excellent practice ground for your communication and interviewing skills, the job interview warrants special attention for two reasons. First, decision makers conduct job interviews—the folks that determine whether or not you'll work there—the folks that with a nod of their head can put money in your checking account. Obviously, job interviews are the main event. This is where your performance *really* counts. Second, because you know that the job interview represents the main event, you may put more pressure on yourself, thereby altering your performance. A little stress is good; it improves every kind of human performance. Too much stress—well, it's not good; it has a negative effect on every kind of performance.

Whether it's opening night on Broadway, the World Series, or a job interview, *practice* is the best way to minimize undue stress and to prepare to perform at your peak during a big event. Try this. First, thoroughly review your career objective, résumé, Vocational Identity Summary, accomplishment statements, and the twenty difficult questions from Appendix D. Next, find an interview practice partner, such as a friend or spouse. Give that partner a copy of

your résumé and a copy of the interview questions from Appendix D. Ask your partner to use these materials to prepare a *tough* 20- to 30-minute job interview. Give the interview partner at least a day to prepare for the interview. Then have the partner take on the part of a decision maker and role-play a job interview. You should not see the questions prior to the practice interview. Figure 31 at the end of the chapter summarizes the steps you should take to prepare for the interview.

Your responses should be crisp and succinct. This is *very* important. Many a person has blown an interview with lengthy, wandering answers. Throughout your practice and during the actual interview, *remember that your answers should take no more than about 30 seconds to 2 minutes maximum*. Have your interview partner keep track of the amount of time you use in responding to questions. You'll find that using a video or audio recorder provides a good way for you to evaluate your own performance. You and your partner can use the evaluation questions from the Post Interview Report form, shown later in this chapter, to critique your interview performance. For additional practice, you can do this multiple times with the same partner, or ask additional partners to assist.

PERFORMING WELL DURING THE INTERVIEW

In 1990 I worked as an internal consultant for one of the Fortune 500's top twenty firms in the upper Midwest. My department was enjoying a good deal of success, and senior management determined that we needed to increase the size of our staff to meet customer demands. We ran an advertisement in a trade journal and received about seventy-five résumés. Several of us read the résumés, rank ordered them, debated those rankings, and selected five people to interview by phone. After conducting phone interviews, we selected our top three candidates. We then invited the three candidates to come to our office for face-to-face interviews.

We set up the interviews and staggered the candidates' travel schedules over about a two-week period. I was to meet the first candidate at his hotel for breakfast. After eating, I planned to bring him into the office for a round of interviews with my staff, several of my peers, and some senior functional executives. When I arrived at his hotel about 7 a.m., the candidate greeted me with a firm handshake, a smile, and a very serious pair of nearly knee-high industrial-strength galoshes. Now, I don't remember the exact date, but I recall very distinctly that the weather on that fall morning was sunny and about 65 degrees. The forecast called for more of the same for the rest of the week.

The candidate and I (and the galoshes) sat down for breakfast. I mentioned, as politely as possible, how nice the weather was. The candidate agreed, ordered eggs, and continued to smile. In the car on the way to my office, I again commented about the weather and told the candidate that he could leave the galoshes in my office during the interviews if he would like. Looking surprised, he said, "No, thank you, I really like to be prepared for things, just in case." Believe it or not, the day got quite a bit stranger from there.

Image may not be everything, but it is a lot! You should arrive 10 to 15 minutes before your scheduled interview time, greet your inter-

viewer with a firm handshake, and smile. Do not smoke at any point in the interview, even if invited to do so. Chewing gum is also not a good idea, but you should take along some breath mints or spray. Throughout the meeting, use a lot of direct eye contact.

GENERAL GROOMING

Of course, your manner of dress is also quite important. In most cases, you should dress conservatively for the job interview. However, each company, industry, and geographic region has its own "style." You need to understand the specific expectations of any company where you will interview. I know of a computer programmer who recently received a job offer for $65,000 with a comprehensive relocation package. He wore a black Harley-Davidson T-shirt and blue jeans to the interview. This company's culture would consider a conservative business suit pretentious and out of fashion. Again, your research can yield information about the company's expectations in this regard.

Regardless of a company's style, personal hygiene is, of course, always very important. Shower, shave, brush your hair, brush your teeth, put on deodorant, trim and clean your fingernails—enough said. Again, the overarching rule is to dress according to the interviewing organization's standards. One common approach is to dress like the person to whom you would report. Ask someone knowledgeable about business dress to give you honest, candid feedback about your appearance and choices for interview attire. It's a good idea to wear a watch to all interviews because this shows that you are sensitive to time—an extremely valuable commodity to your potential employer.

Here's one last bit of image advice. Upon your arrival at the interview location, before the interview begins, go to the rest room and check your appearance in the mirror. An upturned collar, unbuttoned shirt, or a small piece of broccoli boldly displayed in your charming smile will undermine all of your *dress-to-impress efforts*.

If conservative dress is appropriate—for men

If the interviewing organization's expectations are for conservative dress, wear either a navy blue or a light- to dark-gray two-piece business suit (not a European or designer cut). Either a solid or narrow pinstriped suit is fine. With most business attire, natural fiber looks much better than synthetics. A 100 percent cotton long-sleeved white or light-blue dress shirt with medium to heavy starch presents a good business image. Your tie should be made of silk and have a conservative pattern (don't wear funny things on your tie: no Tabasco sauce bottles, no Warner Brothers or Disney characters, or anything from the great outdoors). Because the appropriate width of men's ties changes fairly often, I suggest that you take a trip to the local mall and look at what is currently most acceptable. Don't even think about wearing a bow tie to an interview—hey, it cost Senator Paul Simon a shot at the Presidency. Black or cordovan-colored tie or tassel leather dress shoes look best with a navy or a gray suit. Your belt should match the shoes. Wear navy or black socks that you know will stay up. Also, make sure the socks are long enough so that when you cross your legs your skin doesn't show.

If conservative dress is appropriate—for women

As with men's recommended conservative interview attire, women should wear a business suit. A basic suit in a dark color such as navy, blue, gray, or black is a safe choice. Whether you choose a solid color or a classic business plaid, the suit should be a high-quality wool blend (which will look great and wrinkle less than 100 percent wool). The skirt length should be a little below the knee and never shorter than just above the knee. The blouse should be long sleeved and either 100 percent cotton or silk. Women have a greater range of color options in blouses than do men in shirts. White, pale blue, gray, and light pink are all acceptable. As with men though, I believe the safest choice is white. A tasteful silk scarf that complements your business suit and blouse can add drama to your outfit without any danger of detracting from the professional image. Select a neutral color of pantyhose in a skin tone. Black, navy, brown, and burgundy shoes are all acceptable. Do not wear high heels. Leather closed-toe pumps are a safe choice in terms of style. An open toe with a closed heel is a second choice. Your belt color should match the shoes. With accessories and jewelry, less is more. A wedding ring (if applicable) and a simple bracelet are enough. Take either a purse or a briefcase (but not both) to the interview. Black, brown, and burgundy leather cases all look very professional. Wear as little makeup to the interview as you can—just enough to feel comfortable.

Confidence, the cornerstone of performance

Throughout this book I've mentioned the importance of confidence. Believe me, the interview is the most important time during job hunting to demonstrate your belief in yourself. Review and practice the *Ten Ideas for Developing and Maintaining a Winning Attitude* from Chapter 1. During the interview, speak loudly and clearly when responding to interviewers' questions. Pausing a moment and smiling when asked a question gives you a few seconds to gather your thoughts and causes you to appear confident. Listen intently to the interviewer's questions. Nod your head as he or she is speaking and rephrase and restate any question that is unclear. For example, an interviewer might ask, "What aspects of your last job did you find most disheartening?" If you're not quite sure what she is really asking, you could say, "To make sure I understand your question, are you asking what parts of my last position were demotivating?" If you have the right meaning, the interview will say something like, "Yes, that's it." More often than not, however, the interviewer will slightly modify your rephrased question, giving you a little more insight into what he or she is really after. Having the wherewithal to clarify meaning shows confidence, is wise, and will be appreciated.

That "can-do" attitude

As in the screening interview, you should appear energetic and enthusiastic in order to demonstrate a "can-do" attitude. Always be positive in your attitude and don't speak badly about others. This may be particularly challenging if you had a very difficult employment situation in the past. The more recent this experience, the more difficult it will be to remain positive in your interview responses. The interviewer will probably ask you what it was like to work there, however. I don't care how bad, how ridiculous,

or how unfair the situation was, if you complain during the interview you reduce the likelihood that the company will offer you a job. Fair or unfair, you raise questions when you respond negatively: "Was the situation as he or she describes it, or was it really this person's fault? I wonder if this person has problems getting along with others and understanding how to fit inside an organization's rules and boundaries?"

Morgan McCall, a leadership researcher at the University of Southern California, has shown that most managers have worked for a bad boss at some point in their careers. What separates successful managers from those less successful is how they deal with the difficult experience. Successful managers are able to extract positive learning experiences from their bad bosses, while less successful managers are not.

I'm not suggesting that you mislead anyone, but regardless of how bad it was, you can put a positive spin on the experience if you extract the lessons the experience provided. Think back to the situation and discover what you learned about yourself; maybe how *not* to do something, or how the experience added to your technical skills. When the interviewer asks you about an unpleasant employment situation, point out the positive elements. Perhaps you can say something like, "While we had some philosophical differences, I had an opportunity to grow significantly in my accounting skills," or "Although it was personally challenging at times, I am grateful for the many things I learned. I'm now very focused with my career objective." If you still find it impossible to put a positive spin on a bad work experience, try saying as little as possible about it.

Ah, yes, the salary issue

If at all possible, you should not discuss salary until the interviewer makes you an offer. Your strongest negotiating position occurs after the company decides it wants you and extends an offer, but you have not yet accepted. If an interviewer asks you about your salary requirements during the interview, you can say that you are sure that the company will pay you fairly. You could then ask, "What is the salary range attached to this position?" The most important point is this: you should never be the first to mention a salary figure. Chapter 12 deals exclusively with how to negotiate your best deal.

Determining how close you are to receiving an offer

During the first part of the interview, the interviewer will ask you about your past. In essence, the interviewer is looking for past behaviors that will predict your success in the future. At this point in the interview, you are the salesperson. However, once the interviewer begins to strongly consider you for the position, two things will change. First, rather than focusing on the past, the interviewer will become more future oriented. The interviewer will begin to discuss how your skills and experience might impact the organization in the future. With the second change, the sales role shifts from you to the interviewer. Listen carefully; when you hear the interviewer beginning to discuss the future and describe the benefits of belonging to the organization, you are almost certainly being strongly considered for the job. However, after the company decides that you are the right person for the job, considerable role reversal takes place. The interviewer begins to sell you the company.

Thank you very much; we'll call you

At the conclusion of the interview, the interviewer may offer you a job. Usually, however, it doesn't work this way. Instead, the company wants to look at all of the candidates and then choose the one to hire. If the interviewer does not offer you a job, the end of the interview still presents you with several opportunities. First, you can do what salespeople call "asking for the order." When the interviewer asks you if you have any last questions, you can say, "Yes, will you offer me this job?" or "When may I start?" (Again, you do not need to use my words. Come up with your own way to ask the interviewer if he or she is prepared to make a job offer.) The interviewer will respond in one of

	FIGURE 31
√	**Pre-Interview Checklist**
	Company research complete
	Résumé completed and three quality copies ready
	Thoroughly reviewed Vocational Identity Summary
	Memorized all my accomplishment statements
	Practiced tough interview questions
	Practiced 30-second verbal ad (Chapter 10)
	Practiced stating career objective
	Prepared questions to ask the interviewer
	Portfolio ready with materials: breath mints, pen, notepad, three quality copies of résumé, and interview evaluation form
	Clothes picked up from the dry cleaners
	Exact company and interview location is known

three ways. First, this question will cause the interviewer to make a job offer (this does happen a surprising number of times). Second, the interviewer will not offer the position, but will give you valuable information about the rest of the hiring process. Third, the interviewer will let you know that the company will not be offering you the position.

If you get the first response—a job offer— let me be the first to say congratulations! If you receive the more likely second response, listen carefully. You can ask for further clarification about what to expect and timing issues. If the interviewer gives you dates, you can ask "May I get back in touch with you after (the date)?"

If you receive the third response and learn for certain you are no longer a candidate for this position, all is not lost. You can ask if the company has any other positions that fit your skills and background. If not, ask the interviewer to provide honest and candid feedback about your résumé and interview performance. Let the interviewer know that not only would you welcome feedback, but also that you would truly value his or her insights. Also, as in the advice meetings, ask the interviewer for referrals. Ask, "Who else should I contact?" and "What other companies are likely to show an interest in me?" Because the interviewer is familiar with your background and the job market, any referral you receive is likely to be a good one.

> "Keep the faculty of effort alive in you by a little gratuitous exercise every day. That is, be systematically ascetic or heroic in little unnecessary points, do every day or two something for no other reason than that you would rather not do it, so that when the hour of dire need draws nigh, it may find you not unnerved and untrained to stand the test."
>
> William James

After each interview, you should evaluate your performance. What did you do well? What could you improve on next time? The Post-Interview Report Form provided in Appendix A will assist you in this evaluation.

Answering those tough interview questions

In the end, employers only want the answer to one question: "How will this organization benefit by hiring you?" I call this the fundamental interview question. Every aspect of an organization's selection process aims at solving this fundamental question. To answer this one question, interviewers certainly take many different approaches. Although this is what they *really, really* want to know, interviewers almost certainly will not ask you this question. Instead, they'll inquire about many other issues. Some of the issues make a lot of sense, some clearly don't. The interviewer will listen, probably take notes, meet with others involved in the hiring process, discuss what you said and how you acted, and then answer the fundamental interview question himself.

To understand better how and what interviewers try to accomplish through their questioning, I reviewed several hundred difficult interview questions. I discovered that although there are a lot of different "tough interview questions," I could sort virtually all of them into the following nine categories:

- The most difficult question of all: So, please tell me a little about yourself.
- How well do you get along with others?
- Your work history and your current situation
- Why should we hire you?
- Why do you want to work here?
- Illegal questions
- Welcome to the hot seat
- Do your personality and work style fit our needs?
- Let's talk about money

I selected twenty of the most common and most difficult questions to include in this book. You'll find these twenty questions in Appendix D organized under the nine categories just mentioned. Following each question, you'll see three sections to help you prepare to answer the tough questions: *What the interviewer wants to know, Your basic strategy* for responding, and *Possible words to use.*

LAST AND CERTAINLY NOT LEAST— FOLLOW UP

The *next* day following the interview, send a brief thank-you letter and include any particularly strong points that you discovered as you completed the Interview Report Form. You will find a sample thank-you letter in Appendix C. Although the interviewer or others in the organization may tell you to telephone to follow up on the status of the position, be cautious. If you call too frequently you may appear overly anxious and unsure of your value. Once again, remember the important role that confidence plays in the process.

PART

3

CONDUCTING YOUR JOB SEARCH

C H A P T E R

11

Launch Your Job Search Campaign

··

Climb high
Climb far
Your goal the sky
Your aim the star.
Inscription on Hopkins Memorial Steps,
Williams College, Williamstown, Massachusetts

READY, SET—GO!

Congratulations, you've just been hired as the CEO of *Your Job Search, Inc.* This is obviously a very important position for you and for the companies in real need of your unique skills, abilities, and vocational personality. As CEO, you created the marketing plan and have the decision-making authority to determine the amount of time and effort to expend on job searching. You are also responsible for establishing the criteria for evaluating job offers: acceptance or rejection of an offer is totally up to you. In addition to these important strategic responsibilities, as CEO of *Your Job Search, Inc.,* you must also manage the job-hunting cam-

paign on a day-to-day basis. Building a solid job searching plan was crucial, but your ultimate success (finding that best job) depends on effective *execution* of the plan.

Before your shoe leather hits the job-hunting pavement, I need to let you know that there's some good news and some bad news. If you use all of the strategies contained in this book to manage your job search campaign, here are some truths you'll likely encounter:

- You'll find that some people really don't care about your need to find a new job.
- A lot of people will not return your phone calls.
- Many people will find very creative ways *not* to Do What They Say They Will Do.

- Many companies won't even reply to your letters and résumés.
- Some people will be more cooperative and helpful than you can imagine, or even understand.
- You will come in second for a job you really wanted.
- And in the end, *you'll find a very good job.*

With careful planning, shrewd decision making, and attention to administrative detail, you can bring your marketing plan to life. Remember, you have a plan, and it makes a lot of sense. Stay focused on the last bullet—it *will* happen. I can't tell you if it's tomorrow, next month, or a year from now, but it will happen.

Two important factors serve as hallmarks of an effectively managed job search campaign. Making good choices about how you spend your time is the first factor. The second factor is carefully keeping track of all of your job-hunting activities. This chapter provides the basic ingredients for efficient time management, so that you have a good handle on the first factor. I'll also give you a number of proven ideas for keeping track of your activities, so you can manage the second.

In addition to managing time and keeping track of activities, this chapter tells you how to look for work while still employed, get a fast start in the new job, and stay ready for job searching throughout your career.

THE NEED FOR TIME MANAGEMENT

Whether you're employed or unemployed, married or single, or have seven children or none, we all have more time-taking opportunities than we have time available. The dilemma resides in the impossible justification of two competing realities: infinite possibilities and our finite resources.

I have heard it said lately that the currency of the late 90s is *time.* To help us save time, book writers, seminar gurus, new high-tech products, and infomercial pitch men seem to be coming out of the woodwork. To assuage modern society's often-heard cry, "If I only had more time," these various sources respond with a soothing promise: More time. Soothing, yes, but *more time* is a promise that no one can deliver.

Time is the great equalizer. Every one of us gets the exact same portion of that precious commodity called time: a 24-hour allotment each day. While each day gives us tens of thousands of hours of possible activities to purchase, our time budget always remains fixed at 24 hours. We receive 24 hours and we expend 24 hours. We cannot increase it or save it. Managing time effectively is really about making good choices among your various desires and demands. It's about choosing wisely what you will do, and more important, what you will not do.

You've already faced a couple of time decisions related to job searching when you built your marketing plan. I gave you a common job-hunting rule of thumb earlier: It takes about one month of searching for every $10,000 of salary you're expecting. In developing your marketing plan, you decided how much total time you will invest in job searching each week. You also determined the type of job-finding activities you'll engage in with that time investment.

When you launch your job search campaign, you quickly move from the conceptual to the practical. It's one thing to plan to spend 30 hours a week networking and quite another to do it. Each day the *urgent* attempts to push out the *important*. As I said, no matter who you are or what you do, you cannot get more time. However, you can certainly manage your decisions about how to spend time in ways that reflect your priorities and lead to your desired outcomes.

A process for making time choices

At the heart of all good time-management strategies, you'll find a system for prioritizing and organizing daily tasks. Essentially, an effective time-management system allows you to keep track of all important tasks and contacts with others, and determine which activities you'll attend to and in what order. The best time-management systems also consider the larger issue of purpose, or life's mission, when prioritizing tasks. At times, it is only by considering your purpose that you can make good decisions among the multitude of competing time demands. I'll present some basic ideas for managing time under these five points:

- Get a calendar—get rid of the legal pad
- The early morning *daily* planning meeting
- Managing tasks throughout the day
- The end-of-the-day evaluation
- The Sunday evening *weekly* planning session

Get a calendar—get rid of the legal pad

I've seen a lot of homegrown time-management systems. Many of these systems work fairly well until they're stretched. In other words, a lot of systems can keep up with low demands, but

may fall apart when the number of tasks, contacts, and so forth become too great. Three-by-five note cards, tiny spiral notebooks, legal pads, and the like are examples of common homegrown time-management tools. As CEO of *Your Job Search, Inc.,* your time demands may be greater than for any other job you've ever held. Even if this is not true in terms of work quantity, it is certainly true in terms of personal importance. Fail to execute your strategic marketing plan effectively or to do what you say you'll do (DWYSYD), and you will look for work longer than you would otherwise.

Unless you already use a calendar-based time-and-task management system, please get rid of whatever you're currently using for at least the duration of the job search. Go to the store and purchase a calendar. I don't think it's particularly important what brand you buy, but look for these things. The calendar should be in a book form. It can range from pocket size to notebook size, but select one that has two pages per day and allows room to write daily tasks and appointments on one page and to take notes on the other. Also, the calendar should have a place for you to carry a mechanical pencil. You can buy this sort of calendar at any office supply store, Franklin-Covey retail outlets, or in many catalogs.

Here are two of the most important principles for effectively managing time: Write daily tasks and record phone calls only in your calendar, and always have your calendar with you. You should not decide whether to write something on a notepad, a 3 x 5 card, one of those little stickies, or in your calendar. Always write important information in the calender—*Always!* And you should not look around the table during a lunch appointment searching for a matchbook to record important information. It looks unprofessional and you'll lose the matchbook. Have your calendar with you—always!

When you telephone someone, or when someone calls you, record information about the call on the calendar's note page for that day. To make sure that I have plenty of room for the day's activities, I personally use a large 8" by 11" calendar. Most people find smaller calendars more convenient because they're easier to carry with you. Regardless of the size calendar you choose, record the time of the call, the caller's name and job title, the phone number, and any particularly important points discussed in the call.

Example

Date: November 30, 199X

Note Page

10:45a.m. Bill Smith—Acme, Inc.—Human Resource Manager
555-555-1234

I called Mr. Smith. He was in a meeting and his secretary (Susan) said he would call me back before the end of the day.

You can image how useful this information will be next week when you need to call Mr. Smith again, or when he calls you.

In addition to tracking phone messages, the calendar should serve as the primary tool you use to manage daily tasks. Record daily tasks as they occur to you, and prioritize them each day during your early morning planning meeting.

The early morning daily planning meeting

Before you make your first phone call, type your first letter, or go to your first meeting, *set aside about 10 minutes for planning.* Although you will spend only a few minutes organizing and prioritizing each day's activities, you will make some very important decisions. From a time-management perspective, these are the most important moments of the day.

Find a quiet place where you will not be interrupted. Lay your calendar on a table or desk, and take about 3 to 5 minutes and list all the activities you would like to accomplish today. Actually, these are not all new tasks because, as you will see, you are adding to several activities carried over from previous days. The list may be quite long. It may appear impossible. It may indeed be impossible. Your job during the early morning planning meeting is to make some decisions and some choices. You must decide which items on the day's task list are most important. This is a job that only the CEO of *Your Job Search, Inc.,* can do.

After listing the day's most important tasks, you need to prioritize these items. Spend another 5 to 8 minutes thinking about which items are most important. You'll take two cuts at this prioritization. During the first cut, you should determine your top priority items; those things that must be done today. The mathematician Pareto, among others, has shown that we achieve about 80 percent of our results with about 20 percent of our efforts. To find this critical 20 percent, divide the number of items on your list by five. These are your top priority (TP) items. For example, if you have twenty tasks for the day, you probably have about four TP items. After this calculation, place a TP next to your most vital tasks for the day.

After you identify your TP items, it's time for the second cut. In this second cut, number the tasks in order of their importance. Begin with the TP items and give the most important task a 1 rating, the next most important a 2, and so on until all of your day's tasks are ordered. You have now completed your early morning daily planning meeting, and it's time to put your plan into action.

Managing tasks throughout the day

Although it's not always possible, you should generally try to attack the most important tasks first. In other words, get the TPs done, then move on to the other tasks. At times, you can complete a nonTP task very quickly. Perhaps a phone call or an e-mail is all that is required. Even if you have remaining TP tasks, you may decide you'd like to get a lower-priority task out of the way quickly. However, remember that time spent on one task is time away from another.

As you complete a task, place a check mark next to it. If you decide not to complete a task, that is, to *drop it*, place a D next to it. If you choose to *move* a task to another day, put an M next to this task and a note as to where you move it.

Each time you address a task, you should place one of these three symbols next to it on

FIGURE 32
Time-Management Symbols

√	**I've completed this task**
D	I've decided I'm not going to do this task
M	I've moved this task to a new date (write that date next to the task)

the task list. When you encounter a new task during the day, either include it in the current day's task list or write it on another calendar day.

The end of the day evaluation

Okay, it's 5:30 p.m., time to stop the day's job-hunting activities—almost. Before you stop for the day, review the task list one more time. Make sure that at the end of the day, every item has either a √ for completed tasks, a D for those things you decided to drop, or an M for those tasks you moved forward to other dates. Additionally, list any items you wish to complete at a later time on future calendar pages. The following example shows a calendar with tasks and phone calls managed using these techniques.

Example
Calendar Using Time-Management Techniques

SATURDAY—OCTOBER 3, 199X

Status	Priority	Task		Appointments
			7:30	
			8:00	
√		Morning planning	8:30	
M (10/4)	TP 2	Complete résumé	9:00	Interview with Mark O. at Acme
M (10/5)	5	Mail 10 target letters	9:30	
√	TP 1	Call Susan E.	10:00	
√	6	Work out	10:30	
√	7	Met painter for estimate	11:00	
M (10/7)	4	Return Rick's mower	11:30	
√	TP 3	Check on airline tickets	12:00	Lunch with Susan E. — Networking
D	11	Call Jim W. for meeting	1:00	
√	10	Pick up dry cleaning	1:30	
√	8	Mail follow-up letters	2:00	Networking meeting with Al R.
D	9	Contact local colleges	2:30	
			3:00	
			3:30	Meet painter for estimate
			4:00	
			4:30	Work out at the Y
			5:00	
			5:30	
Expenses:			**Evening**	
				Kids' soccer game — Wilson field 6:00

Example
Calendar Using Time Management Techniques

SATURDAY—OCTOBER 3, 199X

Notes

10:00 Susan E., Vice President of Operations 555-1234

Susan was out, got her voice mail, asked that she please return my call at her convenience.

10:52 Susan E. — Returned my call and we agreed to meet on 11/14 at 9:45 a.m.

10:30 Milton D. — Responded to my cover letter and résumé!

We set up a phone interview for Friday. Seems very interested in my background and sounds as

if they need to make a decision as quickly as possible.

With just these few basic ideas, you can manage your time fairly well. However, it's still easy to lose track of some important strategic issues unless you hold a Sunday evening planning meeting.

The Sunday evening weekly planning session

This session will take you only about 15 minutes and will prove worthwhile for ensuring the strategic nature of the decisions you make during the upcoming week. You will need four items to begin the session: your calendar, the Vocational Identity Summary (VIS), your Strategic Marketing Plan, and the Weekly Planning Worksheet. First, from the VIS, read your Life's Mission Statement carefully and thoughtfully. Ask yourself, "Is this still me; is this what I really believe?" If not, modify the statement so that it more accurately represents your truest feelings. Second, briefly read through the rest of the VIS. Third, review the formal Strategic Marketing Plan you created in Chapter 9. Fourth, consult your calendar and review last week's activities. Now ask yourself these four questions:

- (After the first week) Did I do what I said I would do in last Sunday's strategic planning session? (DWYSYD)
- Did last week's activities move me toward my life's purpose?
- Did last week's job-hunting activities reflect my vocational identity?
- Were last week's job-hunting activities consistent with my Strategic Marketing Plan?

Example
Weekly Plan

Monday					
Research	**Networking**	**Answering Ads**	**Employment Agencies**	**Mailings**	**Internet**
Walt Disney	Bill Williams (1) Susan Evans (1) Rick Thomas (1) Melvin Harper (1) Rex Valenta (2)	Regents Specialties (3) Harper Wells Company (3) Piedmont, Inc. (3)		Williams Company (5)	Research

Tuesday					
Research	**Networking**	**Answering Ads**	**Employment Agencies**	**Mailings**	**Internet**
Home Depot Paradise Time Share	Cindy Jenkins (1) Mark Pierce (1) Sam Parsons (1) Brian Rice (2)		Contact the Sullivan Company (1)	Walt Disney (4)	1 hour searching job listings

Wednesday					
Research	**Networking**	**Answering Ads**	**Employment Agencies**	**Mailings**	**Internet**
	Kevin Meeks (2) Wanda Jackson (2) Will Stieger (1) Walt Stack (1) John Hawk (1)		Jason Howard (2)		1 hour reviewing job listings

Thursday					
Research	**Networking**	**Answering Ads**	**Employment Agencies**	**Mailings**	**Internet**
	Gerri Beeson (2) Joe Kalkman (1)			Northwest Airlines (4)	Post résumé with at least one service Research Northwest Airlines through Hoovers.com

Friday					
Research	**Networking**	**Answering Ads**	**Employment Agencies**	**Mailings**	**Internet**
Plantation High Tech Ceramics	Employment Agencies				

Saturday					
Research	**Networking**	**Answering Ads**	**Employment Agencies**	**Mailings**	**Internet**

Sunday					
Research	**Networking**	**Answering Ads**	**Employment Agencies**	**Mailings**	**Internet**
		Review the Sunday classifieds			4 hours searching job postings

Key:

1—Telephone call 2—Meeting 3—Ad response, letter, and résumé
4—Targeted letter and résumé 5—Follow-up mailing 6—Job interview

Other things to do or to keep in mind this week:

Review résumé distribution list to see if any additional follow-up is needed.

Fifth, based upon your answers to these three questions, ask one last question: "What will I do this week to improve my answers to these questions next Sunday evening?" Summarize your answer to this last question on the calendar's note page for the next Sunday. This week's answer becomes next week's first question.

Finally, develop your plans for this week by filling out the Weekly Planning Worksheet. You can see an example of a completed weekly plan on the previous pages. Appendix A provides a blank Weekly Planning Worksheet. As with all the forms in Appendix A, make as many copies as you need for your personal use.

Well, there you have it: the basics of time management. These ideas are all that you will need to manage time effectively during the job search. However, all time-management systems can fail without a commitment to follow through faithfully with all of the techniques. The number one time-management rule is to "use the system."

If you would like a more in-depth treatment of time management, Franklin-Covey provides the best seminar I know of. To find information regarding pricing and availability in your area, contact Franklin Covey at 800-767-1776, or online at http://www.FranklinCovey.com.

A warning: Time management and multiple job offers

I recently spoke to a senior executive (I'll call him Rick) in the midst of a job search. In his first few sentences, both the tone in his voice and his choice of words indicated that he was frustrated and struggling with his self-esteem. I asked him how long he had been looking for work. He replied that he was just entering his seventh month. He then told me that only within the last few weeks had he begun to look for work on a full-time basis. Of course I asked why it had taken so long for him to get serious about finding a job. He then described a common scenario that I want to warn you about.

Rick had lost his job when his company restructured the management staff. He immediately found a temporary consulting job. Almost as quickly, one of his former company's competitors made very strong hiring overtures to him. He began to walk through the hiring process; first a screening interview, then second- and third-round interviews. It didn't stop there. Over a two- to three-month period, the company interviewed Rick eleven times! Of course, Rick was sure that any company expending this much time and energy would soon extend a job offer. Additionally, he was in no immediate financial need because of the ongoing consulting work. I'm sure you've guessed the story's outcome by now. The company decided not to fill the position, the consulting work came to an end, it's been seven months since Rick lost his job, and he is just now getting down to the nitty-gritty of daily job hunting.

It's easy to count too heavily on one company. A lot of job hunting is not particularly fun. If your job prospects appear extremely bright with an organization, it's easy to get complacent and stop all the other hard work associated with job finding. The moral to Rick's story is this: You must *never, never, never* stop job hunting until after you accept a job offer. You must continue to execute your marketing plan full force, generate as many interviews as possible, and hopefully create multiple job offers. A job offer from one company often motivates another company to extend its own offer. Also, your self-esteem, and consequently your confidence, is dramatically higher when you have a number of interviews and offers working simultaneously.

KEEPING TRACK OF YOUR ACTIVITIES

Keeping track of your networking contacts, distributed résumés, and other job-hunting activities is, of course, very important to the campaign's success. Throughout the book, I've provided a number of forms for you to utilize in tracking your activities during the campaign. You will find clean copies of all the forms in Appendix A. Again, feel free to make as many copies of these forms as you would like for your personal use. Of course, please obey all copyright laws and don't give the forms to anyone else.

You could effectively manage and file these forms using many different schemes. Here is one suggested method for managing the paper-

FIGURE 33
A Suggested Filing System

Hanging File	Name on Manila Folder	Contents of Manila Folder
Administrative and Planning Tools	My Marketing Plan	Marketing Plan
	Networking Contact Sheets	Networking Contact Sheets
	Phone Interview Forms	Phone Interview Forms
	Post-Interview Report Forms	Post-Interview Report Forms
	Résumés	Copies of Résumés
	Résumé Distribution List	Résumé Distribution List
	Target Company List	Target Company List
	Used Weekly Planning Worksheets	Used Weekly Planning Worksheets
	Weekly Planning Worksheets	Weekly Planning Worksheets
Networking	List of Possible Networking Contacts	List of Possible Contacts
	Name of Contact	Networking Contact Sheet
Self-Assessment	My Values	Values Assessments and Purpose Statement
	My Marketable Job Skills	Skills Assessments
	My Vocational Personality	Personality Assessments
	Vocational Identity Summary	Vocational Identity Summary
Target Companies	Company Name (for each company)	Company Profile
		Correspondence
		Completed Post-Interview Forms
		Phone Interview Form

work. Go to your local office supply store and purchase a few hanging files and about 100 manila folders. Label four of the hanging files with the following titles from the first column of Figure 33:

- Administrative and Planning Tools
- Networking
- Self-Assessment
- Target Companies

Column 2 of the table provides the titles for the manila folders to place inside the hanging files. Column 3 describes the contents of the manila folders. This very simple filing system, coupled with the time-management process, should allow you to keep up with all of your job search activities. The Résumé Tracking Form is the only form I haven't introduced to you yet. You'll find an example of a completed Résumé Tracking Form below and a blank form in Appendix A. Always be sure to record the date when you distribute your résumé, to whom,

any comments, and your plans for follow-up. You should also note the follow-up plans on your calendar.

HOW TO LOOK FOR WORK WHEN YOU'RE STILL EMPLOYED

If you desire to change jobs and you're currently employed, the job search campaign presents some special challenges. In your case, some of the campaign management advice I've given doesn't make a lot of sense. For example, if you're employed, how can you possibly dedicate 40 hours a week to job searching? Simple answer: you can't. What you must do is to maximize the time you do have. You may find that it takes longer to find the right job since you can only give the search a part-time effort. However, because you're under much less financial pressure than if you were unemployed, you can afford a lengthier job search. Along with this constraint, you also have an advantage. Many people believe that it's easier to get a job

FIGURE 34
Résumé Tracking Form

Company/Contact	Date Dis-tributed	Comments	Follow-up Plans
Acme Title Company	10/1	Response to classified	10/10 with phone call
Meador Construction	10/1	Response to classified	10/10 with phone call
Susan Williams	10/3	Referral from S. Thompson	3 to 4 weeks by letter
Northwest Airlines	10/5	Internet Posting	By e-mail 10/10
Dial Construction Company	10/5	Targeted mailing	By phone 10/10
M. Robbins	10/5	At advice meeting	Next week meet again for feedback 10/11
C. Hicks	10/5	Referred by M. Robbins	By phone 10/10

when you have a job. There is some truth in this. Employers, like the rest of us, often want what others seem to want. When you're working, your current employer serves as a strong endorsement of your benefits. However, this endorsement factor works best for employed job hunters who wish to stay in the same field, but change companies. It's much less true for people wanting to make significant changes in occupational fields.

You must job search during those times that are available to you if you are employed. For example:

- At lunchtime
- In the evenings
- At night
- On the weekends
- Vacation days

Because it will require deception on your part, I cannot recommend that you call in sick in order to look for a job. I know that you have precious little "free" time, but it's simply a matter of integrity. It's also not something that an interviewer will appreciate learning.

I have one cautionary note about responding to published ads. Remember that if you respond to blind published advertisements, you cannot be sure who will learn about your job-hunting efforts. Likewise, if you decide to work with an employment agency or headhunter, make sure the firm understands the need for confidentiality.

GETTING A FAST START IN THE NEW JOB

A smooth transition into your new job is the last phase of a successful job search. First impres-

sions are extremely important. These impressions will become a part of your reputation at your new company. Good, bad, or in between, they will follow you for some time. You can do several things to get a jump start on your new job. First, review all of your company research before beginning work (e.g., company profile, brochures, annual report, and so forth). Second, ask your new boss for any reading materials that he or she thinks would be helpful for getting you up to speed quickly. Also, ask for a job description if you don't already have one. Third, make sure you know exactly where and when to report on that first day. Get exact directions and arrive a few minutes early.

As soon as possible, meet with your new boss. Any time you meet with your boss, particularly when you are new, make sure you are well organized. In the meeting, ask him or her the following questions:

- What do you see on the horizon for this company and for our department?
- What are the most important goals for the company and for our department?
- What barriers do you see to achieving these goals?
- What can I do to make the most immediate impact?
- Who are key people that I should meet right away?

Spend time introducing yourself to your new colleagues. Accept and extend lunch invitations. It's important that you learn what they do and how their jobs interface with your new responsibilities. Be sure to ask them, "Since I'm new here, can I call you when I have a question?" They'll say yes, you'll probably need their help soon, and you'll begin to build relationships that will be vital to your long-term success.

STAY READY

A couple of years ago, a very good friend of mine (I'll call him Samuel) was working as a senior executive at a very well known organization. Things seemed to be going very well for Samuel's career: pay increase after pay increase, ever-increasing job responsibilities, and a very good reputation throughout the organization. Things were going so well that one of the organization's most senior executives asked Samuel to hire a talented direct report that he could quickly groom as his replacement. As soon as the replacement was ready, hopefully in about a year, Samuel could move up to an even more senior position. Clearly this was an exciting opportunity, and, with exuberance, Samuel took to his task of finding a direct report.

After an extended national search, he found the person he wanted, and he hired his future successor. However, things are not always as they seem. About four weeks after the direct report came on board, the same senior manager who told Samuel that he soon would take on more responsibilities called him into his office and delivered an unbelievable message. "Surprise—you no longer have a job, but thanks for hiring your replacement." This is not a direct quote, but the message is accurate.

Obviously, this is a pretty ugly story whose major theme is deception. After considerable consternation, tears, and in his case, much prayer, Samuel went to work looking for a new position. After a number of emotionally difficult months, he did find a new position, making more money, with more responsibility, and a better working environment. A few weeks after Samuel started his new job, I asked him, "What one thing stands out as your greatest lesson from this whole experience?" His reply is outstanding advice for all of us: "I will never again allow my network to become cold. I will constantly stay in touch with others in my field and in my industry. I will listen when recruiters call, keep my résumé up to date, and never again have to start the job-finding process from scratch."

We live in a very turbulent time for careers. Job security no longer comes from organizations, but instead resides in the marketability of your skills and your ability to market yourself. After you find your new job, continuously seek ways to increase your value, not only for your new employer, but in the larger marketplace. Keep honing your job searching skills by seeking networking opportunities and constantly building relationships. While indeed turbulent, for those with the right job skills and the ability to market them, these times offer unparalleled opportunities to find career treasure.

12

Get the Offer and Negotiate Your Best Deal

"Negotiating hard for your interests does not mean being closed to the other side's point of view. Quite the contrary. You can hardly expect the other side to listen to your interests and discuss the options you suggest if you don't take their interests into account and show yourself to be open to their suggestions. Successful negotiation requires being both firm *and* open."

Roger Fisher and William Ury

MONEY, MONEY, MONEY, MONEY

"Your qualifications are certainly impressive, and I'm convinced that you will fit in very well around here. I'd like to offer you the position. Now, how much will it take to hire you?" Congratulations, you did it! It's been a long, sometimes frustrating road, but here it is—a real live, honest-to-goodness job offer. It's time to be very careful. Please, whatever you do, don't forget what you set out to find at the beginning of the job search journey.

You've worked hard to understand yourself better and to find a career that is deeply satisfying. Please, don't give up the search for career treasure at the same moment you receive an offer. For some reason, once the interviewer extends an offer, it's easy to shift from looking for job satisfaction to the salary negotiation game. The object of this game is to drive as hard a bargain as possible. You know you've done really well in the game when you get a little more money than the employer was initially prepared to pay.

Of course, SALARY IS IMPORTANT. I want you to receive the highest paying job offer possible, so I'll give you plenty of ideas about how to negotiate your salary. However, the number one issue I'll ask you to keep in mind is this: *The job offering the highest salary may not represent your best deal.*

Almost every week I work with executives who are terribly unhappy in their careers; some make in excess of $100,000 a year, a few are millionaires. They often confide in me that they really "want to find a way out." When they do, I always ask them a very simple question: "Well, why don't you leave?" They usually tell me that they can't leave their current position because "the money is too good." I then respond with something like, "I'm sorry, I'm a little confused. Let's see if I've got it. You want to leave your job because you're unhappy. You're paid extremely well, but the money doesn't make you happy; however, you can't leave because the money is too good. What's wrong with this picture?" Obviously, at its core, this kind of career dilemma is about values. The question is simple, the implication profound: What is it that really matters to you?

Whether or not you're a highly paid executive, as you evaluate the offer during the negotiation process below, consider the offer's ability to meet all of your vocational identity needs, not just salary. Please keep searching for your best deal; keep searching for career treasure.

THE SEVEN-STEP CAREER NEGOTIATION PROCESS

There are seven sequential steps to the career negotiation process. Each step is vital and builds upon the previous step. Here they are:

- Get the financial facts
- Secure the offer
- Clearly understand the job
- Respond to the initial offer
- Determine the offer's total value
- Negotiate
- Reject or accept the offer

Step 1: Get the financial facts

In order to negotiate intelligently and to evaluate an employer's job offer, you must know your *financial needs and desires*, and understand the *job's value* to the employer and in the marketplace.

Your financial needs and desires

You should calculate three figures to determine your financial needs and desires. The first figure represents the minimum amount of money you need to feel comfortable. For each of us, and at various times in our lives, this figure is different. I suggest that you review Exercise 10 in Chapter 6 to help you determine your financial needs. In all likelihood, you will share this number with no one, but you need to know it. This figure is your "gotta have," or you will walk away from a job offer regardless of any other factors. Don't become fixated on the number, however. Instead, think about the principle associated with this number: I must be able to support my family and myself. This "gotta have" can come in many forms, and I suggest you hold firmly to the principle, without holding as firmly to the number. I'll say more about this kind of thinking during the discussion of negotiation in Step 6.

EXERCISE 11
Total Compensation Worksheet

Compensation	Value
Base Salary	
Bonus	
Stock Options	
Deferred Compensation, Stocks, etc.	
Benefits (20 to 40% of base salary)	
Company Car or Car Allowance	
Educational Benefits (Tuition, books)	
Other Perks, e.g., Club Dues, etc.	
Total Compensation	

The next figure you should calculate is your current financial situation (if employed), or the amount you're accustomed to receiving (if unemployed). Employers know you are unlikely to leave your current situation for the same or less money, or for less than you're accustomed to receiving. For executives, this figure includes stock options, deferred compensation, and the like. As with the first figure, I will discuss how to use this number in Step 6. For now, complete the Total Compensation Worksheet to determine your current, or accustomed, total compensation.

The third figure for you to calculate is your dream figure. It's the kind of figure that you would be absolutely ecstatic about receiving. It should be within the realm of possibility, but just barely.

These three numbers, your "gotta have," your current situation, and your dream figure, are good touchstones for the negotiation process. Of course, they're only part of the mix. These three numbers tell about your side of the equation. Effective negotiation also requires knowledge of the job's value in the marketplace.

Know the job's value

Some career experts suggest that after you receive a salary offer, you can dramatically increase the offer by persuading the company that you will provide enormous economic value in the future. In other words, because you're so talented and hard working, the company should pay you much more than the initial offer. It sounds good, but there's one problem. It just doesn't work this way in companies that have personnel departments.

The reason this strategy can't work or can work only to a very limited extent is because hiring managers do not set salary ranges, the personnel department does. And the personnel department uses an external equity approach to establish salary ranges, not an internal equity approach. Here's the distinction. With an internal equity approach, the company asks, "What is the position's economic value relative to other positions in this company?" For example, is a secretarial job worth the same as, or more than, a welding job in terms of delivering financial benefit to the organization? Interesting idea, but no one uses this approach to establish salary ranges. With an external equity method, the company asks, "What is the market value of people doing this kind of work?" The personnel department's compensation experts spend considerable time and energy conducting salary surveys to find out what other organizations are paying for similar jobs. They then develop salary ranges for each position, such as $23,000 to $26,500 for Position A, $25,000 to $28,500 for position B, and so on.

In addition, while the personnel department doesn't use the internal equity approach to set salary ranges between different jobs, it is extremely diligent about maintaining pay equity within job titles. Every personnel professional's worst nightmare is having one Associate Class 1 making $24,500 and another Associate Class 1 making $42,600; they're just not going to let it happen.

Instead, the personnel department determines the job's value based upon the salaries of similar positions in the marketplace. And personnel establishes fairly narrow salary ranges to represent this value. Additionally, the company will keep people doing the same work, with the same job title, within the same salary range. Thus, researching the salary range that companies in your area or industry attach to similar positions is your first task during the negotiation process.

While the rules about salary ranges still hold somewhat true for executive positions (those over $60,000), it's a lot less true for several reasons. Executive positions are much more difficult to compare to one another and

the pool of applicants is much smaller. A vice president does not necessarily equal a vice president. Personnel's influence for senior positions is considerably less than it is for lower-level jobs, as well. The corporation's senior leadership is much more likely to insert itself in the hiring of key executives. When this occurs, all bets are off.

The rule of thumb for the amount of salary range flexibility is this: The more money you make, the more negotiable the salary and perks. Below about $25,000, little negotiating room exists; between $25,000 and $60,000 or $65,000, you'll find more flexibility; and above $75,000, companies will exercise *much* more discretion in determining salaries.

I'll talk more about how to negotiate within this system in Step 6. For now, you need information about the market value of the position for which you're applying, for a couple of reasons. First, this information will help determine if an offer is a fair one for the position you're considering. How can you begin to negotiate without a good idea about what is reasonable in the marketplace? Second, if a hiring manager really wants to hire you, he or she may wish to pay you more, but will need market data to persuade the personnel department. You may be able to help the hiring manager persuade personnel to reevaluate the position if you can supply good salary information from objective sources. In Appendix E, you'll find nine sources for gathering salary information.

Step 2: Secure the offer

Here are two salary negotiating rules that you should never forget. *Rule 1: Never be the first one to mention salary during the hiring process. Rule 2: Try not to discuss salary before the interviewer offers you the job.* How important are these two rules? Well, on a scale from 1 to 10, I'd rate them both about an 11. Yes, they're *really, really* important. Here's an exception to rule number 2. If a recruiter calls to entice you into leaving your current position, I suggest that you quickly inquire about the position's salary range. That way you'll know if it's even worth considering. The recruiter knows you are highly unlikely to leave your current position for less money, has a lot of interest in convincing you to leave your current situation, possesses little to no financial interest in saving the hiring company any money, and will not take any salary questions personally. Just ask.

So, are they going to offer me the job or not?

How do you know when you're about to get a job offer? Several factors strongly indicate an impending offer. You will know that the company is seriously thinking about offering you a position when it brings you back for second or third interviews. As already mentioned, when the interview moves from discussing your work history to the present, and then to how you'll benefit the company in the future, the interviewer is strongly considering you. Another very strong indication occurs when you observe a sharp role reversal between you and the interviewer. In the beginning, you are the salesperson and the interviewer is the buyer. After the company decides it wants you, the interviewer becomes the salesperson and you become the buyer. When you hear the interviewer begin to sell you on all the wonderful benefits associated with the organization, you know that the roles have changed 180 degrees; the organization wants you. Also, if the interviewer begins

to inquire about very practical issues associated with beginning employment, such as when you could begin work, or take a physical or drug screen, a job offer is probably imminent. Once a job offer occurs, move immediately to Step 3 before you beginning negotiating the specifics.

Before I move to discussion of Step 3, however, I need to address two extremely common salary-related interview questions that can occur anytime during the hiring process.

What are your salary requirements?

At any point during the screening interview or during subsequent job interviews, a company representative my ask something like "What are your salary requirements?" or "How much will it take to hire you?" Remember salary negotiating rules 1 and 2. Do *not* answer this kind of question with a number. You can respond in a variety of ways, but your goals are to have the hiring organization reveal the salary range associated with this position and to move them toward making a hiring decision. You can say something like, "Well, I'm most interested in finding a situation where my skills and abilities can be fully utilized and where I can make valuable contributions. I'm certain that if (company name) extends a job offer to me, that you will pay me fairly for the work that I do. Are you offering me this position?"

At this point the interviewer will either say yes, or indicate the he or she is simply trying to determine your financial needs. If you receive a yes, it's time to move on to Step 3.

If you get the second response from the decision maker, perhaps something like "No, not yet, we're just trying to understand your financial requirements," you'll need to respond in a manner that causes the interviewer to reveal the salary range associated with this position. You might say, "Once again, I'm certain that (company name) will make a fair offer for someone with my experience and skill level. What is the salary range associated with this position?" When they give you a figure, "Between $32,000 and $35,000," I suggest that you pause for about 5 to 10 seconds (it will seem like 20 minutes!), think about the number, and reply, "Well, I'm sure that's workable." I like the word "workable" much more than saying "Let's negotiate." It's softer, but gets you to the same point. Also, just pausing a few seconds will sometimes cause the interviewer to increase the offer: "We can do a little better than that, say, $1,500 more."

If the interviewer asks for your reaction to the salary range, for example, "Is this figure good enough?" you should again indicate that, "I'm sure it's workable; it's in the ballpark. Let me make sure I understand all the job's requirements." With this statement it's time to move on to Step 3 and begin clarifying the position's requirements.

At the time you receive a salary range from the interviewer, you may also want to review mentally your minimum, current, and dream figures you calculated in Step 1. Assuming the salary range is above your minimum, and you have market data to support your position, you may want to add to the previous statement by giving your own range that overlaps with the interviewer's range. For example, with the $32,000 to $35,000 range just mentioned, you might say, "I'm sure that number is workable. I really want between $34,000 and $37,000." At a minimum, you should be able to negotiate toward the top of the range with this approach. Also, sometimes employers do not

reveal the true top of the range with their first figure and may have negotiating room above the initial top figure. In either event, you are no longer talking about $32,000.

What are you making now? or What are you accustomed to making?

Watch out for this one. In many ways this question is irrelevant. The job has a value. Personnel determined its value through marketplace research and it created a salary range. You have marketable knowledge, skills, and abilities. On the basis of this knowledge and these skills and abilities, you either can or cannot do the job. If you can do the job, and if the company wants you, it should offer you some figure within the salary range associated with the job. You should then decide if you want to work for the figure offered and either accept, reject, or negotiate the offer. This is logical—but, as you know, life is often not logical.

The interviewer has asked you a specific question. Of course, the *last thing* you can say is "That question is irrelevant." Your task, in most instances, is to divorce earlier salaries from the current situation. Here are three strategies for dealing with this question.

Strategy 1 (If you are currently making very little): For a variety of reasons, you may currently be working for very little. For example, you may be a recent or soon-to-be college graduate working part-time until you graduate. Maybe economic necessity forced you to accept a low-paying job until something better came along. Perhaps you created your own business, which is now struggling. Regardless, the last thing you want your next employer to do is base your salary on your current earnings. One strategy that has proven effective is to say, "My current salary is laughable compared to this position. My (wife/husband/fiance) and I have a number of financial goals we plan on reaching in the next five to ten years. This is one of the main reasons I'm seeking a change in my employment. As far as my salary expectation, well, I hope to be paid fairly in relation to my skills and abilities and my commitment to work extremely hard. Also, I know (company name) will pay me fairly for the requirements demanded for this position. What is the salary range associated with this position?"

Strategy 2 (If you must give them a figure but you think the number is lower than what this position is worth): The second strategy is very straightforward. Look the interviewer in the eye and say "My current total compensation is $X, but I'm not sure how this number relates to this job since they are so different." (The number you should give is the total compensation figure from the worksheet in Step 1.) "What I am sure of is that I really want to be paid in relation to my skills, abilities, and overall contribution. I'm willing to work very hard, and I know this job plays an important role in the company's success. (This is where your homework will really come in handy.) I've done some research, and I've learned that other organizations value this kind of position at between _____ and _____."

Strategy 3 (When your current salary is very good, maybe better than the employer thought): If you're currently employed paid very well for the work you're doing but considering changing positions for some other reason, this strategy may be for you. Perhaps a recruiter has contacted you about a new exciting-sounding position. This strategy is particularly

effective if the interviewer acts surprised when you share your current total compensation. To respond, simply hand the recruiter or decision maker the worksheet from Step 1 and say, "I've put some numbers together to reflect my current total compensation." You don't need to say any more at this point about your compensation. You should then immediately move on to ask them about some current business need or some other specific about the job. The company will either let you know that your current salary is beyond its possibilities, or it will go back to the drawing board to try to get more money. I first got this idea from John Lucht's book *The Rites of Passage at $100,000+*. I've found it a useful tool for conveying the specifics of your financial needs and wants without having to play hardball or other nonproductive games.

Step 3: Clearly understand the job

Once you receive an offer, you should ask a number of questions and confirm information you learned earlier. It is very important that you are certain about the job's accountabilities, scope, and responsibilities; the company's culture; and any other factors that are important to you. Having an exact understanding of these issues is important for three reasons. First, you absolutely need to know what you're signing up for. Many a person has changed jobs only to learn that his or her expectations did not match reality. This can be incredibly painful for all involved. Second, understanding all the particulars will help you decide whether to accept, reject, or negotiate the offer. Third, these agreements should form the content of an offer letter that contains all of the expectations important to you. I'll discuss getting these expectations in writing in Step 7.

Simply go over the expectations in detail with the interviewer. For example, "Okay, I understand the job's title is (say the job's title). I will be responsible for (state the responsibilities as you understand them). The amount of travel required is between (xx percent and xx percent). My base salary is (base salary)." Of course, if you are negotiating an executive package, also spell out the other total compensation factors, then continue. "I will report to (job title of the person to whom you'll report), and you would like me to start on (requested start date)." Once you're sure of the particulars, move on to Step 4.

Step 4: Respond to the offer

Regardless of how you feel about the offer, it's best to ask for some time to evaluate the offer. Ask for a day, a couple of days, or even a week. They'll let you know if a week is too long. Explain that "I do not make decisions like this lightly. I'd like to have a day or two to consider this offer (if appropriate—and discuss it with my spouse)." After reaching agreement about when you'll respond, set up a face-to-face meeting, if possible, or a phone meeting to return and discuss the offer.

If the interviewer presses you for an immediate decision ("I really must know today") I would decline. Careers are big deals; asking for an immediate decision is unreasonable and shows a lack of understanding about human nature and common courtesy. This is the romance stage. If they treat you like this now, it's only going to get worse after employment.

There are several other reasons you should ask for a little time to consider the offer. First, it will indeed give you time to evaluate the offer. So many things go into the decision—location, money, career path, company culture, and on

and on—that asking for a day or two is reasonable and wise. Second, a job offer in hand is one of the best leverages you will ever have to motivate other buyers. If you contact the other companies who are interviewing you and let them know that another company has extended you a job offer, they just may come through with their own offer immediately. If not, you've lost nothing. Third, between the time of the offer and the scheduled date to get back together, you can put together a carefully considered strategy for negotiating the offer.

Step 5: Determine the offer's value

Value: "Relative worth, utility, or importance: degree of excellence." (Thank you, Mr. Webster.) Here it is, the sin qua non of job hunting. To what degree does the job offer deliver excellence? To what degree does the offer yield career treasure? That's what you're after, right?

During the day or two before you return to the decision maker's office, or contact her by phone, you need to do two things. First, determine how closely the job offer matches your vocational identity and financial needs. Second, decide how you will negotiate the initial offer to reflect more closely your vocational identity and financial needs.

To analyze an offer's value, you'll need three things: your Vocational Identity Summary, the three financial figures you calculated in Step 1, and the Job Offer Evaluation Matrix. You'll find a sample of a completed Job Offer Evaluation Matrix to assist you in evaluating the offer on the following page. As with all the forms in this book, you'll find a blank form in Appendix A. Column 1 lists Vocational Identity and Financial factors to consider. Column 2 allows you to weigh the issues in terms of importance. As you read each item in Column 1, decide how important it is to you on the following scale:

1—Very unimportant
2—Unimportant
3—Important
4—Very important

Example
Job Offer Evaluation Matrix

Vocational Identity Factors	Importance (Multiplier 1–4)	Current Job or Last Job	Job Offer	Job Offer 2
Life's Purpose	4	2 × 4 = 8	5 × 4 = 20	
Career Objective	4	2 × 4 = 8	5 × 4 = 20	
Vocational Personality/Job Fit	4	1 × 4 = 4	4 × 4 = 16	
Treasure-Yielding Skills	4	1 × 4 = 4	5 × 4 = 20	
Accomplishment Skills	3	1 × 3 = 3	3 × 3 = 9	
Other Skills	2	3 × 2 = 6	3 × 2 = 6	
Personal Values	4	2 × 4 = 8	5 × 4 = 20	
Work Values	4	2 × 4 = 8	5 × 4 = 20	
Lifestyle—Travel	4	1 × 4 = 4	5 × 4 = 20	
Lifestyle—Location	2	5 × 2 = 10	5 × 2 = 10	
Lifestyle—Commute	1	4 × 1 = 4	5 × 1 = 5	
Company Culture	4	1 × 4 = 4	4 × 4 = 16	
My Boss	3	4 × 3 = 12	2 × 3 = 6	
Other Company Issues	4	2 × 4 = 8	5 × 4 = 20	
Other Factor	4	2 × 4 = 8	5 × 4 = 20	
Other Factor	4	2 × 4 = 8	5 × 4 = 20	
Subtotal		85	185	

Rate Items on the following scale: 1—Very Inadequate; 2—Inadequate; 3—Adequate; 4—Very Adequate; 5—Ideal

Financial Factors	Importance (Multiplier 1–4)	Current Job or Last Job	Job Offer	Job Offer
Base Salary	2	5 × 2 = 10	2 × 2 = 4	
Bonus	2	5 × 2 = 10	0 × 2 = 0	
Stock Options	2	5 × 2 = 10	0 × 2 = 0	
Deferred Compensation	2	4 × 2 = 8	0 × 2 = 0	
Benefits	2	4 × 2 = 8	0 × 2 = 0	
Vacation	2	2 × 2 = 4	0 × 2 = 0	
Relocation				
Job-Finding Services for Spouse				
Other Perks				
Club Memberships, etc.				
Other				
Subtotal—Page 1		85	185	
Subtotal—Page 2		50	4	
TOTAL		135	189	

Rate Items on the following scale: 1—Very Inadequate; 2—Inadequate; 3—Adequate; 4—Very Adequate; 5—Ideal

As you survey the VIS and your financial needs, wants, situation (current), and dreams, place your ratings on the matrix. For your current job, list the ratings in Column 3. Rate job offers in Columns 4 and 5. Each time you read an item in Column 1, rate the item's ability to deliver career treasure on the following five-point scale:

    1—Very Inadequate
    2—Inadequate
    3—Adequate
    4—More Than Adequate
    5—Ideal

After rating the item, multiply your answer by the importance weighting in Column 1. After rating all items and multiplying them by the importance number, sum the scores to get an overall Career Treasure evaluation. If you're employed, you can complete the matrix for Column 3 to evaluate your satisfaction with your current job and to diagnose what aspects you like best and least.

When you're evaluating a job offer, be sure to go back to any items you rated 1 (Very Inadequate), and decide if it's a knock-out factor. In other words, if the job's ability to meet this need is so poor that you would not consider the job unless this item changes dramatically, mark this item with a highlighter or colored pen.

This is not the time to decide whether or not to accept the initial offer, because you do not yet know what the company may do to improve the deal. This is the time to determine what things you would like to change and by how much. However, recognize that some issues can be changed through negotiation and some cannot. As you review the items on the matrix, it is important that you determine which ones are changeable. For example, if the company culture is very uncomfortable, you had better pass; no amount of negotiation on your part will help this issue. Once you decide what to negotiate, it's time to move on to Step 6.

Step 6: Negotiate

Here's some advice you may not get from anyone else. If, after careful evaluation against market salary standards, your vocational identity, your family's needs, and your hopes and dreams, you determine that the job offer is *ideal*—take it. Don't go back and ask for a little bit more. Just thank God, show your appreciation, and take it. There is a good chance that if you do go back and ask, you'll get a little more, but that's not the point. As you'll see when you read the rest of this section, I believe that the most effective negotiation concerns itself with finding win/win agreements that deliver mutually satisfying solutions to all parties' needs. You're seeking career treasure and fairness. If you've found it, you're there. If you go back for more, when in fact you're already very satisfied, you're negotiating from a win/lose rather than win/win perspective. Only take this advice when you're absolutely sure that your salary is at or above market value and every other aspect of the offer thrills you. It happens rarely—but it

FIGURE 35
Cooperative Versus Competitive Approach to Negotiation

Cooperative Approach	Competitive Approach
How negotiators treat each other	
Partners in a problem-solving process—both can win	Adversaries—there will be only one winner
What you negotiate	
Principles—such as fairness or market value	Positions—such as $32,500 and a bonus
The goal	
A good outcome for both parties	A victory
Strategy	
Learn your partner's interests and seek mutually acceptable solutions	Have a bottom line and make offers; make concessions only when you have to do so

does happen. Now, on to dealing with the other 99 percent of job offers.

Competition versus cooperation

You can approach any negotiation in one of two ways: competitively or cooperatively. In competitive negotiating, one side wins, one loses. I'm not talking about being a tough guy versus being a wimp. In competitive negotiation, tough guys anger their opponents and wimps loose. And whether you play the wimp or the tough guy, when the negotiations end, you have not laid the groundwork for a long-term mutually satisfying relationship.

If you elect to use a cooperative approach, however, more than one party can win. This is the idea of seeking a win/win agreement. Figure 35 displays several of the most important differences between the cooperative and competitive approaches.

You'll be best served if you approach all negotiations as a problem-solving partner, focused on principles, concerns, and interests, and employ a strategy of mutual gain. Look for solutions to barriers to agreement rather than staking out a position. Doesn't it just make sense that it will be easier, and more satisfying to both parties, to gain agreement about paying you fairly (at market value) than to argue over a particular dollar figure? Once you agree in principle, you can then move toward satisfying the principle with objective information and creative solutions.

What if the other party won't play? Doesn't the employer try to hire employees for the least amount possible, while employees try to get the most they can out of the employer? If so, isn't this a competitive approach from the outset? Yes, it usually is; but you can change the game.

Here is an example of an employer initially focused on competitive negotiation and a job searcher with a cooperative approach. In this example, the personnel department has determined that the job's salary range is $28,000 to $32,500. The decision maker has extended a job offer of $29,000 and wants to get the employee for as little more than that as possible. The job seeker has learned that some employers are paying as much as $37,000 for the position. On the basis of this information and her financial needs and goals, the job seeker would really like $35,000.

Employer: How do you feel about $29,000?

Job Seeker: *Let me ask you a question: What is most important to you regarding this offer?*

E: I want to make a fair offer and receive your hard work in return.

JS: *So fairness is key, and you expect my hard work as well?*

E: Yes.

JS: *Well we're in agreement. I'm also looking for a fair offer, and as my track record shows, I'm committed to working hard for my employer.*
How do you determine fairness in pay issues?

E: Our personnel people do a lot of work studying the marketplace and pulling these numbers together.

JS: *Well, I agree that the marketplace is the best way to determine value. Would you agree that it is reasonable for me to base my salary expectations on the marketplace?*

E: Yes, of course.

JS: *So we agree that fairness is key and the marketplace is the best source of information.*
I've done some research on my own and your salary range of $28,000 to $32,500 is certainly

realistic. However, many other companies in the same industry pay as much as $37,000 for this position. (You will, of course, need real data.)

Given the market's range of $28,000 to $37,000, my salary goal is $35,000. (You will always need a reason for any position or proposal.)

E: *Is that your bottom line?*

JS: *I don't have a bottom line; I'm seeking fairness based upon market factors.*

What can we do to achieve my goal but maintain the idea of fairness, which is important to both of us?

E: *Well, that's out of the question. The top of the range as determined by personnel is $32,500.*

JS: *How could I move to a different range that still maintains the concept of fairness?*

E: *What did you have in mind?*

JS: *I believe my skills and experiences qualify me for the next level position. What salary range is associated with the next position? (A number of other solutions exist, e.g., signing bonus, vacation days in lieu of cash, etc.)*

E: *The salary range for that position is $32,500 to $39,000, but we're not hiring for that position for another six months.*

JS: *Would I qualify for that position?*

E: *Yes, I think you would.*

JS: *What if I accept the first position at the top of the range, and then assuming good performance, move to the next position in six months at my goal salary? Is this solution consistent with your concerns about market value and fairness?*

E: *Yes, I think that will work for both of us.*

Of course, it's infinitely easier for an author to generate hypothetical examples that always turn out well than to actually do it. This is why understanding negotiating principles is much more valuable than learning rote responses to

specific situations. The following principles will serve you well regardless of the exact circumstances:

- Be a problem-solving partner, not an adversary.
- Be courteous to people in the process, but tough as nails about the issues and barriers.
- Learn what principles, concerns, and interests are most important to your problem-solving partner and share the principles, concerns, and interests most important to you.
- Reach agreement about the principles involved, e.g., fairness, economic value, etc., then seek creative solutions to overcome any barriers so the result is mutual gain.
- Lay all the issues on the table at one time. Explain all the principles or concerns at the same time. Otherwise, you will appear to always have "just one more issue."
- *Avoid having a bottom line* and *stay open* to creative solutions to overcome the barriers to reaching you, and your problem-solving partner's principles.
- Use data to find objective solutions.

I've drawn many of my ideas about effective negotiating from the work of Roger Fisher and William Ury of the Harvard Negotiation Project. If you would like a more detailed discussion of the cooperative approach to negotiating, I highly recommend that you read their book, *Getting to Yes*. Also, William Ury's book *Getting Past No* is excellent for learning how to deal with particularly difficult negotiations.

Lots of options

When you're seeking creative ways to overcome barriers and problems, remember that items

FIGURE 36
Money, Benefits, and Perks

Money	Benefits	Perks
Base salary	Medical insurance	Car
Bonus	Life insurance	Car allowance
Stock options	Tuition reimbursement for you	Club membership dues
Deferred compensation	and your family	
Sign-on bonus	Your development—outside	
Dollars in lieu of benefits	courses and conferences	
	401(k) plan	
	Immediate vesting in retirement	
	plan	
Severance Agreements	**Relocation**	**Personnel Issues**
Employment contract	The dollars for moving expense	Move your first performance
Letter agreement for severance	Guarantee to make up for any	review forward, thereby
package—outplacement	loss on sale of current home	giving a quicker increase in
and salary for some period	Temporary housing allowance	salary
of time	Dual house payments	The job's title
	Job-finding assistance for	Work schedule, e.g., flexible
	spouse	hours
		Support staff
		Amount of vacation

other than base salary may hold the key to a solution. Figure 36 illustrates other items to consider.

Here is an increasingly common option for executives. In today's world of restructuring and downsizing, executives increasingly ask for, and get, a severance package built into their job offer. It is not at all unusual for an executive to receive eighteen months of severance built into the job offer. If you would like an outstanding discussion about executive employment contracts and severance agreements, read Chapter 17 of John Lucht's *Rites of Passage at 100,000+*.

Common barriers to agreement

I've said that understanding principles and having a negotiation process is more important

than learning responses to specific questions. However, several barriers to agreement are so common that I want to alert you and provide some ideas about how to handle them. I've already discussed two such issues: "What are your salary requirements?" and "What are you making now?" or "What are you accustomed to making?" In Appendix D's twenty tough interview questions, I've included the following compensation issues with suggested responses:

- The salary you're requesting is outside of range.
- I'm sorry, but we just don't have room in our budget to pay the salary you're asking.
- We can't pay you that much because our other (job title)'s don't make that much.

- Your past salary just doesn't justify what you're asking.
- What do you think you're worth?
- What is the minimum amount you need to support your family?

How you start is how you'll end

Finally, realize that the way you approach any agreement sets a precedent for later agreements. If you decide to play the traditional competitive negotiation game, remember that if you play the wimp in one instance, they'll expect you to play the wimp in all later negotiations. If you play the tough guy early on, they'll expect you to play the tough guy throughout, and they'll build their strategies to respond. If you take on a competitive approach at one point, don't expect the potential employer to accept a cooperative approach later on.

Step 7: Reject or accept the offer

You've negotiated, and now you must decide: yes or no. Update the job-offer matrix and review it in detail. Ask yourself if this job represents your best deal. In other words, given your economic needs and the condition of the marketplace, does this job match your vocational identity well enough to say yes? Now that you've done this careful, factual, black-and-white analysis, ask yourself one more very important question: "Does it feel right?" That's right, just as you did when you

> "In most instances to ask a negotiator, 'Who's winning?' is as inappropriate as to ask who's winning a marriage. If you ask that question about your marriage, you have already lost the more important negotiation—the one about what kind of game to play, about the way you deal with each other and your shared and differing interests."
>
> Roger Fisher and William Ury

began thinking about career treasure, forget analysis for a moment. Determine what your heart is telling you about this job offer. When an offer is right, it should *feel* right. I know that this advice doesn't sound particularly scientific, but I believe it's one of the most important suggestions in the book. If the offer doesn't feel right, ask yourself, "Why?" You'll probably recognize the reason pretty quickly. Usually when an offer *feels* wrong, one or more of the job's aspects are exactly what you wanted, perhaps even dreamed. These aspects are so wonderful that you're willing to forget about that one little issue. However, that little issue is always there in the background; it just keeps nagging ever so gently. As many an unhappy worker has found, great parts of the job will not always make the awful parts go away. For example, a great salary or a wonderful location will not make up for an organizational culture that you really dislike. If it doesn't feel right, and you can deal with the financial consequences of rejecting the offer, do yourself a favor and walk away.

If you decide to reject the job offer, do so with class. Thank the organization for its interest and job offer, verbally and in writing.

Get it in writing

If your careful analysis revealed a job offer worth accepting *and* it feels right, congratulations! There's just one more item: Get it in writing. Most organizations today provide official offer letters summarizing your agreement. This is very important and indeed can serve as a legal contract in the event that the organization did not live up to its agreement. At a minimum, the letter should contain your job title, start date, salary, and any special condition you negotiated, such as relocation allowances, more vacation time, and so on. If for some reason the organization refuses to put the offer in writing, ask if you can summarize the agreement in your own letter. Mail the letter to the decision maker and make sure that you keep a copy of any correspondence detailing the offer for future reference. Once again, congratulations!

13

WHAT TO DO IF YOU DON'T GET THE PERFECT JOB OFFER

"Winners find a beginning to every ending."
Steve Spurrier
Coach, University of Florida

BUT WHAT IF . . .

Before starring in movies, actor Steve Martin's many hilarious stand-up routines made him a favorite in comedy clubs and on late-night television. I recall watching Martin on NBC's *Tonight* show one evening. Johnny Carson, then the show's host, began his program by outlining the show's celebrity lineup, which included Martin. Carson strongly encouraged viewers to stay tuned for something very special. Steve Martin would be his first guest, and he had promised Carson that he would tell everyone watching *how to have a million dollars and be happy.*

After the opening monologue, a couple of commercials, and a jazzy number by Doc Severinsen and the NBC Orchestra, Carson introduced Martin, again guaranteeing that he would tell everyone *how to have a million dollars and be happy*. Martin strolled up to the microphone, smiled, and said he would now list the things needed to have a million dollars and be happy. "First, get a million dollars. Second, buy a really nice house. Third, . . ." He went on to describe many things one might do to become happy, but never discussed how to acquire the million dollars in the first place.

Although you wouldn't laugh, I'm afraid you might feel somewhat as the audience did after Martin's routine if I don't provide you with ideas about what to do if you don't get that perfect job. If you've followed all the steps laid out in *The Ultimate Job Search Survival Guide*, you stand a very good chance of finding a great job within a reasonable time frame. Of course, a *very good chance* is not the same as a guarantee. A number of factors outside of your direct control, such as the state of the economy, medical needs tying you to a particular community, or your past, can keep you from finding a good job. That is, you just might not immediately find a job that would be satisfying, a job that would yield career treasure. Additionally, factors within your control, such as your values, a spouse's relocation, or your vocational interests, may cause you to reject the available job opportunities, but not allow you to find a position that would deliver career treasure. Added to the overall complexity of job hunting, financial realities may be pressuring you to make a decision sooner rather than later.

When and how do you decide that your job search campaign is not working? This is a really tough question. The difference between the dogged determination required for job-finding success and just plain stubbornness is quite small. Give up too early on your campaign and you may miss a wonderful opportunity that lies just around the next job-hunting bend. Cling too long to a failing strategy and you run significant financial and perhaps even emotional risks. Only you can decide when a campaign is stalled. Remember the job-hunting rule of thumb I explained earlier: On average, it takes about one month per $10,000 in salary to locate new employment. For some job fields and industries, such as high tech, or in some economic climates, like that of central Florida,

it usually takes much less time. For some fields and economies, however, the estimate is higher.

How do you know when it's time to make changes in your marketing campaign or career objective? First, listen to the answers you receive in your networking advice meetings. When you tell network contacts that you are preparing for a campaign that might last as long as X months, find out if they believe this timetable is realistic. Second, in addition to hearing your contact's advice, listen to your heart and emotions. When you're ready to give up, have no more ideas or contacts, when you're nearly completely out of hope, *double your effort* with your current campaign for another two to four weeks. At the same time you begin to double your effort, begin to consider the options presented in this chapter for modifying your current strategy. At the end of this two- to four-week period you'll need to choose how you will move forward with your career journey.

CONSIDER CHANGING YOUR MARKETING STRATEGIES

If you believe that your marketing strategy is not working, the first thing you should do is evaluate whether you're executing your job-finding campaign as you originally intended. Revisit the Strategic Planning Worksheet and your written strategic plan from Chapter 9. Also, review your weekly plans and consult your calendar since the job search began (Chapter 11). Often, after reviewing these items, job hunters are unable to determine their strategic plan's effectiveness because their day-to-day actions have not reflected the original strategy. For example, a job searcher's marketing plan may call for her to spend 75 percent of her time networking. However, she may learn by reviewing her calendar that over the last two months she actually spent only 50 percent of her job-hunting time networking. In this example, the job searcher does not know how well her original plan might have worked because she never implemented it.

After evaluating the degree to which your actions have matched your marketing plan, you can decide how faithfully you've executed the original plan and then determine how well you think your current marketing strategy is working. As the common joke says, "One definition of insanity is doing the same old things and expecting different outcomes." If what you're doing is not working, do something else! You can either rededicate yourself to the original strategy or, if you believe the original marketing plan is ineffective, change it. Reread Chapter 9, and then modify your marketing strategy to reflect what you've learned about the marketplace and about yourself.

PART-TIME AND TEMPORARY WORK

Beginning in the mid to the late 1980s, and continuing through today, many organizations strategically reduced their number of full-time employees and replaced them with both part-time and temporary workers. The reason is simple: they save enormous amounts of money. First, the companies saved millions of dollars because part-time workers do not receive benefits. Even the money above workers' salaries that companies pay to temporary agencies doesn't compare to the high cost of employee benefits. Second, with temporary and part-time

employees, companies can expand and contract the size of their workforce to match product and service demands as needed without taking on permanent employment costs. Third, companies save millions upon millions because they will not be paying retirement benefits to their part-time and temporary workers.

While part-time or temporary work may not fit your long-term career objective, it's an option that presents you with two opportunities. The first has to do with the length of time you can afford to hunt for a job, and the second relates directly to finding a job.

When you evaluated your financial situation in Chapter 6, you got a picture of how long you could reasonably look for work without creating significant negative consequences. Both part-time and temporary work can greatly extend this length of time. For example, instead of perhaps ninety days of financial stability, part-time or temporary work might allow you to continue job hunting for six months while remaining financially secure. If things are beginning to become financially difficult, calculate the minimum amount of money you would need to continue searching. Explore part-time and temporary opportunities to determine if this option will meet your minimum financial needs. This kind of work often provides a very flexible work schedule. This flexibility should allow you to continue looking for the job you really want.

Here is the second opportunity that part-time and temporary work sometimes provides. While I certainly don't suggest that you count on it as a primary marketing strategy, it is not unusual for companies to offer full-time employment to part-time and temporary workers who impress them with skill and effort.

You may feel somewhat put off by the idea of working for a temporary agency. For many people, clerical positions are the only thing that comes to mind when they hear the term "temporary agency." At one time, this was pretty much the case, but no longer. When companies restructured their workforces to be more flexible, the need for temporary workers skyrocketed. Temporary agencies raced to meet this need and began to offer almost every kind of employee on a part-time or temporary basis. Along with clerical workers, accountants, lawyers, factory workers, engineers, and virtually every other kind of occupation imaginable now comprise the part-time and temporary workforce.

According to the Bureau of Labor Statistics, as much as one third of the U.S. workforce now works in either a part-time or temporary capacity. If you feel your campaign is stalling or your finances are becoming very tight, consider this option for the two benefits mentioned above: it can greatly extend the amount of time you can look for the job you really want, and it can demonstrate your worth to potential employers in a very tangible manner.

START YOUR OWN BUSINESS

Ah, yes, the great American dream. Tired of the 8 a.m. to 5 p.m. grind, the insane commutes, and a boss who thinks that *Dilbert* is an instructional manual rather than a comic strip? Maybe you're considering the world of self-employment. Who hasn't said at least once, "I'm shucking the whole darn thing and heading out on my own?" Isn't it the entrepreneur who creates most of the new jobs in America? Why, the small business owner is what made this country

great. Herbert Dow was a nobody with a crazy idea when he moved to Midland, Michigan, and started Dow Chemical. Who was Henry Ford before the Model T? "If they can do it, so can I!" you may be thinking.

A realistic job preview for the would-be entrepreneur

United States government statistics show that sixty-five out of every 100 new businesses fail within the first year. If you decide to try self-employment at home, realize that home-based workers make 30 percent less than their office-bound counterparts. Also, you may find that you're not whom you used to be when you start your own business. Let me explain this last point.

If you've worked for a well-known firm, and you had any sort of reasonably impressive job title, people were glad to meet you at Chamber of Commerce meetings, lots of folks sent you those beautiful holiday greeting cards each year, and people *always* returned your phone calls. In almost every case, if you start your own business, your number one need will be to *sell* products or services. When you shift from buyer to seller, or from business contact to seller, things change. When you move from employed person with a well-known firm to a self-employed person needing business, be prepared for a humbling experience, particularly in the beginning. The holiday cards will stop arriving, except from your printer. Upon seeing you at the Chamber, some of the folks will head quickly, but skillfully, to the other end of the room. And the phone calls—whew! You're going to get heavily screened by the secretary, or transferred to voice mail when you call. They're not going to call you back, so you'll have to call seven times to make contact. When you do finally get through to inquire about your business proposal, your contact will say something like, "Yes, yes—it sounds like a great idea. I'm going to think very seriously about it next year after we get the new budgets." Still thinking about how difficult it was to get a phone call through to this person, you'll say something to yourself like, "Hey, what happened to this guy? He used to be so professional." Then it'll hit you: "Next year—new budgets? How am I going to eat between now and the new budgets?"

Damn the torpedoes, full speed ahead!

"Sure," you say, "I know all that, but I still really want to give it a go!" Good for you. If the thought of working for yourself sounds enticing despite the risks and the difficulties inherent with self-employment, the options and the opportunities are nearly unlimited. If you decide to pursue self-employment, you have three major decisions to make:

- What are you going to do?
- Where are you going to do it?
- How will you make it happen?

What are you going to do?

As you explore self-employment, one of the first things you must decide is the type of work you will do. It's important that you make a sharp distinction between the first two questions above: the what and where of self-employment. Simply changing from a company-employed to a self-employed worker may not provide the career treasure you're looking for. Likewise, moving from an office-based to a home-based environment may not improve your career satisfaction. These are considerations of where you'll work, not what you'll do.

To answer the first question, please continue to keep the idea of finding work that you love in mind. If you dislike being an accountant for *The Big-Name Accounting Company*, you may very well dislike being an accountant for yourself. As you decide what you will do, please don't just ask, "What do I know how to do?" "What is the best business to start today?" or "Where is there a market for what I've done in the past?" These questions may tell you something about the marketplace, but they'll tell you nothing about your ideal career destination. As with all career-choice questions, if you decide to work for yourself, make certain that the type of work you choose is consistent with your vocational identity.

Where are you going to do it?

Once you know what you're going to do, you must decide where you're going to do it. This is essentially a question about whether you'll work at home or if you will spend the money to set up an office. For most people, working at home makes the most economic sense. With a fax, telephone, computer, and cell phone, you can communicate with almost anyone in the world at any time. In addition, local telephone companies now offer very sophisticated phone mail systems to small businesses for modest fees. For a few thousand dollars, you can have your business up and running at home. The possible disadvantages of a home-based office include a lack of meeting space for customers and clients, the perception that you are not as legitimate as office-based businesses, and the conflict between family and work demands that is constantly present.

How will you make it happen?

Whether you will work as a consultant, a freelancer, an inventor, a telecommuter, or a seamstress, you should take the time to write a business plan. Many colleges and universities offer assistance in preparing a business plan. You can also contact the local Small Business Administration (SBA) office or call 800-827-5722 to find the location nearest you. The SBA offers business plan outlines and free consultation. The SBA's Directory of Business Development Publications lists a number of booklets useful for learning about various topics important for business start-ups. Additionally, many community and county governments offer free small-business guidance.

As you move toward self-employment, you will need to make some basic decisions about whether to operate as a corporation, proprietorship, partnership, etc. Bookkeeping is also a very important aspect of starting your own business. For many entrepreneurs, a good attorney and an accountant are well worth their fees to help you decide about such issues. Increasingly, computer software offers small-business owners viable alternatives to professional services. For example, accounting programs such as Quick Books do a very good job of managing the finances of small businesses.

Once again, do your homework!

Before you decide to become an entrepreneur or consider whether to seek a loan, use professional services, set up an office at home, or make any other self-employment decisions, you must do some research. After you form your basic idea, you will need to determine your potential market's size, trends, and so forth. Go to the library and review the kinds of sources provided in Chapter 8, and write a one-page summary of what you found. *Now it's time for the most important homework.* Find several self-employed workers who are already doing work that is the same as, or similar to, what you'd like to do. Set up an informational meeting with them. If you find that small business owners in your community are reluctant to talk to their soon-to-be competition, you can contact owners in a community a few miles away. At a minimum, ask these owners the following four questions:

- What are the three biggest challenges in your business?
- What kind of skills and personality does it take to be successful in this business?
- If you could do it all over, what things would you do differently in terms of starting your business?
- What do you see on the horizon for your business in the next two to three years?

After completing your informational interviews, do some very serious soul-searching. Look at your financial situation and consider your vocational identity. Given what you know about yourself, the market, and the business you're considering starting, decide whether or not self-employment is for you. While it's anything but easy, working for yourself can be the most satisfying of all possible career options—if it truly fits who you are.

VOLUNTEER

Yes, I mean working for free. Surprisingly, you may find it more difficult to give your time away than you might think. Nevertheless, while many companies will turn you down, some will take you up on your offer. A number of good things can come out of volunteering your time. First, for some job hunters, the routine of returning to work provides improved self-esteem. Second, you will increase your number of contacts and, assuming you do terrific work, your professional reputation. Third, sometimes after observing your work, a company will learn that they just can't get along without you, and offer you a job. Please don't count on getting a job offer this way, but it can happen. Fourth, if the company allows you to do some kind of meaningful work, you may actually develop transferable job skills and thereby increase your marketability. And last, with some employers you can exchange your volunteered time for an employed status. The following brief story demonstrates the value of this last point.

I know of an individual who is currently a very successful medical practice business manager. A few years ago, however, he was seriously unemployed. It began one afternoon, when Tom's (not his real name) employer abruptly fired him. He didn't panic and assumed he would find new employment shortly. He put together his résumé, read a number of job-finding books, and headed out on the job-hunting trail. However, the days quickly turned to weeks, and the weeks turned to months, and the months into a year. More and more often, interviewers asked Tom why he had not yet found employment. It had become a vicious circle: employers didn't hire him because no employer had hired him.

Tom knew of an acquaintance who had a small but quite successful consulting firm. Tom made the firm's owner a proposition. He would volunteer his time answering phones and provide some other basic administrative services, if he could have the title of business manager and list the firm as his current employer. Of course, Tom also said that he would continue to seek full-time permanent employment. The consulting firm owner agreed, and Tom *went to work*. His new status as an employed business manager, along with his educational and experiential background, soon landed him his current position. Since that time, he has received a number of significant raises and other medical groups and consulting firms regularly recruit him. For Tom, volunteering was the window through which career opportunity entered.

RELOCATE

"But I like it here." Fine. But at some point you may have to think earnestly about your values and ask yourself this: Do you "like it here" more than you like being employed? I personally understand what it's like to have a strong attachment to a community or to a region of the country when employment is difficult. I've been there and done that. Unfortunately, sometimes the place we love is not where the work we love to do is available. Of course, no one except you and your family can decide if relocation is a reasonable option, but I will tell you that a change in the availability of jobs often accompanies a change of scenery.

It's not only the number but also the types of jobs that vary by location. Knowing a location's unemployment rate will tell you only part of the story. You must also understand a bit about the location's economy base. For example, the unemployment rate may be about the same in Lubbock, Texas, and Orlando, Florida. However, the demands for petroleum engineers and for tourist guides are radically different in each location. If you're a tourist guide living in Lubbock or a petroleum engineer residing in Orlando, my guess is that regardless of the quality of the job search marketing plan you've put together, you're probably unemployed. Perhaps it's time to consider geographically broadening your job search.

RETOOL: GO BACK TO SCHOOL

Maybe you've considered this option for some time. Perhaps your forays into the marketplace have shown you that the work you really want to do will require additional education. Regardless, in my decided opinion, this is the only option that is always a reasonable possibility, irrespective of your circumstance. While this chapter's other options are means to an end (a job), education is a rewarding end, in and of itself.

Sure, you will increase your marketability if you increase your job skills through education. Indeed, you may find that only through more education will you get the job you really want.

But stretching and challenging yourself and gaining knowledge through education will provide benefits to every aspect of your life, not just your career.

Almost every technical school, junior college, and university provides assistance to those considering the pursuit of education. The services they provide include information about where to seek financial aid as well as academic advice.

THE LONG AND WINDING ROAD

I intentionally chose the metaphor of a journey to begin the book. Careers are journeys; full of twists and turns, deep heartbreaks, and great joys. Absolutely no journey is full of constantly smooth sailing. It's during the side trips, the difficult times, when the ship's captain does his most important work. Staying focused on the journey's mission—career treasure—and molding creative solutions out of difficult problems is challenging, but unbelievably rewarding. Because the captain knows that these side trips are an inevitable part of reaching the ideal destination, he never loses heart and always looks ahead.

14

SPECIAL JOB SEARCH JOURNEYS

···

"That low man seeks a little thing to do,
Sees it, and does it;
This high man, with a great thing to pursue,
Dies ere he knows it.
That low man goes on adding one to one,
His hundred's soon hit;
This high man, aiming at a million,
Misses a unit.
That, has the world here—should he need the
next,
Let the world mind him!"

Robert Browning

IT'S EXACTLY THE SAME BUT DIFFERENT

At 3:30 p.m. one Friday afternoon, four good friends gathered around their employer's water cooler for a little "decompression." What a week it had been: two project deadlines, the secretary resigned, and the maintenance people somehow managed to keep the temperature at a constant 86 degrees. But they made it. The clients are happy, the boss is happy, and, hopefully, the former secretary is now happy as well.

The four friends decide it's time for a little relaxation. They agree to meet at their favorite Italian restaurant about 7:30 p.m., have a drink, and then walk next door to the Mega Movie 16 Theater Complex and catch a film. After the movie, they will return to the restaurant for dinner.

The first two friends arrive at the scheduled hour, greet each other, take a seat, and order a drink. At 7:50 p.m. their other two friends still have not arrived. They determine their comrades must have gotten tied up in traffic, so they decide to walk over to the theater and hopefully meet their friends there. They survey the sixteen possible movies and learn that the film they want to see starts in 5 minutes. Not wanting to miss the beginning of the film, they purchase their tickets and hope to catch up with the others at the restaurant afterward.

Returning to the restaurant after the movie, they locate their friends. They did indeed get tied up in traffic, but arrived in time to attend a different movie that started a few minutes later. The two friends who arrived at 7:30 begin to discuss their impressions of the film they saw.

"Wasn't that quite a film?" said Friend 1. "It certainly was," replied Friend 2. "I've never seen more ridiculous drivel in all my life!" "What?" asked a somewhat shocked Friend 1. "I thought it was wonderful."

"It's too bad that you didn't see our movie! You'd have no disagreement—our movie was great!" chirped Friend 3. "It certainly was wonderful, wasn't it?" said Friend 4. "That was the best acting I've seen in a while. "Ugh," said Friend 3, "I thought the acting was mediocre, but the story line was fantastic."

Perception is all we know of reality

Even when we go through the same basic situations, two factors create unique experiences in each of us. First, even when the context is the same (for example, going to the movies), the specifics may differ. Both the first and second set of friends found themselves in the same context: They both attended a movie. However, obviously the specifics were different because these two sets of friends saw different movies. Second, even when the specifics are the same, our unique personality causes us to interpret events differently. Although Friend 1 and Friend 2 saw the same movie, one believed it was great and the other thought it was terrible. Friend 3 and Friend 4 agreed that the film they attended was terrific, but couldn't agree on the reason why.

Job hunters' interpretations of job searching experiences are just as unique as those of the amateur movie critics. All job searchers face the same basic context (looking for work), but different specifics create unique experiences. Additionally, regardless of the specifics, each job searcher will interpret his or her experience uniquely. This chapter will address both of these issues. First, I will describe three special job-finding situations: dual-career families, changing careers at midlife, and moving from a military to a civilian career. These situations are like the different movies viewed by the two sets of friends. Second, I will discuss the commonality among all job hunters' experiences, as well as how all job hunters have truly unique interpretations of these experiences.

DUAL-CAREER FAMILIES—THE CHALLENGES OF RELOCATION

Families know that it's never easy managing two careers—today more than 65 percent of relocating families have dual careers to consider. How do you find balance? What is quality time, anyway? And which one of you is going to stay home when little Jimmy is sick and one of you has an extremely important client meeting and the other a key departmental presentation? The challenge of managing both careers becomes especially acute when one partner is offered a position in a new geographic location. Dual-career families know that an exciting new job opportunity for one partner often presents considerable career challenges for the other. And making a decision about accepting a job in a new location forces couples to face a tough question: "Whose career is most important?" Additionally, regardless of how they answer this question, many couples fear that they will lose economically in a relocation. A recent study conducted by the University of Tennessee and Right Associates showed that there is good reason for their concern, even if a promotion is involved. More than half of the spouses who find work after relocating take a cut in pay and in benefits. Sadly, dual-career families are twice as likely to suffer a decrease in their standard of living after relocation than families with only one working partner.

Few of life's events create more stress than moving; add changing jobs and the stress increases even more. Employers consistently find that spouses' concerns over relocating rank among the top reasons employees turn down relocations. I believe that many of these negative consequences result from poor job-finding techniques as much as from the relocation itself. The study I cited in the previous paragraph also asked spouses of relocating employees to describe how they looked for employment. Not surprisingly, only about 15 percent engaged in networking and most of them sought work from the classifieds. As you know from reading Chapter 9, these percentages are exactly the opposite of what they should be!

Managing the dual-career job search

Just like all job searches, a number of core factors will increase your ability to find a good job in a timely fashion:

- Treat dual-career job hunting as a full-time job.
- Write an effective resume using OAR statements (Chapter 7).
- Conduct company and industry research (Chapter 8).
- Prepare well for the job interview (Chapter 10).
- Use only the best job search techniques (Chapter 9).
- Build a formal marketing strategy that allocates most of your time in the most productive activities (Chapter 9).
- Make networking the centerpiece of your job hunting.

It's the last bullet that presents the most unique challenges to the dual-career spouse who relocates. Relocating spouses will have the most job-finding success through networking, as networking is still the only way get to the hidden job market. Ah, but now relocating spouses are faced with a couple of challenges that are indeed unique to geographic transitions: long-distance networking and finding business contacts in a new area. If you've already moved, you probably do not know many people in the new community, and those you do know, you don't know very well. On the other hand, if you've yet to move, making contacts in the new area from long distance is somewhat difficult. Here are a number of suggestions for overcoming these two obstacles and some general ideas for managing your dual-career job search.

- First, read, or reread Chapter 9 and write your formal marketing strategy.

- As you plan your networking strategy, list any A contacts in your new area.

- List at least ten A contacts in your current/former location. Meeting with these people will provide feedback about your ideas and presentation, allow you to practice your networking skills, provide social support, and perhaps gain you a B contact in the new location.

- Ask your spouse to refer you to at least five coworkers in the new location. Not only will these coworkers be able to provide you with additional B contacts from their networks, but their spouses also possess networks of their own.

- Recognize and accept that you will necessarily rely more heavily upon B contacts in a dual-career relocation situation than if you were to seek a new job in your current/former area.

- Although you may not know many people in the new community particularly well, this is not necessarily a disadvantage because most people welcome the opportunity to meet with newcomers to the community. Seek out community and religious leaders, neighbors, local politicians, and others to serve as networking contacts. Each of these people has her or his own network and can provide advice and information. You will also find that you will jump-start your relationships in the community in a quite natural way. Some of these people will become your A contacts of the future.

- Do not immediately disregard any potential contact; you never know whom he/she might know and to whom he/she may be willing to refer you.

- Plan to extend any house-hunting trips for several days to leave time for conducting early networking advice and information meetings. At a minimum, you should be able to meet with several of your spouses' new colleagues. Don't discount these contacts; often they and their spouses know the community very well. Of course, be sure to ask for two or three referrals as outlined in the advice meeting agenda in Chapter 9.

- Conduct advice and information meetings with as many of your spouse's company's human resources staff as possible. These people constantly network with other personnel people in the community and often know who's hiring. Ask them for referrals to other human resource people and business people.

In addition to the points above, you should ask your spouse's employer to supply spousal employment assistance. Unfortunately, only about 25 percent of companies provide spousal career assistance as part of their standard relocation package. I'll discuss the importance of *asking* for relocation benefits in the next section. Fortunately, you have *The Ultimate Job Search Survival Guide.* Follow this book's job-finding ideas and techniques faithfully and you'll quickly establish a strong network in the new community.

Companies' discretion and relocation assistance

Although it's a pretty well kept secret, there is often much more relocation assistance available than you might think. Did you notice the phrase *standard relocation package* in the previous paragraph? For the vast majority of organizations, the human resource department and the hiring manager have at least some flexibility in providing relocation benefits. In many instances, what you get depends upon what you ask for. This is especially true today. In the past, organizations moved people primarily for promotional reasons. Today, most companies' rationale for moving employees is different. Primarily because of last decade's corporate restructuring, companies now move people for strategic business reasons, not for promotions. This means that if your company has asked you to move, a very good chance exists that it *really* needs you in the other location. The implication: If your company has asked you to transfer, you probably have some negotiating leverage, so when it comes to your relocation package—ASK!

Because the average move costs companies about $40,000 to $45,000, they're rightly concerned with controlling these costs. Therefore, instead of publishing all the possibilities, the company controls costs by granting some of the most expensive items on a case-by-case basis. Although you may not see them in the company's standard relocation policy, these items are often available nevertheless. Of course, I don't know if your particular company commonly grants the relocation items listed below. I will tell you, however, that most larger organizations commonly provide these items on at least a limited basis. Typically, one's level in the organization, or the need for an employee's special skills, dictates what kind of assistance the company is willing to offer. Here are a number of items you may receive if you ask:

- At least two fully funded house-hunting trips
- Temporary housing costs until your permanent housing is ready
- Travel between both locations until permanent move is made
- Cost of moving household items
- Temporary storage for household items if needed
- Payment of all realty fees and closing costs (on both ends of the move)
- Loss protection on real estate sale
- Cost for new car tags
- Spousal job-finding assistance

IT WASN'T SUPPOSED TO BE LIKE THIS: OUTPLACED AT MIDLIFE

You've paid your dues: You've worked hard, taken the good with the bad, and given up a significant part of your life for your job. And you've played by the rules: You went to school, showed up on time, and did what they asked. Now here you are, facing a career change at midlife. It wasn't supposed to be like this. By this time you should be able to relax a bit and to feel secure in your career because of what you've accomplished and because of the considerable skills you've amassed. You were supposed to be financially comfortable as well. For many, it's not like this at all.

What changed?

Over the last two decades (and particularly within the last ten years), dozens of factors have conspired to change the employment landscape forever. As early as the 1940s, organizational theorists began trying to persuade managers that they could improve productivity and worker satisfaction by pushing down decisions from the top of the organization to lower levels. Not much happened initially, however, and these ideas about high-involvement management, or democratizing the organization, remained largely in the classroom for four decades.

Shortly after World War II, it was hard for organizational leaders to recognize a need to change anything. The economy grew steadily, companies were profitable, and returning soldiers—and soon their children—were enjoying life in the modern organization. The company exchanged job security for loyalty. While it wasn't always fun and often not very fulfilling, the contract for *lifetime employment* was hard to turn down.

Then came the 1960s and 70s, and the times (as described in the Bob Dylan song of the era) they were a-changing. The world seemed to grow smaller as other economies, such as Japan's, became powerhouses. A global economy developed, accompanied by extremely fierce global competition. Around the world, organizations looked for new ways to gain productivity and competitive advantage. Suddenly, organizations—first in Japan and then in the rest of the world—began to reconsider workplace democracy, process improvement, and reorganizing in more efficient ways. When organizational leaders saw these ideas as merely philosophical theories, little happened. But when companies realized that they could cut enormous costs out of the organization by eliminating layers of management and redundant services, they adopted the ideas vigorously. The explosion in the availability of relatively cheap desktop personal computers added considerable fuel to the downsizing

fire, because companies could do so much more work with so many fewer people.

What changed? A lot! We live in a global economy, organizations have many new ways to organize work, and computers are pervasive. The results have been nothing short of staggering. Since 1979, 43 million U.S. jobs have disappeared. One third of the population have a family member who experienced a permanent layoff and 40 percent of us know a relative or friend who lost his or her job through downsizing. The trend toward restructuring continues today and will likely be with us from now on. I've heard the new world of work described as *permanent white water*. The contract has changed forever.

What you may be feeling

I've observed that middle-aged workers respond somewhat differently than younger workers when they lose their jobs. Instead of the despair and depression that younger workers feel, older workers' first reactions to job loss tend to be closer to confusion and denial. Unless the company provided outplacement, older workers often don't immediately begin to look seriously for work. Instead, they may take a vacation, play a little golf, and act as if everything is just fine. This is especially true of middle-level managers and executives who may have the financial wherewithal to survive several months without suffering significant economic hardships. They also tend to be overly optimistic in the beginning, assuming that they'll pick up the phone, let their contacts know that they're now available, and have a job in days, or at worst, in a few weeks.

By the time I usually see these people, it's been three to four months since they lost their job and their naive optimism has been replaced by thinly veiled despair and low self-esteem. Through all their years of work, education, and other kinds of life experiences, nothing prepared them for job searching. Time and again I hear them say, "But I've never really had to look for a job." They tend to follow one job lead at a time, use poor networking techniques, and look for work only a few hours a week. Of course, this means the job search will drag on longer than it should. Long job searches can cause self-esteem to plummet lower, and low confidence will lead to poor performance during any job interviews that do occur—it's not a pretty picture.

At midlife and facing a job change: Here's what to do

The number one piece of advice I have for you is this: start now. Second, you can, and should, consider this time in your life as a great opportunity. You have the opportunity to consider carefully what you *really want to do with the rest of your life*; that's a blessing that our work-a-day world often doesn't allow. Before you go looking for another job basically like the last one, consider exploring options that could give you even greater career satisfaction. The sooner you begin to consider your options, write a career objective, build a solid marketing strategy, and implement it, the sooner you'll be working again. In other words, job searching at midlife is exactly like searching for a job at any other time—with one exception. Some people may think you're too old. Guess what? Most won't. Forget those that will, focus on those that won't, and move forward. You may know a lot about a lot, but you probably don't know

much about job-finding techniques and strategies. If you want results, read this book cover to cover, complete all the exercises, write a well-thought-out marketing plan, and give your job search your full-time effort. Yes, job searching at midlife is sometimes difficult, but *many* people report that they are happier after a midlife career change than before. Carpe diem!

MOVING FROM A MILITARY TO A CIVILIAN CAREER

Learning to package your marketable job skills represents perhaps the biggest hurdle in making the transition from a military to a civilian career. Of course, some military job titles and skill sets readily transfer to civilian work environments; for example, nurse, other healthcare jobs, and police officer. However, some jobs do not; for example, the Navy's ship driver and signal man, or the Army's tank driver. Some bases offer at least limited career counseling. These counselors should be able to help you convert military job titles into civilian titles and learn the basics of job finding. Your military branch's personnel manual will help you with this conversion as well. Just because a military job title doesn't transfer to the civilian world doesn't mean that you don't have marketable job skills. Read Chapter 4 and complete the exercises. You will see that regardless of your military job title, you've acquired a number of marketable skills. By creating OAR statements (Exercise 7) and presenting them in attractive packages (your resume and verbal advertisement—Chapter 7), you'll maximize your marketability.

Some of the challenges concern culture more than job skills. I asked Willy Waggoner, a career counselor at a Navy base currently undergoing a shutdown, what he felt his clients' biggest job-finding challenges were. Mr. Waggoner said that many longtime military personnel "have a very difficult time taking off the uniform." The military is a subculture, with its own language and cultural rules. After several years, military personnel gain a great deal of comfort with those rules; they know how to operate effectively within the military subculture. If you're moving from the military to civilian work, you should place special emphasis on getting rid of the military jargon as quickly as possible. After you inventory your skills with Chapter 4's exercises, refer to your skills using the exercises' language rather than military acronyms and jargon. As with all job searches, the basics are the same:

- Treat your job hunting as a full-time job.
- Write an effective resume using OAR statements (Chapter 7).
- Conduct company and industry research (Chapter 8).
- Prepare well for the job interview (Chapter 10).
- Use only the best job search techniques (Chapter 9).
- Build a formal marketing strategy that allocates most of your time in the most productive activities (Chapter 9).
- Make networking the centerpiece of your job hunting.

EVERY JOB SEARCH IS A UNIQUE JOURNEY

Whether you have a dual-career situation, face midlife career transition, or are moving from the military to a civilian career; whether you are gay, a minority, a Baptist, a Jew, or an atheist; whether you are an outplaced executive or a laid-off factory worker; whether you are well-educated or illiterate; whether you are well-heeled or barely getting by; or whether you just got fired or just received a promotion, you face the same basic set of challenges as every other job hunter.

No matter who you are, some people will want to see you and some won't; some will believe you can provide value to the company and some won't. I'm not trying to minimize the fact that some journeys will be more difficult than others. If the bill collector is at the door, you may need to take any job you can get to deal with your immediate financial needs. Here is my point: regardless of who you are, the job-finding issues and processes are the same. Focus on the things you can control, such as your attitude and the quality of your job-finding efforts. Don't concern yourself with the things you can't control, such as others' attitudes or the state of the economy. Your next job may be your ideal job. If not, it can still be a valuable leg of the journey on the way to your ideal destination. Keep listening to the call, and in the end, your own unique and very special job search journey will deliver career treasure.

APPENDIX

A

JOB SEARCH FORMS

Vocational Identity Summary (VIS)

Career Objective (From Exercise 9 on page 98) _____

MY SEVEN *GREATEST* ACHIEVEMENTS (FROM EXERCISE 6 ON PAGE 46)
1)
2)
3)
4)
5)
6)
7)

TRANSFERABLE SKILLS (FROM EXERCISE 5 ON PAGE 41)			
Skill	Rating	Skill	Rating
1)		11)	
2)		12)	
3)		13)	
4)		14)	
5)		15)	
6)		16)	
7)		17)	
8)		18)	
9)		19)	
10)		20)	

TREASURE-YIELDING SKILLS (FROM EXERCISE 6 ON PAGE 46)			
Skill	Rating	Skill	Rating
1)		8)	
2)		9)	
3)		10)	
4)		11)	
5)		12)	
6)		13)	
7)		14)	

Vocational Identity Summary (continued)

TREASURE-YIELDING SKILLS (FROM EXERCISE 6 ON PAGE 46)			
15)		18)	
16)		19)	
17)		20)	

VALUES	
Personal Values (From Exercise 1 on page 21)	
5 Most Important	5 Least Important
1)	1)
2)	2)
3)	3)
4)	4)
5)	5)
Work Values (From Exercise 2 on page 22)	
1)	1)
2)	2)
3)	3)
4)	4)
5)	5)

WORK ACCOMPLISHMENTS (OAR—EXERCISE 7 ON PAGE 49)	
1)	6)
2)	7)
3)	8)
4)	9)
5)	10)
11)	12)

PERSONAL MISSION STATEMENT (EXERCISE 4 ON PAGE 30)	PERSONALITY/INTERESTS (EXERCISE 8 ON PAGE 64)
PURPOSE	Three Letter Personality Code Interest Code _____ _____ _____
	MY SINGLE FAVORITE SKILL (EXERCISE 6 ON PAGE 46)
	Favorite Skill:

Résumé Worksheet: Chronological

Name:	
Street:	
City, State, Zip Code:	
E-mail:	

CAREER OBJECTIVE

SUMMARY STATEMENT

WORK HISTORY

Company Name:	
City, State:	
Dates: From:	To:
Job Title:	

Responsibilities:

ACCOMPLISHMENTS (FROM EXERCISE 7 on page 49)

1)

2)

3)

Résumé Worksheet: Chronological (page 2)

WORK HISTORY
Company Name:
City, State:
Dates: From: To:
Job Title:
Responsibilities:

ACCOMPLISHMENTS (FROM EXERCISE 7 on page 49)
1)
2)
3)

EDUCATION
School Name:
City, State:
Graduation Date: Degree:

OTHER ITEMS
Foreign Language: Level of Proficiency:
Community Service:
Professional Memberships:
Professional Licenses:

MISCELLANEOUS AREAS OF ACCOMPLISHMENT THAT SUPPORT YOUR CAREER OBJECTIVE

You need to complete three work history and accomplishment sections. Make a copy of this page to complete the worksheet in full.

Résumé Worksheet: Functional

Name:	
Street:	
City, State, Zip Code:	
E-mail:	

CAREER OBJECTIVE

SUMMARY STATEMENT

ACCOMPLISHMENTS (FROM EXERCISE 7 on page 49)

Name of Functional Grouping:

1)
2)
3)

ACCOMPLISHMENTS (FROM EXERCISE 7)

Name of Functional Grouping:

1)
2)
3)

ACCOMPLISHMENTS (FROM EXERCISE 7)

Name of Functional Grouping:

1)
2)
3)

Résumé Worksheet: Functional (page 2)

WORK HISTORY
Company Name:
City, State:
Dates: From: To:
Job Title:
Job Title:
Company Name:
City, State:
Dates: From: To:
Job Title:
Job Title:
Company Name:
City, State:
Dates: From: To:
Job Title:
Job Title:

EDUCATION
School Name:
City, State:
Graduation Date: Degree:

OTHER ITEMS
Foreign Language: Level of Proficiency:
Community Service:
Professional Memberships:
Professional Licenses:

MISCELLANEOUS AREAS OF ACCOMPLISHMENT THAT SUPPORT YOUR CAREER OBJECTIVE

Résumé Worksheet: Combination

Name:
Street:
City, State, Zip Code:
E-mail:

CAREER OBJECTIVE

SUMMARY STATEMENT

ACCOMPLISHMENTS (FROM EXERCISE 7 on page 49)

Name of Functional Grouping:

1)
2)
3)

ACCOMPLISHMENTS (FROM EXERCISE 7)

Name of Functional Grouping:

1)
2)
3)

ACCOMPLISHMENTS (FROM EXERCISE 7)

Name of Functional Grouping:

1)
2)
3)

Résumé Worksheet: Combination (page 2)

WORK HISTORY
Company Name:
City, State:
Dates: From: To:
Job Title:
Responsibilities:
Company Name:
City, State:
Dates: From: To:
Job Title:
Responsibilities:

EDUCATION
School Name:
City, State:
Graduation Date: Degree:

OTHER ITEMS
Foreign Language: Level of Proficiency:
Community Service:
Professional Memberships:
Professional Licenses:

MISCELLANEOUS AREAS OF ACCOMPLISHMENT THAT SUPPORT YOUR CAREER OBJECTIVE

You need to complete three work history sections. Make a copy of this page to complete the worksheet in full.

Networking Contact Sheet

Contact Name:	Classification A/B/C:

GENERAL INFORMATION

Company Name:	Phone Number:
Mailing Address:	Fax Number:
	Internet Address:
	Secretary's Name:
Date of Advice Meeting:	Date to mail thank-you letter:
Location of Advice Meeting:	Telephone follow-up data:

INDUSTRY INFORMATION

Strengths, Weaknesses, Potential Threats:

COMPANY INFORMATION

Strengths, Weaknesses, Potential Threats:

ADVICE/FEEDBACK FROM CONTACT

REFERRAL NAMES

Name:	Company:	Phone #:
Name:	Company:	Phone #:
Name:	Company:	Phone #:

MY GENERAL IMPRESSION	ADDITIONAL FOLLOW-UP ACTIVITIES

Phone Interview Form

Date:	Interviewer's Name:
Company:	Direct phone number:

GENERAL NOTES

MY QUESTIONS

How would you describe this position's ideal candidate?

Where would I be able to make the most immediate and valuable contributions?

What are the department's/organization's biggest current challenges?

Post-Interview Report Form

Company Name:	Date of Interview:
	Date of thank-you mailing:
Address:	
Inteviewer's Name:	Telephone Number:
Information about the Interview:	

Evaluation
1—Needs Improvement; 2—Was Okay; 3—Outstanding

	1	2	3
My appearance was very professional during the interview	1	2	3
I was composed and acted confident	1	2	3
I showed a good knowledge of the company and industry	1	2	3
I asked well-thought-out questions regarding the company	1	2	3
I did not answer questions too quickly	1	2	3
My answers lasted no more than 30 to 90 seconds.	1	2	3
I showed enthusiasm and displayed a "can do" attitude.	1	2	3
I was honest, authentic, and genuine throughout the interview	1	2	3
I did all of my interviewing prework.	1	2	3
Overall, I did very well in this interview	1	2	3

ISSUES THAT MOST INTERESTED THE INTERVIEWER:

Weekly Plan

Monday					
Research	Networking	Answering Ads	Employment Agencies	Mailings	Internet

Tuesday					
Research	Networking	Answering Ads	Employment Agencies	Mailings	Internet

Wednesday					
Research	Networking	Answering Ads	Employment Agencies	Mailings	Internet

Thursday					
Research	Networking	Answering Ads	Employment Agencies	Mailings	Internet

Friday					
Research	Networking	Answering Ads	Employment Agencies	Mailings	Internet

Saturday					
Research	Networking	Answering Ads	Employment Agencies	Mailings	Internet

Sunday					
Research	Networking	Answering Ads	Employment Agencies	Mailings	Internet

Other things to do or to keep in mind this week:

Job Offer Evaluation Matrix

Vocational Identity Factors	Importance (Multiplier 1-4)	Current Job or Last Job	Job Offer 1	Job Offer 2
Life's Purpose				
Career Objective				
Vocational Personality/Job Fit				
Treasure-Yielding Skills				
Accomplishment Skills				
Other Skills				
Personal Values				
Work Values				
Lifestyle—Travel				
Lifestyle—Location				
Lifestyle—Commute				
Company Culture				
My Boss				
Other Company Issues				
Other Factor				
Other Factor				
Subtotal				

Rate items on the following scale: 1—Very Inadequate; 2—Inadequate; 3—Adequate; 4—Very Adequate; 5—Ideal

Job Offer Evaluation Matrix (page 2)

Financial Factors	Importance (Multiplier 1-4)	Current Job or Last Job	Job Offer 1	Job Offer 2
Base Salary				
Bonus				
Stock Options				
Deferred Compensation				
Benefits				
Vacation				
Relocation				
Job Finding Services for Spouse				
Other Perks				
Club Memberships, etc.				
Other				
Subtotal—Page 1				
Subtotal—Page 2				
TOTAL				

Rate items on the following scale: 1—Very Inadequate; 2—Inadequate; 3—Adequate; 4—Very Adequate; 5—Ideal

APPENDIX

B

SAMPLE RÉSUMÉS

Chronological Résumé
Customer Service Representative

John Hunt
1234 Some Boulevard
My Town, My State 33333
444-555-9876

SUMMARY A reliable and responsible team player with excellent organizational and leadership skills seeking an opportunity to contribute prior experience and demonstrated hard work.

PROFESSIONAL BACKGROUND

July 1993 to Present **WE SHIP IT!, INC.,** *Winter Park, Florida*
Packing and shipping company

Manager—Responsible for overall store management. Responsibilities include customer service, quotes, bookkeeping, and proper packaging and shipping of a wide variety of items as well as supervising personnel.

- Implemented a customer satisfaction policy that increased customer satisfaction by 70% and sales by 15%.

- Redesigned company bookkeeping procedures, which resulted in an efficiency increase.

July 1990 to July 1993 **PROFESSIONAL SHIPPING,** *Orlando, Florida*
Packing and shipping company

Shipping and General Clerk—Duties included high-volume packing and shipping as well as heavy data entry. Involved in fast-paced invoicing and answering phones as well as filing and sorting of numerous items.

- Redesigned and solely implemented a new packaging process for my department that improved completion time by approximately 25%.

EDUCATIONAL BACKGROUND

Winter Park High School, Winter Park, Florida—1993

Chronological Résumé
Personal Banking Officer

Joan Hunt
1234 Some Boulevard
My Town, My State 33333
444-555-9876

Summary

A goal-oriented individual dedicated to meeting company and client needs. A solid list of accomplishments from eleven years of experience. Particular strengths include:

- Strong organizational skills
- Exceptional communication skills
- Expertise in selling bank products
- Extensive knowledge in deposit and loan products

Experience

SunTrust Bank, N.A.   1986—Present
Atlanta, Georgia

Personal Banking Officer—Responsible for obtaining new accounts, loans and meeting sales goals set forth by management. Maintain client relationships by resolving problems using win/win negotiating skills. Lead branch in loan campaigns. Provide back-up support to safe deposit and SunService Manager.

- Ranked number one personal banker in peer group for 1996 with highest dollar amount in commissions and $4.3 million in new money.
- Reduced annual supply expenses by 16% while in charge of branch ordering.
- Exceeded company set goal for investment referrals by 53%.
- Generated 257 credit card applications exceeding bank goal by 162%.
- Nominated by market manager for Personal Banker of the Year in 1996.
- Devised system to more accurately process stop payments on line of credit checks; reduced processing time by 50%.

Education
B.A.—Business Administration, Emory University, Atlanta, Georgia—May 1997

Changing to a Training and Development Professional

John Hunt
1234 Some Boulevard
My Town, My State 33333
444-555-9876
jbhunt@aol.com

Objective

To acquire a training and development position in the utility industry.

Summary

A bottom-line driven, highly energetic professional with fifteen years of utility experience and ten years of management experience. Numerous accomplishments demonstrate ability to train, lead, problem solve, and build lasting client relationships.

Work History

MACKINAW UTILITIES, *Mackinaw, Michigan*   *1983—PRESENT*

Supervisor—Responsible for customer service operations including leading others, coaching, employee training, performance appraisals, and cross-training employees.

- Improved customer service by decreasing the customer hold time from 5 minutes to less than 1 minute by redesigning the telephone prompts.

- Designed program for the meter readers that increased productivity by 40% by reducing field trips.

- Increased productivity and morale by implementing a program that generates ideas and involves all employees.

EDUCATION

B.S.—Organizational Communication, Saginaw Valley College, Saginaw, Michigan—1983

Restaurant Manager

JOHN HUNT
1234 Some Boulevard
My Town, My State 33333
444-555-9876

SUMMARY

A business-oriented professional with five years' sales and three years' management experience. A strong list of accomplishments that demonstrate abilities to lead, train, and problem solve.

EXPERIENCE

BRANDYWINE RESTAURANTS   **1994—Present**
Miami, Florida

General Manager—Responsible for all restaurant operations including leading others, coaching, management training, and general accounting.
- Improved employee morale and performance standards leading to an increase in sales of an average of 8% for 13 consecutive months.
- Earned bonus for 14 out of 16 months as general manager by initiating special training for managers and implementing systems that decreased costs by 12%.

FINANCIAL SERVICES, INC.   **1990—1993**
Jacksonville, Florida

Director of Marketing—Responsible for gaining new clients, writing and presenting proposals, and contract negotiation.
- Marketed new services to clients and prospects that increased revenue 27%.
- Increased speed and accuracy of data management by designing and implementing new electronic data transfer techniques.

RATEWISE CORPORATION   **1985—1989**
Jacksonville, Florida

Marketing Manager—Marketed services to prospects. Serviced and marketed diversified financial services to an existing client base.
- Implemented SPIN sales techniques and achieved an 89% revenue increase and delivered a $212,000 (107%) increase in profits.

Education
B.S.—Business Administration, Florida State University, Tallahassee, Florida—December 1984

Finance Manager Seeking Banking Career

JOHN HUNT
1234 Some Boulevard
My Town, My State 33333
444-555-9876

SUMMARY

A results-oriented professional who has high standards and a sense of team. More than twenty years of consumer credit and sales experience. Major strengths in the areas of business development, customer relations, training, credit evaluation, risk control, and leading people.

EXPERIENCE

REX HOWARD AUTOMOTIVE GROUP   1994—Present
Spokane, Washington

Finance Manager—Responsible for generating income through the sale of aftermarket products and insurance, qualifying consumer applications for credit purchases, maintaining relationships with lenders, providing executive reports of revenue generated by all departments, maintaining the computer database with current bank finance information, and training and motivating salespeople.

- Designed administrative procedures that reduced turnaround time for contracts in transit by 43%, thereby reducing variable expenses.
- Collected $750,000 of uncashed finance contracts in 60 days, which helped reduce a $2 million backlog of account receivables.

MARK WILLIAMS AUTOMOTIVE GROUP   1991—1994
Spokane, Washington

Finance Manager—Responsible for generating finance department income, qualifying consumer credit, building and maintaining lender relationships, and training and motivating salespeople.

- Increased finance income by more than 17% during a period of 14 months.
- Developed new finance strategies that helped to increase sales volume by 8%.

JOHN HUNT
Page 2

TRUST LIFE INSURANCE COMPANY   1990—1991
Spokane, Washington

Insurance Agent—(Debit Agent) Responsible for the sale of life, health, fire, and property insurance and for servicing and maintaining the insured's policies.

- Increased the debit size by 6% by reducing the lapsed policy ratio by over 28%.

ABC VEHICLE LEASING, INC.   1987—1990
Boston, Massachusetts

Regional Sales Manager—Responsible for roll-out of the Bank of New England's vehicle indirect leasing program in the target market areas of Orlando, Tampa, Jacksonville, and West Palm Beach, Florida.

- Enrolled more than 50 franchised new car dealers to originate leases on behalf of ABC Vehicle Leasing, Inc. These sources produced more than $10.8 million in volume.

COMMERCE NATIONAL BANK   1980—1987
Baltimore, Maryland

Senior Leasing/Office Manager—Responsible for introducing and operating the bank's indirect vehicle leasing program in New England. This involved administration of the office budget, managing the support staff, and maintaining and servicing the customer base.

- Provided leasing and credit expertise that resulted in the sign-up and development of more than 80 automotive dealer customers that produced in excess of $2 million per month in lease originations.
- Reduced credit card delinquency by 1.63% for $21 million in MasterCard outstandings while training and monitoring the activities of the 7 full-time and 10 part-time collectors.

EDUCATION
A.A. Liberal Arts, Essex Community College, Baltimore, Maryland—June 1978

Medical Practice Business Director

John Hunt
1234 Some Boulevard
My Town, My State 33333
444-555-9876

OBJECTIVE

Position as an administrator for a large medical practice, MSO, or IPA.

SUMMARY

A well-organized manager and administrator with experience in managing a multi-location medical practice and eight years of hospital experience within multi-hospital systems. Solid accomplishments in the following areas:

- Managed care strategy
- Contract negotiation
- Cost control
- Marketing and sales

- Finance
- Budget preparation
- Hospital contracting
- Staff management

EXPERIENCE

MEDICAL ASSOCIATES OF THE MIDWEST   1993—Present
Chicago, Illinois

Administrator—Manage and direct all nonclinical aspects of 12-physician, five-office group practice with special emphasis on strategic planning, managed care negotiations, marketing, and financial oversight.

- Managed the accounts receivable balance to an average of 50 days in accounts receivable.
- Recruited 2 new physicians and 4 nurse practitioners.
- Negotiated contracts with 17 HMOs.
- Saved $320,000 in premiums by changing physician life insurance policies.

MEDCARE, INC. (An HMO)   1993
Detroit, Michigan

Hospital Contracts Administrator—Planned, negotiated, and maintained all contracts with hospitals, hospital-based physicians, and skilled nursing facilities for this commercial and Medicare HMO. Responsible for negotiations with physician–hospital organizations.
- Organized and contracted capitated specialty networks in ophthalmology and orthopedics that covered three counties.

HEALTH CARE SOLUTIONS   1992—1993
Ann Arbor, Michigan

Consultant—Performed market assessment studies, developed provider networks, revenue recovery projects, and other consulting engagements in the managed care field.
- Gathered information to build the first capitated cardiology network in central Florida.

DOCTORS GENERAL HOSPITAL   1989—1992
Saginaw, Michigan

Special Projects Coordinator—Researched new product lines and services and conducted surveys, focus groups, and other marketing projects to determine feasibility and viability.
- Conducted review of all grants received by Doctors General and its affiliated hospitals and identified $1.2 million in uncharged expenses.

EDUCATION

Master of Business Administration—The University of Michigan, Ann Arbor, Michigan—May 1988
Master of Health Science, Health and Hospital Administration—The University of Michigan, Ann Arbor, Michigan—May 1985
B.A., Chemistry—University of Central Michigan, Mt. Pleasant, Michigan—June 1979

APPENDIX

C

SAMPLE COVER LETTERS

Response to Published Ad: Blind

1234 Some Boulevard
My Town, My State 33333

October 3, 199x

Human Resource Director
105 Treasure Street
Ideal Destination, TX 54321

Dear Human Resource Director:

I read your advertisement in the October 2 edition of the *Dallas Morning News* for a (the job title in ad) with great interest. I feel that my background and interests make me a strong candidate for such a position.

During the past seven years I have worked as both a project engineer and an engineering supervisor. I am seeking a new challenge and an opportunity to further my career growth as a manager of engineering. I have a solid list of accomplishments that demonstrate my willingness to work hard to make a difference. Here are two examples of recent contributions:

- Led a cross-functional project team that made process improvement changes that resulted in a 7% increase in plant efficiency.
- Redesigned manufacturing process that reduced error rates on the production line by 32%.

I welcome an opportunity to meet with you personally to better describe my abilities. I look forward to hearing from you soon.

Thank you for your careful consideration.

Sincerely,

John Hunt
444-555-9876

Enc. résumé

Response to Published Ad: Open

1234 Some Boulevard
My Town, My State 33333

October 3, 199x

Larry Powell
Vice President
Information Services
Next Employer, Inc.
105 Treasure Street
Ideal Destination, NY 54321

Dear Mr. Powell:

I am writing in response to your October 2 advertisement in the *New York Times*. I am very interested in the position of computer specialist.

Your advertisement caught my attention because my background seems to match the job's qualifications extremely well. As the advertisement required, I have a B.A. degree in computer science and I have two years of work experience with major computer languages, various types of software and tools, and with database management.

Next Employer, Inc.'s plans to open three new facilities in the next two years will require a committed effort from everyone in the Information Services group. The accomplishments listed in my enclosed resume demonstrate my history of making meaningful contributions. For example, last year I earned the highest customer service rating of any computer specialist in my company.

I hope you agree that my background and accomplishments make me an excellent match for this position. I would like to have an opportunity to meet you personally so that I could more fully describe my background and achievements.

Thank you for your consideration. I look forward to hearing from you.

Sincerely,

John Hunt
444-555-9876

Broadcast Letter

1234 Some Boulevard
My Town, My State 33333

October 3, 199x

Larry Powell
(Job Title)
Next Employer, Inc.
105 Treasure Street
Ideal Destination, CO 54321

Dear Mr. Powell:

If you have need for someone with a solid track record of performance as a (your profession or educational background), please consider some of my recent accomplishments (List several of your OAR Statements):

- Designed variable compensation program that reduced fixed costs and increased employee satisfaction.
- Implemented pre-employment testing program for sales personnel that increased sales by 9% in first year.
- Led successful labor agreement negotiations with the IBEW Union.
- Developed succession planning process that reduced the need for outside hires by 85% over five years.

I am confident that a personal interview would allow me to more fully demonstrate my ability to (your overall benefit to companies).

Thank you for your careful consideration.

Sincerely,

John Hunt
444-555-9876

Enc. résumé

Letter to employment agency

1234 Some Boulevard
My Town, My State 33333

October 3, 199x

Linda Powell
(Job Title)
Next Employer, Inc.
105 Treasure Street
Ideal Destination, GA 54321

Dear Ms. Powell:

I am seeking (your career objective) in the (list industries of interests if any) industry.

My eight years of administrative experience include three years as assistant to the president of a 500-person manufacturing company. I am a highly organized person with excellent written and oral communication skills. As you can see from my enclosed résumé, I have experience with word processing and spreadsheet software. I enjoy a fast-paced environment, and I am capable of managing multiple priorities.

I have enclosed my résumé for your review. If you can provide assistance to me in locating an administrative assistant position, please contact me at 444-555-9876.

Sincerely,

John Hunt

Follow-up letter after an advice and information networking meeting

1234 Some Boulevard
My Town, My State 33333

October 3, 199x

Linda Powell
(Job Title)
(Company Name)
105 Treasure Street
Ideal Destination, OR 54321

Dear Ms. Powell:

Thank you again for meeting with me on (date). I see why (the name of the person who referred you to this contact) thought I should talk to you. Your advice about my marketing plan and your insights about the (name of contact's industry) were extremely valuable.

I especially appreciate your suggestions regarding (mention one or two suggestions that the contact gave you). I will certainly incorporate these ideas into my marketing plan.

Once again, thank you. Of course, I would appreciate hearing of any opportunities that you believe fit my background and career objective. I will stay in touch and keep you updated regarding my progress.

Sincerely,

John Hunt
444-555-9876

Follow-up letter after a job interview

1234 Some Boulevard
My Town, My State 33333

October 3, 199x

Linda Powell
(Job Title)
(Company Name)
105 Treasure Street
Ideal Destination, MO 54321

Dear Ms. Powell:

Thank you for the opportunity to interview for the (job title). I enjoyed meeting you and learning more about the job and (company's name).

I felt strongly that my job skills and interests were a good match before my visit. Now that I know more about (the company's name) (something you learned during the interview), I am even more excited about the position.

I am confident that I can make significant contributions to (company's name). Again, thank you for the interview opportunity. I look forward to our next discussion.

Sincerely,

John Hunt
444-555-9876

Acceptance letter: Did receive offer letter

1234 Some Boulevard
My Town, My State 33333

December 2, 199x

Larry Powell
(Job Title)
Ideal Destination
105 Treasure Street
Ideal Destination, AZ 54321

Dear Mr. Powell:

This letter serves as my acceptance of your offer to join (name of company) as (job title). I accept all terms of your letter dated (offer letter's date).

I resigned (resignation date) from my current position at (name of company). They agreed to accept a four-week notice so I will be able to report to work on (start date) as you requested. I will contact the Human Resources department to schedule the mandatory drug screen and physical exam at the earliest date possible.

I appreciate the confidence you have shown in my abilities. I am excited about the future and eager to get started.

Sincerely,

John Hunt
444-555-9876

Acceptance letter: Did not receive offer letter

1234 Some Boulevard
My Town, My State 33333

December 2, 199x

Linda Powell
(Job Title)
Ideal Destination
105 Treasure Street
Ideal Destination, PA 54321

Dear Ms. Powell:

I am delighted to accept your offer to join (name of company) as (job title). As we agreed, my salary will be $xx,xxx.xx and my start date is (start date). I will receive three weeks of vacation and will be eligible this year for a prorated bonus.

I will inform (current company) of my acceptance of this offer as soon as you receive my letter. I am not sure about the specifics of my departure, but I should have no difficulty with the January 3 date. I will call you later this week to confirm your receipt of this letter. I will then contact the Human Resources department to schedule the mandatory drug screen and physical exam at the earliest date possible.

I am confident that I will make contributions to (company name). Thank you for all of your courtesy throughout this process. I am looking forward to fulfilling the trust you have placed in me.

Sincerely,

John Hunt
444-555-9876

APPENDIX

D

INTERVIEW PRACTICE QUESTIONS

THE MOST DIFFICULT INTERVIEW QUESTION OF ALL

1. So, please tell me a little about yourself.

What the interviewer wants to know—This may be the most common of all interview questions. It isn't at all clear what the interviewer is hoping to learn from this request; that is why this is one of the toughest of all interview questions. This question is asked most often by unprepared and untrained interviewers; I think the reason is because it's an easy way for the interviewer to begin the questioning. However, if you're unprepared, it could be anything but easy for you.

Your basic strategy—Good news! If you created a verbal ad in Chapter 7, you're almost completely prepared for this one. The 30-second verbal advertisement offers a very good way to respond to the interviewer's request. The only thing you'll need to add is a direct link to the company at the end of your statement.

Possible words to use—*Well, I have been blessed with a number of wonderful career experiences. During my six years of engineering experience, I've had the privilege of working as both staff engineer and supervising engineer. I've had a chance to work with a number of terrific people in both well-established plants and start-up situations. Through those experiences, I've certainly learned a lot about engineering. But more important, I've learned how to work effectively as part of a team while meeting business goals. For example, I created a cross-functional project*

team that increased our plant's overall productivity by 7 percent. I'm currently seeking an opportunity to use my experiences in a position as a supervisor of engineering. This career objective is what has led me to (the name of the company).

HOW WELL DO YOU GET ALONG WITH OTHERS?

2. Who is the worst boss you've ever had? What did he or she do that made you feel this way?

What the interviewer wants to know—This is not a question about one of your former bosses. The interviewer is concerned that you may not work well within the organization's structure or that you may have a difficult time accepting direction from others. And here's an unfair, but true, fact: any negative comment about a former boss can be interpreted as a failing of yours. For example, if you say "my boss wouldn't give me enough responsibility," the interviewer may wonder if you were unable to handle important decisions. If you say "My boss was always arguing with me," the interviewer may wonder why you can't get along with your superiors.

Your basic strategy—Case 1: If you're one of the fortunate few who have really never had a poor boss, just say so. Be sure to indicate that you recognize how fortunate you are to be able to reply like this. **Case 2:** If, on the other hand, you've had one or more poor bosses, do NOT dwell on the negatives. Indicate that things were not awful (no matter what, they could have been much worse), briefly and objectively comment about the boss, and leave it at that. Regardless of your feelings about the boss, respond calmly, not emotionally. Most important, show that the difficulty with a former boss is not part of a pattern of your behavior. You can do this by finishing your answer by describing the good relationships you've had with other managers.

Possible words to use—Case 1: *I'm one of the very fortunate people in this world because I can truly say that I've never had a bad boss. I know I'm lucky, but I've always had great respect for and good relationships with all of my supervisors.*

Case 2: *Like most people, I had one boss who was a little difficult. We had a few philosophical differences, but we always managed to get the work done and keep the customers happy. Fortunately, all my other bosses have been fantastic. I've had a number of supervisors who have helped me grow in my career, treated me fairly, and given me a great deal of credit for my work.*

3. How would your current/former colleagues describe you?

What the interviewer wants to know—Some interviewers simply want to learn more about your public reputation. Frankly, this question is so transparent that almost everyone says something to the effect of "Oh, they all think I'm wonderful." Truly savvy interviewers ask this question for a slightly different reason. They want to know how insightful you are about yourself. In other words, do you really know yourself and how others perceive you?

Your basic strategy—As with all questions, be honest and genuine; but at the same time put your best foot forward. Review your Vocational Identity Summary, and select one to three of your strengths. You may want to mention one strength that others may perceive as somewhat unfavorable but the employer will find desirable. This will show that you understand yourself and how others might view you and provide another selling point in your favor.

Possible words to use—*I believe my work colleagues would say that I'm very hardworking, honest, and very creative. I'm such a perfectionist when it comes to my work, however, that they might say I'm a little too hard on myself sometimes.*

4. When you encounter conflict with others, how do you handle it?

What the interviewer wants to know—The interviewer may be after any or all of three things; one obvious, two not so obvious. First, the interviewer indeed wants to learn what you do when you encounter conflict: how do you react, how do you handle it, and so forth. Second, the interviewer is listening for subtle clues as to how often you have difficulties getting along with others and if you are a source of difficult personal relationships. Third, the interviewer may wish to evaluate your ability to successfully resolve conflict.

Your basic strategy—I assume that you can honestly indicate that you seldom encounter interpersonal conflict. Describe the importance of listening to others and the role understanding others' perspectives plays in avoiding the creation of conflict. Next, describe a real situation where you encountered and addressed a conflict that ultimately led to a positive outcome.

Possible words to use—*I don't experience a lot of conflict. I believe that listening to others and understanding their point of view before I present my perspective helps me avoid a lot of tough situations. Like everyone else, I have seen conflict at work, though. I once worked with a woman who was talking behind my back and was trying to undermine my relationships with other workers. I had received a promotion that I knew she had wanted badly. I sat down with her and described what I had seen. I showed her one of the memos she had written that contained some false information about me. I then told her that it was important that we work it out because we both needed to focus on our jobs for the good of the company and for our careers. Although she became a little angry at first, I just listened. It was like she just needed to get it off her chest. We agreed to discuss any differences we had with each other before we aired them elsewhere. And here's the best part: Not only did we end up working the business part out; today I'd call her a friend.*

YOUR WORK HISTORY AND YOUR CURRENT SITUATION

5. You've changed jobs a lot in a very short period of time. Is this a reflection of how long you will stay with us?

What the interviewer wants to know—The company is considering investing a lot of money in you, and it wants to know if you will stay long enough to provide a return on that investment. Changing companies fairly often is much more common today than in the past. In fact, some career experts now suggest carefully planned "job hopping" as a wise career management strategy.

Your basic strategy—The two main objectives you must accomplish are to provide a rationale for your career movement and to demonstrate that you're a wise investment. **Case 1**—If you've always moved for increased pay and/or responsibility, your task is fairly easy. **Case 2**—However, if your career path is erratic, you'll have to address this head-on. In both cases, if your skills and experiences prepare you to hit the ground running, explain that you will be adding benefit almost immediately after you start. Finally, assuming that it's true, express that you desire to find a position and a company that you can stay with for some time.

Possible words to use—**Case 1:** *My career is very important to me. I focus on performance that delivers results. Because of my track record, I've been given the opportunity to move to a number of positions, each one providing more responsibility and rewards. This varied experience and my commitment to hard work to deliver results means that I will require very little start-up training and will begin making contributions immediately. I really want to find a company that will allow me to make important contributions and to grow within the organization.*

Case 2: *My career is very important to me. I must admit that I've had some difficulty in the past clarifying my career objective. Although I've always delivered results, I've tried a number of different* *things looking for the best place to make significant contributions. Recently, I've gone through a lot of self-assessment, looked at my interests, skills, abilities, and talents, and explored a number of options—and I've done a lot of soul-searching as well (Part 1 of this book). Now I'm confident that I know where I want to head with my career. I truly believe that my varied experience and my commitment to hard work and results mean that I will require very little start-up training and that I can begin making contributions immediately. I really want to find a company that will allow me to make important contributions and to grow within the organization.*

6. Why do you want to leave your current employer?

What the interviewer wants to know—The interviewer wants to learn three things. First, are you leaving because you can't get along interpersonally with others? Second, are you leaving because you have to—that is, they've asked you to leave? Third, is your desire to change capricious, or do you have a rationale for moving on? Obviously, failure to get along with others, being asked to leave, or changing jobs just for the sake of changing jobs does not bode well for your job prospects.

Your basic strategy—This can be a very tough question. If you're unhappy, I mean *really* unhappy, this can be an extraordinarily difficult question. No one leaves a job that's just right. Undoubtedly you're seeking a different position for a reason. If you're angry about whatever this reason is, your anger may show when you respond, regardless of your words. This is

the first major point in answering this question: You must not let your emotions get out of hand when you respond. The second point is this: Do not spend time focusing on the negative or whining about how unfair things are. True or not, it does your job candidacy harm, maybe mortal harm. Here are some reasons for leaving that you *can* talk about: seeking more responsibility or money, wanting a new location, looking for new challenges, wanting to find a position that allows for more professional growth, or wanting to work for a bigger, better-known, or more prestigious company.

Possible words to use—*I like a lot of what I do in my current position. I've had the opportunity to learn a number of things and to achieve some accomplishments that I am quite proud of. I just believe that it's time for me to look for new challenges. I'd like to find a position that provides more responsibility and that will allow me to continue growing professionally.*

7. What would you do if . . .

What the interviewer wants to know—Interviewers often ask candidates to describe how they would react to some given hypothetical situation. These situational questions usually pose some dilemma that you must analyze and then choose a course of action to resolve. This type of question can cover a nearly limitless number of hypothetical situations. The interviewer is trying to determine if you have a sufficient experience base to draw upon and if you exercise good judgment.

Your basic strategy—First, do not answer too quickly. It's important that you take a few seconds to think through the described situation. Second, make sure you understand the question. You may want to rephrase and then repeat the question to the interviewer. You can start your rephrased question with, "Let me make sure I understand your question," or "What I heard you ask was. . .Is that correct?" Third, think back over your career and see if you've had a very similar experience. Perhaps one of your OAR accomplishment statements will address a similar situation. Nothing provides a more powerful response to a hypothetical question than a real-world example. Fourth, if (and only if) you have no idea how you might address the hypothetical situation, you might say that you would seek counsel with your peers, team, or boss before acting. You may not feel that seeking advice is a strong demonstration of your abilities, but it certainly beats a response that shows very poor judgment.

Possible words to use—*Let me make sure I understand your question. (State your rephrase of the interviewer's question.)* (Interviewer: *Yes, that's it.) That's a very interesting situation. I faced a similar challenge (or situation, problem, dilemma) when I was with Acme. Here's what I did (describe your actions). If possible—Indeed, I feel like it led to one of my best accomplishments (say one of your OAR statements).*

8. What are your three greatest strengths as an employee?

What the interviewer wants to know—This is one of the most common questions asked by interviewers. The interviewer simply wants to learn the ways you can add value to the organization in the future.

Your basic strategy—Most people respond with a short laundry lists of attributes. While this response is fine, if you would like to provide a more compelling case, build your response around one of your OAR accomplishment statements. Select an OAR statement that required you to use three or more of your strongest attributes. List these attributes for the interviewer, and then provide the OAR statement as an example of how they delivered benefit to a former employer.

Possible words to use—*First, I'm a very hard worker. I pay great attention to detail. And I'm good at coming up with very creative solutions to problems. I've used these strengths many times to deliver business results. For example, (say OAR accomplishment statement) in my last job I suggested and implemented new ideas in purchasing that resulted in reducing the amount of time in processing orders by 50 percent.*

9. What are your three greatest weaknesses as an employee?

What the interviewer wants to know—The interviewer wants to know two things: First, whether you have any weaknesses that would keep you from succeeding in this job or at this company. Second, he or she is looking to find out if you're a forthcoming, honest person. If you say "I don't have any weaknesses," either you possess little personal insight or you're lying. Obviously, neither of these two interpretations does your prospects any good.

Your basic strategy—Again, start with your strengths. Identify your three greatest strengths.

While these are your best selling features, all strengths are weaknesses in certain contexts. You'll need to be honest in your response, but at the same time accentuate the positive. The example below uses the three strengths from question 8 above. CAUTION: Be prepared to provide concrete examples of these weaknesses. The interviewer may very well follow up with "Can you give me an example of when this was so?" Finding an acceptable example should be very easy as long as what you're saying is true and accurate.

Possible words to use—*Well, my three greatest weaknesses relate to my three greatest strengths. As I said, I'm a very hard worker. However, at times I have to really work at keeping a balance in my life and not spending all my time at work. Second, while I like to pay attention to detail, I can become frustrated with others if they seem not to care about dotting all the i's and crossing all the t's. And third, while I've had some great success with creative ideas, occasionally I haven't been able to make them work. Then I've had to work doubly hard to come up with another solution.*

Your basic strategy—This is another one of those questions that allows you to really shine, if you link your marketable job skills (Chapter 4) and your values (Chapter 3) with the results of your market research (Chapter 8). You should only answer this question after you have a good idea about the job's requirements. If the interviewer has yet to detail the requirements, you should say something like, "What I know so far is very appealing, but I'd like to know more about the job before I answer. Could you please briefly outline the job's requirements and the qualifications needed?"

Possible words to use—*First of all, I'm excited about how well this position's responsibilities match my experience and my skills and abilities. My strong technical skills, attention to detail, and creativity will allow me to make important contributions. Also, I'm impressed that (Company's name—and at least one positive thing learned in your research) Acme is the leader in ABC technology. The company has a strong reputation in terms of customer service and honesty, and this fits my values very well.*

WHY DO YOU WANT TO WORK HERE?

10. What appeals to you about this position?

What the interviewer wants to know—The interviewer is curious about your level of understanding regarding the job's requirements and the company. He or she also is trying to determine how well you fit with the job and the company.

11. What do you know about our company?

What the interviewer wants to know—It's pretty simple: The interviewer wants to know if you did your homework.

Your basic strategy—"Thank you, thank you, thank you," should be your first thought when you hear this question. Because you've done the market research in Chapter 8 and prepared a company profile describing this company, you're going to stand head and shoulders above the other job candidates vying for this position. In about one minute, you can demonstrate that you are a person who does his or her homework.

Possible words to use—*I've learned that (Company's name—then a sentence or two from the Company Profile summary). You were founded in (date of founding) by (founder's name). Your main customers include (largest customers and/or types of customers). The current (CEO or Owner) is (name). Last year the company's revenues were (financial performance in dollars). There are (number of employees). One of the things I found most appealing was in your mission statement. You state that (something you found interesting from the mission statement).*

12. So, do you have any questions you'd like to ask me?

What the interviewer wants to know—Often the interviewer doesn't want to know anything and only extends this question as a courtesy. In other cases, the interviewer is checking to see if you know how to gather and analyze information when making important decisions.

Your basic strategy—In either case you should always ask at least one very good question. Even if this is the eighth interview of the day, never say, "No, I think you've covered about everything." This question provides the opportunity to learn some key things about the organization. Equally important, because this question usually signals that the interviewer has come to the end of the questioning, you can leave a final strong impres-

sion: You are a person who makes good decisions because you gather all the relevant facts. Of course, you should ask for further explanation of any items that you feel need further elaboration. Additionally, you should ask at least one or two questions from the list below, first provided in Chapter 10.

Possible words to use—*Yes, I do have a question (or a couple of questions). Why is this position open? How much overnight travel is involved? To whom will I report? What is the career path? May I meet those with whom I would be working? How do the responsibilities of this position fit into the company's overall strategy? What are the biggest challenges facing this organization over the next three years? How could I best make an immediate contribution? How is employee performance measured? What are the biggest advantages of working for this organization? Are there any disadvantages? What is the company's employee turnover record?*

WELCOME TO THE HOT SEAT

13. Have you ever been fired or asked to resign?

What the interviewer wants to know—This can be one of the toughest questions to handle. The interviewer may already know the answer to this question. If so, this may be more of an integrity test than anything else. If he or she doesn't already know, then the interviewer is looking for personality flaws or patterns of poor behavior that suggest you will not succeed in the future.

Your basic strategy—You need to tell the truth, put the best spin possible on it, be brief, and move on. Above all, do not become emotional, don't blame others (even if they deserve it), and don't look shocked if the interviewer asks this question.

Possible words to use—Case 1: *No.*

Case 2: *I was one of (number of people) 350 people who lost their job as part of a corporate restructuring/downsizing effort.*

Case 3: *When I was with Acme, my boss and I had a philosophical (or strategic or business) difference of opinion, and we both agreed that it was best for me to move on.*

Case 4: *Yes. I made some mistakes. I was unsure about my career direction, and didn't focus my attention on my job the way I should have. I've learned from my mistakes, and now I'm sure about what I want to do. I'm looking for an opportunity to move my career forward and to give a company 100 percent of my effort for that chance.*

14. If your boss asks you to do something that you believe is wrong, what would you do?

What the interviewer wants to know—The interviewer is trying to learn if you are willing to take direction even if you don't like what you've been asked to do.

Your basic strategy—You must show that you understand that you need to do what your supervisor asks but not appear as though you are an unthinking robot. In today's flatter organizations, everyone needs to provide input into decision making.

Possible words to use—*Well, I would certainly express my opinion. I'd try to make a case for my point of view and provide information or data that supports it. In the end, if I could not persuade my boss of my point of view, I would do it his or her way. But I'd try to gain agreement that we would reevaluate the situation after a short while to see how well it was working.*

15. Can I call your references?

What the interviewer wants to know—The interviewer wants to know if you're what you appear to be. Sometimes this question is used just to see if you remain confident about the things you've said in the interview. The good news is that employers do not go to the trouble of actually checking references unless they are very interested in you. The bad news is that a reference can undermine your candidacy in the eleventh hour.

Your basic strategy—Of course, you should reply yes. It is vitally important that you've taken the steps described in Chapter 7 to prepare your references before they are contacted. If you've prepared your references and know how they will respond, you can confidently give these names to your interviewer. Additionally, it's perfectly acceptable for you to request that the interviewer not contact anyone at your current place of employment because of your concern about confidentiality.

Possible words to use—*Yes, of course you can contact my references. For reasons of confidentiality, I would ask that you don't contact anyone at my current employer until after I begin work.*

16. Why have you been out of work so long?

What the interviewer wants to know—Here's the unfair reality: The longer you're out of work, the less appealing you will be to some employers. Yes, unfair—but true.

Your basic strategy—Most important, you cannot show a lack of confidence if asked this question. Be prepared to respond calmly and with honesty. **Case 1:** If you've been out of work for several months, but just started looking, say so. **Case 2:** If you've looked for several months and received a couple of offers, but determined they weren't right for you, say so. **Case 3:** If you've been looking for some time, but received no offers, let the interviewer know that you're selective and looking for a good fit for your skills and background.

Possible words to use—Case 1: *Well, I didn't start looking for work immediately. The truth is, I took some time off to reevaluate my career and I've just started looking.*

Case 2: *Well, I've been offered a couple of positions, but they just weren't right. I'm highly selective and I want my next job to be a great opportunity for me to use my skills and to grow professionally. That's why I'm especially interested in this position. (Be prepared to tell the interviewer which companies offered you what kind of positions; he'll probably ask.)*

Case 3: *Well, I'm not looking for just any job, I'm looking for the right job. The right job is one that allows me to use my years of experience and my skills and abilities to make significant contributions to an organization. That's why I'm especially interested in this position.*

DO YOUR PERSONALITY AND WORK STYLE FIT OUR NEEDS?

17. How would you describe your ideal job?

What the interviewer wants to know—The interviewer wants to learn if your expectations, interests, and motivations match this job and this organization. The employer assumes, and rightly so, that if this job doesn't match these factors, you will not stay highly motivated, and will soon seek other employment.

Your basic strategy—Describe your ideal job. Yes, you may show that you don't fit. But discovering that you don't fit is a win for both you and the employer. Describe the aspects of your ideal job that allow you to use your best strengths and talents.

Possible words to use—*I'm looking for a job that allows me to use my job skills and other strengths. (Describe strengths) I'm very hardworking, value honesty, have a very good technical background, and enjoy creative problem solving. In my ideal job, I will be given increasing responsibilities and decision making latitude so that I can grow in these areas and learn from others.*

18. What do you like most/least about your current/former job?

What the interviewer wants to know—The thing you like least about your current job may be an important part of this job. If so, you obviously will be unhappy here as well.

Your basic strategy—Again, start by selecting one of your strengths. Almost certainly, some factor that keeps you from freely exercising one of your strengths is one of the things you like least about your current job. By describing this factor, you provide a reasonable rationale for why you would want to leave your current employer. At the same time, you showcase one of your best selling features.

Possible words to use—*I'm a person who likes to pay attention to detail. In my current situation, we often focus on quantity more than quality and, frankly, it's uncomfortable for me to let details go unattended.*

19. What is it that you like least about your current/former company?

What the interviewer wants to know—The interviewer is testing to see if you have a tendency to complain or if you're the cynical type that causes everyone around you to feel negative.

Your basic strategy—Throughout the interview, show an upbeat, positive, and confident attitude. When asked this question, describe others in your current/former company who didn't look out after the company's best interest.

Possible words to use—*Some of the people at my company don't seem to understand that we're in a business and that we have to make a profit. They seem to have developed an entitlement mentality as if someone owed them something. They take their benefits for granted, misuse their sick days, and in general just don't seem to care. That really bothers me.*

LET'S TALK ABOUT MONEY

20. The salary you're requesting is outside of range.

What the interviewer wants to know—The interviewer may want to pay you more but feels his or her hands are tied by the salary ranges defined by personnel. As discussed in Chapter 12, maintaining internal equity is very important to the personnel department.

Your basic strategy—You cannot change the company's pay ranges, but you can explore other options. If you've already received a job offer (and you shouldn't be talking about money unless you have!), you know that the company wants you. Remind the interviewer of the benefits of hiring you by reiterating your desire to make significant contributions with your job skills and experience base. Ask the interviewer if he or she has ever been in this situation before. If so, how did they resolve it? Realize that a number of options exist: The company can move you to another job title with a different pay range; pay a sign-on bonus because this doesn't affect the range; move your performance review date forward, which will make you eligible for a pay raise more quickly; give you additional vacation at the three- or five-year level; or suggest a number of other potential solutions.

Possible words to use—*I appreciate the need to pay people consistently within the company. At the same time, I would like to be paid fairly according to the market value of my job skills. I am excited about this company and very much want to go to work making significant contributions to the business. Have you ever run into this issue before—where you wanted to hire someone but the salary they wanted was outside the pay range? How did you handle that situation?* Or simply ask: *What options are available other than my regular salary?* (You can also make suggestions from the list above.)

ILLEGAL QUESTIONS

What the interviewer wants to know—Title VII of the 1964 Civil Rights law makes it illegal for employers to discriminate based upon race, color, religion, sex, or national origin. In 1978, Congress passed the Age Discrimination in Employment Act (ADEA) which, among other things, prohibits age-based employment decisions for those over 40 years old. In 1990, the Americans with Disabilities Act (ADA) made failure to hire people with disabilities illegal unless they cannot perform the job with reasonable accommodation from the employer. The

questions per se are not illegal; however, using the information to make a hiring decision is. Of course, to avoid potential lawsuits and any misuse, any prudent employer will not ask questions that touch on these illegal issues. Some still do ask, however. In some cases, these issues are broached quite innocently in the course of discussion. Other times, however, the purpose is more insidious. These questions can make you feel very uncomfortable; but if you react too strongly, you may spoil your job prospects.

Your basic strategy—You'll have to decide if a question is so distasteful that you don't care whether or not you get a job offer. If so, you can always pick up your things and go home. If you're very uncomfortable with the question but want to continue the interview, you might say something like, "I prefer to keep personal matters such as this to myself." In most cases, however, a short answer that directly addresses the interviewer's question and then quickly returns to a focus on your skills will allow you to "move on" in the interview. You can judge the interviewer's intent after you get back home and have time to reflect on the experience. You can always refuse a job offer, of course. Below are several different ways interviewers sometimes get at the issues covered by Title VII, ADEA, and ADA legislation.

Race/National Origin: *"Say, is that an (Italian, Russian, African) name?" "What is your native language?"* or *"Where were your parents born?"*

Possible words to use—**Case 1**: Just smile and answer very briefly, *"Yes," "Spanish,"* or *"In Poland."* **Case 2**: Smile and say, *"I don't see how that pertains to my qualifications. I'd really* *like to stay focused on my qualifications for this particular job and my abilities to make contributions to the company."*

Religion: *"Do you believe in God?" "Where do you worship?" or "We're a (Seventh Day Adventist, Mormon, Baptist) company. How do you think you'd fit in here?"*

Possible words to use—Case 1: Smile and say, *"Yes, I do," "I worship at the (ABC synagogue, XYZ church),"* and *"I'm sure I would get along very well in this environment."*

Case 2: *I have a strong set of values and beliefs, but I don't attend an organized religious service. I'm sure that I can get along very well in this environment.*

Case 3: *I have a strong set of values and beliefs, but I like to keep them to myself. I'm sure that I can get along very well in this environment.*

Age: "How old are you?" or "What is your birth date?"

Possible words to use—Case 1: *February 28; I'm in my forties. One of the things that draws me to this position is the opportunity to fully utilize my 16 years of experience.*

Case 2: *Old enough to have learned from my mistakes, and young enough to bring considerable energy to work every day!*

Case 3: *"I'd rather not say," or "It's none of your business," or "That's an illegal question."* Then leave.

Disabilities: Do you have any disabilities we should know about?

Possible words to use—Case 1: *No.*

Case 2: *I'm certain I can do the job.*

APPENDIX

E

JOB SEARCH RESOURCES

Research Resources: Publications

ABI/Inform—Updated monthly, this source is an index to more than 1,000 business journals. This index covers a wide range of industries and provides company-specific information including financial and geographical.

America's Corporate Families and International Affiliates—This two-volume work describes information for more than 11,000 parent companies and their affiliates. There are 55,000 companies included in Volume 1; Volume 2 (multinational) provides additional information on 23,000 companies.

Business Organizations, Agencies & Publications Directory—Approximately 25,000 organizations are contained in the directory, which lists company names, addresses, and contact names.

Career Guide to Industries—Published by the Bureau of Labor Statistics. Gives broad career information for forty industries, which account for about 70 percent of all wage and salary jobs.

D & B Industry Norms and Key Business Ratios (Library Code: HF5550.D73)—Provides industry normative information.

Directory of Directories (ISBN 0-8103-2508-X)—Edited by Cecilia A. Marolow and published by Gale Research, Inc., this 2,200-page work is invaluable for locating information sources.

Directories in Print—Another Gale Research publication.

Directory of Executive Recruiters (ISBN 1-885922-03-5)—Published annually by Kennedy Information, this work is *the* guide to working with headhunters. It profiles more than 3,000 firms, and describes their fees and typical clientele.

Dun's Business Rankings (Library Code: HG4057. A1D84)—This publication uses sales or employment size to rank major companies within SIC code.

Dun and Bradstreet's Million Dollar Directory (ISBN 1-56203-477-4)—Lists 40,000 U.S. companies worth $1 million or more. Corporate officers, products and services, and size of the employee population are included.

Dun's Census of American Business (Library Code: HA456.D8)—This publication provides statistical information about a company's sales and employee population size. The information is organized by SIC code and broken down to the county level.

Dun's Consultant Directory—More than 200 specialties and 25,000 consulting firms are covered by this work.

Encyclopedia of American Industries (Library Code: HD 9725.E5)—460 manufacturing and 544 service/nonmanufacturing industries are profiled. Industry and company overviews and trends are presented.

Encyclopedia of Associations (Library Code: AS8. E6)—This is a good source for locating professional associations. The work is a guide to more than 22,000 national nonprofit organizations. It describes their membership, size, and publications.

Encyclopedia of Business Information Sources (Library Code: HF5353.E9)—This work covers a very wide range of topics from business ethics to functionally specific information. In all, more than 1,100 topics are covered.

Encyclopedia of Careers and Vocational Guidance (Library Code: HF5381.E52)—Presented in four volumes, this encyclopedia is published by Rosen Publishing Group, Inc. It presents career articles, history of particular jobs, typical career paths, and resources for learning about training, internships, scholarships, and job placement.

Economic Census Publications (Library Code: HD202)—Presents SIC code statistics to assist in understanding current industry conditions and trends.

Forbes—"Annual Report on American Industry," published annually in the first January issue. The report covers more than 1,100 of the largest public companies in 20 major industry groups. The report ranks companies against their competitors, companies in similar or related industries, and all other companies.

Global Trade Outlook (Formerly U.S. Industrial Outlook)—Published annually by the U.S. Department of Commerce, it covers more than 200 industries. The "Trends and Analysis" section analyzes each industry.

Guide to American Directories—The guide lists and describes more than 6,000 directories.

Hoover's Handbook of American Business (Library Code: HG4057.H62)—This handbook provides one-page summaries on 500 major American companies.

INC. Magazine—"INC. 500 Fastest Growing Private Companies," published in the December issue.

International Directory of Company Histories (Library Code: HD 2721.I68)—This directory presents the histories of 1,250 large companies, both private and public. The information is provided by the companies themselves, compiled from periodicals and books and annual reports.

Job Hunter's Sourcebook (Library Code: HF5382.7.J62)—A comprehensive list of references in one volume. Provides information on sources for classified ads, placement services, handbooks, directories, and numerous other topics.

Market Share Reporter (Library Code: HF5415.2.M3)—By compiling statistics from periodicals, this annual publication presents market share information.

Moody's Industry Review—Provides statistics for approximately 3,500 companies arranged in 137 industry groups. The information is updated twice annually.

Moody's Investors Fact Sheets: Industry Review—Presented in loose-leaf form, this source arranges information into 140 industry groups. It contains key financial data and comparative statistics on about 4,000 companies.

Moody's Manuals—These manuals are invaluable resources describing many organizations in the U.S., Canada, and other countries. Histories, executives, financial performance, locations, and other factors are covered by the manuals.

Occupational Outlook Handbook—Published by the U.S. Department of Labor, this work provides information for specfic occupations including the nature of work, working conditions, employment statistics, qualifications, job outlook, and earnings.

Occupational Outlook Quarterly—Another Department of Labor publication, it is published four times a year and gives the how-tos about today's jobs and those of the future. It discusses training issues and salary trends.

Occupational Compensation Survey: Pay and Benefits—U.S. Department of Labor, Bureau of Labor Statistics.

Predicasts Basebook—This annual publication contains many industry statistics and economic indicators.

Predicasts Forecasts—This quarterly publication predicts both long- and short-range economic conditions for industries and products.

Predicasts F & S Index Plus—Like ABI/Inform, this is an index. However, this index focuses more on industrywide information and is a very valuable research tool. The print version will only give you citations to articles.

Standard & Poor's Industry Surveys (Library Code: HG4905.S74)—Presents industry overviews of 22 broad industry categories. The information is updated annually.

Standard & Poor's Register of Corporations—In this directory, more than 55,000 U.S. companies are presented in three volumes. Both public and private corporations are found here. Information on executives and directors, as well as other important information, is included.

Statistical Abstract of the United States (Library Code: HA202)—This work contains an enormous amount of statistical information, much of which pertains to industry.

The Company's Annual Report—Whenever possible, get a copy of the annual report. It contains valuable information regarding financial performance, values, key personnel, and much more.

The National JobBank (Library Code: HF5382.5. U5)—This series was first published by Adams Media Corporation in 1980. It provides company profiles and employment contact information for thousands of U.S. companies.

Thomas Register of American Manufacturers (Library Code: T12.A2T5)—This work describes over 150,000 manufacturers, their products and services, locations, company profiles, and trade and brand names.

U.S. Industrial Outlook—This is a good source for forecasting industry trends over the next three to five years.

Ward's Business Directory of U.S. Public and Private Companies—(Library Code: HG4057. A1W26)—Prepared by Gale Research Company, this annual ranks U.S. companies within their Standard Industrial Classification (SIC) code.

World Market Share Reporter (Library Code: HF5410.W67)—This is a compilation of global market share data from periodical literature. It ranks companies, products, and services.

Value Line Investment Surveys (Library Code: HG4501.V26)—This publication gives a brief analysis of 100 industries. In addition, company-specific data are included. This loose-leaf publication has weekly additions. Both industry and company data are updated quarterly with weekly additions.

Research Resources: Online (CD-ROM and Internet)

CD-ROM

ABI/Inform (CD-ROM)—This source is an index to more than 800 business journals. The index covers a wide range of industries and provides company-specific information including financial and geographical data.

Dun's Million Dollar Disc Plus (CD-ROM)— Along with providing information on more than 380,000 companies, this is a good source for gathering biographical information on executives.

Predicasts F & S Index Plus (CD-ROM)—Like ABI/Inform, this is an index. However, this index focuses more on industrywide information and is a very valuable research tool. The CD-ROM version provides full text of brief articles.

INTERNET

Search Engines

Alta Vista (http://www.altavista.digital.com)—I've personally had more success with the hard-to-find things with Alta Vista than with any other search engine. However, because it looks through the entire Internet, you'll need to be very specific in your search to limit the number of hits.

C/Net Search (http://www.search.com)—This is a great site! This search service uses more than 250 other search engines. You can access all 250 and search the entire Web by keyword or search by topic. For example, it lists 33 search engines for *employment*.

Excite (http://www.excite.com)—This engine allows browsing by subject through its Net Directory. Check out the Career & Education channel. It gives you access to more than 50 million Web pages, 140,000 preselected Web site listings, and thousands of Usenet postings.

HotBot (http://www.hotbot.com)—This is *Wired* magazine's search engine. The site lets you know that HotBot is the only search engine to receive both *PC Magazine*'s Editor's Choice award and the PC Computing MVP Finalist distinction. Once you get to the site, look under the Business heading and click on Careers. Also, take a look at the Help directory and click on Getting Started; it contains some good advice on limiting searches.

Lycos Home Page (http://www.lycos.com)—Lycos is known for finding arcane information. Its career section is worth taking a look at.

MetaCrawler (http://metacrawler.com)—This search service sends your queries to several Web search engines, including Lycos, Infoseek, WebCrawler, Excite, AltaVista, and Yahoo!. MetaCrawler organizes the results and sends them back to you in a uniform format. It is somewhat slower than other engines, but is more likely to obtain results than any single search engine operating on its own.

WhoWhere (http://www.whowhere.com)—I really like this site. Among many other things, it allows you to find people based upon past or current affiliations like schools, interest groups, and occupations and look up e-mail addresses, phone numbers, and addresses of more than 90 million U.S. residences. It also offers online yellow pages with geographic mapping. For your company research, check out WhoWhere's Companies Online. It claims to be "the most extensive worldwide directory of company whereabouts on the Net."

Yahoo! (http://www.yahoo.com)— A very well organized site. However, its information is more limited than some of the other search engines in this list. The reference area is useful, but you'll find the LDOL CareerNet Reference site easier to use. The

Business & Economy section is good for finding career and company information. Be sure to surf through the reference, professional organizations, and company directories.

Search Engine Links (http://www.wvonline.com/utc/search1.htm) You will find links here to most of the search engines listed above and many more.

Great Web Sites

100Hot (http://www.100hot.com)—Provides links to many of the best sites and lists many directories and companies.

AT & T Toll-Free 800 Directory (http://www.tollfree.att.net/)—You can look up toll-free numbers by company name or by category.

American Society of Associations Executives (ASAE) (http://www.asaenet.org/Gateway/OnlineAssocSlist.html)—Provides a searchable database, organized alphabetically, to many trade associations currently on the Web.

Associations on the Net (AON) (http://www.ipl.org/ref/AON/)—AON is a collection of more than 700 Internet sites. It provides information on many professional and trade associations, cultural and art organizations, political parties and advocacy groups, labor unions, academic societies, and research institutions.

BigBook (http://www.bigbook.com/)—Calling itself "a new kind of yellow pages," BigBook lets you search for any one of 16 million businesses by name, industry group, and/or geography. Along with company names and addresses, you can get a map, although these are sometimes outdated or do not have enough detail.

Bureau of Labor Statistics (www.stat.bls.gov/)—Searchable resources, surveys, and publications. This is a good place to learn about predictions regarding occupations' futures.

Business Week (http://www.businessweek.com/)—This site allows you to search back issues. Once you get to the home page, click Archives.

Business Sources on the Internet (http://www.simsbury.lib.ct.us/business.html)—This site provides many links to approximately 38 popular business and career sites.

Business Job Finder (http://www.cob.ohio-state.edu/dept/fin/osujobs.htm)—Maintained by the Fisher College of Business at Ohio State University, this site is designed to give you information on business careers. Along with listing jobs, it provides a variety of reference material. This is a good place to explore business career options.

BizWeb (http://www.bizweb.com)—Lists hundreds of companies indexed by product.

Catapult (http://www.jobweb.org/catapult/emplyer.htm)—A terrific site with many links to valuable job search, company, and industry information.

DataMasters—1997 Salary Survey (http://www.datamasters.com/dm/survey.html)—This is a good source for information about salaries in the computer industry.

EDGAR Database (http://www.sec.gov/edgarhp.htm)—EDGAR gathers, analyzes, and retrieves information submitted by companies and others who filed information with the U.S. Securities and Exchange Commission (SEC).

Forbes "Annual Report on American Industry" (http://www.forbes.com/forbes/archives/)—Appearing annually in the first January issue, the report covers more than 1,100 of the largest public companies in 20 major industry groups. The report ranks companies against their competitors, companies in similar or related industries, and all other companies.

Free Online Dictionary of Computing (http://wfn-shop.princeton.edu/foldoc/)

Global Trade Outlook (Formerly U.S. Industrial Outlook) (http://www.osha.gov/abstracts/sicser.html)—Published annually by the U.S. Department of Commerce, it covers more than 200 industries. The "Trends and Analysis" section analyzes each industry.

Hoover's Inc. (http://www.hoovers.com)—This is one of the best! An absolutely wonderful site for researching company information. Over 10,000 organizations are searchable by name, ticker symbol, location, industry, or sales. Gives a wealth of information.

IBM InfoMarket Service (http://www.infomarket.ibm.com/)—Contains a lot of detailed information on thousands of companies. This is a fee-for-service site. Unfortunately, it may take you longer to read through all the legalese set out in the user agreement than to find the information you need at another site.

INC. 500 Almanac (http://www.inc.com/incmagazine/archives/14950381.html)—Fully searchable.

Industrial Outlook (http://www.jobtrak.com/jobsearch_docs/indoutlk.html)—Published by the U.S. Government's Department of Labor, the Industrial Outlook "offers you a solid foundation on which to examine various industries and your career options." Includes global economic outlook.

JobSmart (http://www.jobsmart.org/tools/salary/salsurv.htm)—Contains information for more than 150 salary surveys from general surveys and profession-specific salary surveys. This site is updated regularly.

JobTrak College and University and Major Index (http://www.jobtrak.com/newsite/htdocs/emp/emp_index.shtml)—JobTrak is a very active site that receives more than 35,000 inquiries a day. This is a good place to review possible college majors (more than 450 listed) and learn more about educational opportunities.

LDOL CareerNet Reference (http://www.ldol.state.la.us/career1/HP_REFER.HTM)—The Louisiana Department of Labor has provided a lot of useful research information at this site: Search engines, directories, the Internet Public Library, a congressional-bill-tracking database, the ERIC, LOUIS, and CARL databases, and links to a number of really good sites.

Pencom Career Center (http://www.pencomsi.com/java_career.html)—Pencom gives you an interactive salary guide and career advice articles.

Mansfield University Cybrarian (http://www.mnsfld.edu/depts/lib/index.html)—Nicely laid out and easy to navigate, the Cybrarian offers a lot of online information including government documents, links to EDGAR, Hoovers, a number of Internet resources, and much more. A very good general research site.

National Yellow Pages (http://www.ypo.com)—Contains 18 million listings.

NewJour Archive (http://gort.ucsd.edu/newjour/)—You can use this site to locate journals online within your career field.

O-Net (http://www.o-net.org/index.html)—This site is still under construction (at the time of this writing). However, it is obvious that the consortium of government and private industry career experts putting it together may have quite something indeed when it's complete.

Occupational Outlook Handbook (http://stats.bls.gov/oco/oco1000.htm)—Fully searchable, this site describes the nature of the work, working conditions, employment statistics, qualification, job outlook, and earnings.

Occupational Outlook Quarterly (http://stats.bls.gov/empooq.htm)—You can order reprints and view topics, but at the time of this writing the publication cannot be read online.

Sales Leads USA (http:www.abii.com)—A truly wonderful site for conducting company research. Sponsored by American Business Information, you can find at least some information on almost any business in the U.S. Their business profiles include the "company name, address and phone number, name of the owner or top decision maker, number of employees, estimated annual sales, credit rating score,

and primary and secondary lines of business." You can order even more detailed information for a $3.00 fee.

Scholarly Societies Project (http://www.lib.uwaterloo.ca/society/overview.html)—The University of Waterloo created The Scholarly Societies Project to "facilitate access to information about scholarly societies across the world."

Starting Point (http://www.stpt.com/buine.html)—Very nicely laid out, Starting Point gives you a number of directories from which to choose. After you get to the site, click on *Business*, and you can choose from multiple business and career directories.

SunSITE LibWeb (http://sunsite.berkeley.edu/Libweb/)—SunSITE, maintained by Berkeley Digital Library, is a good source for locating academic, public, and national libraries currently on line. Many of these libraries have their own valuable research resources. Again, a very good general research site.

The Company's Annual Report—Whenever possible, get a copy of the annual report. It contains valuable information regarding financial performance, values, key personnel, and much more. You can often find it simply by typing the company's name plus .com. Try the search engines and Hoover's if you don't find it this way.

The Riley Guide (http://www.dbm.com/jobguide/)—As I said earlier, this is one of the best job search sites on the Web! The guide describes Internet etiquette, newsgroups, virtual libraries, and search engines as they relate to job hunting. You should absolutely take a look at this one early.

The Argus Clearinghouse (http://www.clearinghouse.net/)—This is a resource guide to resource guides. The Argus Clearinghouse collects hundreds of resource guides from across the Internet and organizes them in a single location in a way that you can quickly find the type of information you seek.

Thomas Register (http://www.thomasregister.com/index.html)—Describes more than 155,000 manufacturers, their products and services, locations, company profiles, and trade and brand names. The site bills itself as " the world's largest online industrial buying source." The site makes finding product, service, or company information fairly easy.

Wall Street Journal (http://www.wsj.com/)—The interactive version of the WSJ is great, but full text is only available through online paid subscriptions.

Research Resources: Salary Statistics

Bureau of Labor Statistics—Occupational Outlook Handbook—Provides a wealth of information for specific occupations, including the nature of the work, working conditions, employment statistics, qualifications, job outlook, and earnings.

Occupational Outlook Quarterly—Published four times a year, provides "how-to" information about today's jobs and those projected to be in demand in the future. Presents training opportunities and salary trends.

Trade Journals—Many times trade journals have the most up-to-date salary information and are also a source for names of contacts to call for salary information e.g., the president of an association.

Recruiters—*They know*. Salaries are very much a part of what headhunters and employment agencies deal with on a day-to-day basis.

National Business Employment Weekly—This is a weekly publication from the *Wall Street Journal*.

Along with interesting articles and job listings, it is a good source for salary information.

Your Network—This is one of your best resources. The contact you made during your advice and information meetings may be able to give you an idea about salary ranges for the type of position you've been offered. If not, they may be able to refer you to someone who can.

DataMasters 1997 Salary Survey—(http://www. datamasters.com/dm/survey.html) This is a good source for information about salaries in the computer industry.

Job Smart—(http://www.jobsmart.org/tools/salary/ sal-surv.htm) Contains information for more than 150 salary surveys from general surveys and profession-specific salary surveys. This site is updated regularly.

Pencom Career Center—(http://www.pencomsi. com/java_career.html) Pencom gives you an interactive salary guide and career advice articles.

Job Search Sites: Online

4Work (http://www.4work.com/)—You can search 4Work jobs by state, company, and position.

100Hot (http://www.100hot.com)—Will give you links to many of the best sites on the Web. For job searching purposes, select Jobs.

America's Job Bank (http://www.ajb.dni.us/index. html)—Operated by the U.S. Department of Labor's Public Employment service, this site is a clearing-house for 1,800 state employment offices. You can search by keyword or by occupation. To give you an

idea of what you're up against, the last time I accessed this URL, it let me know that the site had been accessed 177,690,841 in the last six months.

C/Net Search (http://www.search.com)—This is a great site for locating job postings. Under Employment, click on Job Search. C/Net will give you more than 30 search engines to use to look for job postings.

Career Magazine Jobline Database (http://www. careermag.com/db/cmag_postsearch_form)— Career Magazine updates this database daily from

Usenet newsgroups postings. You can search by Location, Skill, Title, or Keyword.

Career Path (http://www.careerpath.com)—One of the most famous job sites on the Web, Career Path posts over 500,000 jobs each month from more than 40 newspapers' classified ads.

Career Mosaic (http://www.careermosaic.com/)—Also one of the most famous job-posting sites on the Web, Career Mosaic lists thousands of U.S. and international jobs.

CareerNet (http://www.careers.org)—After you get to the home page, click the Jobs Now! Web Sites button. Also, check out the Career Gems button. It has links to many useful career Web sites.

CareerWeb (http://www.cweb.com/homepage.html)—Focusing on professional, technical, and managerial jobs, CareerWeb lists thousands of jobs in "engineering, information systems, telecommunications, marketing, accounting, health care, and many other fields."

Catapult (http://www.jobweb.org/)—A very good place to find links galore to many of good career sites.

Coolworks (http://www.coolworks.com)—Want a cool job working in the great outdoors? Coolworks lists more than 42,000 jobs on ranches, National Parks, ski resorts, cruise lines, and more.

Comforce (http://www.comforce.com/)—Comforce lists high-tech jobs in "the growing telecommunications, information technologies, and technical market sectors."

Counsel Connect (http://www.counselconnect.com/)—This site lists jobs for attorneys under Employment Listings.

E-Span (http://www.espan.com/)—Like most sites listed here, E-Span lists many jobs. Click on Job Search. One very nice feature: under Employer Listings, you will find important information about companies recruiting on E-Span.

Federal Jobs Central (http://www.jobsfed.com)—Lists thousands of federal jobs.

FedWorld (http://www.fedworld.gov/jobs/jobsearch.html)—If you want to view even more federal job postings, FedWorld will allow you to access 20 different databases.

InfoSeek (http://www.infoseek.com/)—Click on Business, then choose Careers, and finally, select Company Job Offerings.

JobBank USA (http://www.jobbankusa.com/jobs.html)—Undoubtedly, this is one of the best job postings sites on the Web. Once you get to this location, click on Search for Jobs. This will take you to about 20 or more job postings search engines. You can search them individually, or you can run JobBank's MetaSearch that accesses the Internet's largest job databanks.

JobHunt Page (http://www.Job-Hunt.org)—If I were to give you only one site for finding job postings, this would be it. Developed by Dane Spearing while he was in the midst of his own job search, JobHunt offers links to more than 200 sites for job postings on a single page.

JobTrak (http://www.jobtrak.com/)—Once you get to the home page, click on employers and then postings. This site is best for college students or recent graduates. Lists a couple thousand new jobs each day.

MedSearch (http://www.medsearch.com/)—Provides job listings in the health-care field.

National Business Employment Weekly (http://www.nbew.com/)—This is one of my top picks. This weekly provides many jobs and some very interesting articles.

NationJob Network (http://www.nationjob.com/)—This site lets you search its job listings by field, location, full- or part-time work, and salary range.

New Boston Systems (http://www.toner.com/)—Contract computer job listings.

Peterson's (http://www.petersons.com)—Provides information on career resources, including job search, résumés, and internships.

Point (http://www.pointcom.com/)—This is a service of Lycos. Point provides the top 5 percent of sites as rated by Internet experts and reviews. You can then link to the site from there. When you get to the site, choose Top 5%, then click on Business and then select Careers.

SHRM HR Magazine (http://www.shrm.com)—The online version of the human resources magazine. Click on the Table of Contents and select HR Job Openings.

The Black Collegian Online (http://www.blackcollegian.com/jobsg.html)—Besides providing job listings, the site provides information on internships and the top 100 employers.

The Chronicle of Higher Education (http://www.chronicle.merit.edu/)—The online version of *Academe This Week*. The publication lists primarily faculty and administrative jobs in higher education. Jobs can only be searched if you are a subscriber; however, The Chronicle conveniently allows you to subscribe online.

The Monster Board (http://www.monster.com/)—One of the most popular of all job hunting sites. It lists over 50,000 jobs submitted by more than 7,000 U.S. and 1,500 global employers. You can search by location, discipline, and keyword.

TopJobs (http://www.topjobsusa.com)—This is one of my favorite sites for professionals. The only downside is that the geographic scope of most of the jobs seems to be limited primarily to the southwestern part of the U.S.

Women at Work (http://205.219.112.5/)—The National Association of Female Executives (NAFE) maintains Women At Work. It has a great deal of valuable information and advice for working women. You will also find a number of links to job postings.

Ventana Career Center (http://www.vmedia.com/books/business/sec5/index.htm)—Through this site you can find Fortune 500 jobs and get connected to some headhunters.

INDEX

Note: An "f" following page number indicates figure.

Look to Peterson's on line and Peterson's guides when searching for success!

Finding the right job is never easy.

Peterson's Education & Career Center at petersons.com gives you the tools and the help you need to find and win the job of your dreams.

At petersons.com you can:

Search for career opportunities

Find helpful articles to steer your search

Get advice on building a portfolio

And the best part? It's all free!

Let Peterson's be your online guide to the future!

P PETERSON'S
Princeton, New Jersey
www.petersons.com
1-800-338-3282

Wait! There's more!→